Palgrave Studies in Victims and Victimology

Series Editors
Matthew Hall
University of Lincoln
Lincoln, UK

Pamela Davies
Department of Social Sciences
Northumbria University
Newcastle upon Tyne, UK

In recent decades, a growing emphasis on meeting the needs and rights of victims of crime in criminal justice policy and practice has fuelled the development of research, theory, policy and practice outcomes stretching across the globe. This growth of interest in the victim of crime has seen victimology move from being a distinct subset of criminology in academia to a specialist area of study and research in its own right.

Palgrave Studies in Victims and Victimology showcases the work of contemporary scholars of victimological research and publishes some of the highest-quality research in the field. The series reflects the range and depth of research and scholarship in this burgeoning area, combining contributions from both established scholars who have helped to shape the field and more recent entrants. It also reflects both the global nature of many of the issues surrounding justice for victims of crime and social harm and the international span of scholarship researching and writing about them.

More information about this series at
http://www.palgrave.com/gp/series/14571

Louise Wattis

Revisiting the Yorkshire Ripper Murders

Histories of Gender, Violence and Victimhood

palgrave
macmillan

Louise Wattis
School of Social Sciences, Business,
Law
Teesside University
Middlesbrough, UK

Palgrave Studies in Victims and Victimology
ISBN 978-3-030-01384-4   ISBN 978-3-030-01385-1   (eBook)
https://doi.org/10.1007/978-3-030-01385-1

Library of Congress Control Number: 2018956583

Cover illustration: © Andrew Taylor/Flickr

This Palgrave Macmillan imprint is published by the registered company Springer Nature
Switzerland AG
The registered company address is: Gewerbestrasse 11, 6330 Cham, Switzerland

For Kev, Mam and Dylan. And Sheila, still the best criminologist I know.
I would like to dedicate this book to those who took part in the research.
Finally, and most importantly, to the victims and their families.

CONTENTS

CHAPTER 1

Introduction: The Yorkshire Ripper Case—Exploring Recent Crime History

Abstract This introductory chapter provides an overview of the Sutcliffe murders before considering the criminological value of revisiting this infamous case involving the murder of thirteen women by Peter Sutcliffe. It is argued that exploring this case expands understandings of crime, history and place, violence against women, feminist history, struggles over the representation of prostitution/sex work, as well as a closer meditation on the figure of the victim as represented across a range of texts. In addition, the chapter also identifies the book's methodological and theoretical approach as feminist cultural criminology, which stresses the importance of an engagement with history, academic criminology, cultural studies and popular criminology alongside the recognition of the role of gender in shaping violence and its representation.

Keywords Crime history · Cultural criminology · Feminism · The Sutcliffe case

The murder of 13 women in the North of England between 1975 and 1980 by Peter Sutcliffe, who became known as the 'Yorkshire Ripper', can be viewed as a significant criminal event in terms of the level of fear generated and the impact on local communities. The case represents an 'iconic criminal event' or set of events, assuming the notoriety of other high profile cases involving serial murder and becoming the stuff of

© The Author(s) 2018
L. Wattis, *Revisiting the Yorkshire Ripper Murders*,
Palgrave Studies in Victims and Victimology,
https://doi.org/10.1007/978-3-030-01385-1_1

numerous popular criminological texts (Rafter 2007). Writing about the growing popularity of historical analyses of crime and high profile criminal events specifically, Gilman Srebnick and Levy (2005) have noted how, alongside exploring 'cultural meaning', focusing on crime in this way also offers 'a window into issues and themes in the history of society, culture and politics' (p. 3). Likewise, Brown (2003) refers to the utility of crime as a means of reading culture and history.

In essence, these observations on what the academic can extract from particular crime happenings is reflected in the discussions which make up this book where the purpose of the project is to interrogate the murders and use them as a reference point from which to explore a range of related criminological concerns. The following discussions draw upon research findings from oral history interviews alongside analysis of popular criminological texts and academic commentary. The use of the 'Yorkshire Ripper' as a case study may appear somewhat narrow in terms of its criminological potential beyond an analysis of explaining motivation for the violence and the mythologizing and cultural production surrounding the case. However, a closer examination of the case reveals a wider range of interconnected criminological possibilities relating to crime, history and place, violence against women, feminist history, struggles over the representation of prostitution/sex work, as well as a closer meditation on the figure of the victim as represented across a range of texts. Indeed, the nature of this case has much to tell us about feminism, fear of crime, violence against women and serial murder, representations of victims and sex workers, and the relationship between violence, culture and the social imaginary. In addition, I argue that excavating our 'recent criminal history', looking to 'differing spheres of representation' (Brown 2003) and reading across texts presents new ways for understanding crime, violence, gender violence and victimization, which remain relevant within the contemporary context. I present further detail on these themes in the latter part of this introductory chapter. Prior to this, the chapter will provide a summary of the case and discuss themes relating to methodology.

BACKGROUND TO THE SUTCLIFFE CASE

There are a number of thorough overviews of the Sutcliffe case from academic and popular criminology, which provide detailed chronologies of the murders and attacks on women, and the various stages of the infamously flawed police investigation (Yallop 1993; Bilton 2006; Burn

2004; Wilson 2007; Kinnell 2008; Smith 2013; Bland 1992). In addition, David Yallop's (1993) true crime polemic offers sympathetic and in-depth accounts of victims' lives. I have drawn on the aforementioned summaries to provide the following chronology of the murders and attacks for those not familiar with the case:

In August 1975, 14 year-old school girl Tracey Browne was attacked with a hammer by Sutcliffe on a country lane on the outskirts of Halifax, but was excluded from the police investigation to follow because she did not fit the police profile of victims which assumed attacks were linked to prostitution and developed to include women whose behaviour marked them as non-respectable or 'good-time girls'. Upon arrest however, Sutcliffe admitted to the attack. Moreover, Browne provided an accurate description of Sutcliffe, which may have helped apprehend Sutcliffe earlier on in the investigation. Joan Smith (2013) identifies this as a key failing of the investigation.

In July 1975, Anna Rokuljski was attacked in Keighley, but survived; Olive Smelt was then attacked in Halifax in August 1975. In October 1975, Wilma McCann, a Scottish mother of four who lived in the Chapeltown area of Leeds was murdered by Peter Sutcliffe after being picked up in Chapeltown. In January 1976, Emily Jackson a suburban mother of four from a South Leeds village suburb, who began selling sex to manage financial problems, was murdered. Marcella Claxton survived an attack in May 1976. All three women were attacked in Chapeltown, the red-light area of Leeds. Following the discovery of Irene Richardson's body in Roundhay Park in Leeds—again not far from the red-light area, the idea that the police were dealing with a serial killer targeting women connected to prostitution became explicit and henceforth, came to define the investigation. The murder of Patricia (Tina) Atkinson at the hands of Peter Sutcliffe, in her flat not far from Manningham Lane (Bradford's red-light area) in April 1977 likely lent further support to this view of the killer.

It was around this time that the 'Ripper' moniker was applied to the case by police and media. Taking their cue from a number of newspaper reports, police began to draw parallels with the Nineteenth Century White Chapel murders involving five women linked to prostitution by the still unknown killer who signed himself off as "Jack" in anonymous letters sent to the Central News Agency. The comparisons made between the two cases further established the mythology of 'prostitute-killer' in the context of the Yorkshire murders.

Sixteen year-old shop assistant Jayne MacDonald was attacked and murdered by Peter Sutcliffe walking home from a night out in Leeds city centre to her home in Chapeltown in June 1977. Jayne worked as a shop assistant for a local supermarket chain in Chapeltown and was a well-known face in the area. As the first murder victim not linked to prostitution, her death provoked considerably more police, press and public concern and outrage than the preceding murders. Moreover, Kinnell (2008) notes that the outrage was likely intensified because of Jayne Macdonald's youth and physical attractiveness, which frequently shapes representation and responses to victims (Greer 2007).

Two more women would be attacked and survive in 1977—Maureen Long, who was a well-known face around the pubs in the Manningham Lane area of Bradford, and Marilyn Moore in Chapeltown. Scottish mother of three Jean Jordan was murdered in Manchester in October 1977. In a statement following his arrest, Sutcliffe admitted that the murder of Jean Jordan in Manchester was in response to heightened surveillance in Leeds and Bradford from the summer of 1977 onwards. Following her attack, Marilyn Moore provided an accurate photo fit description of Sutcliffe, which prompted Tracey Browne to return to the police and insist this was the same man who had attacked her, but again the police dismissed her as she did not fit their assumed victim profile (Kinnell 2008).

Yvonne Pearson was a well-liked and well-known face in the red-light area of Bradford. She was experienced and well aware of the risks involved working on the streets, having had a friend murdered in London. Yvonne went missing in January 1978. Friends became concerned when she failed to pick up her children—something they claimed she would never do, but when her disappearance was reported to the police, they dismissed it, labeling her as a feckless mother and assuming that Yvonne had left the area to avoid a court appearance for soliciting (Kinnell 2008). Her body was found stuffed under a disused sofa on wasteland in Bradford two months after she had disappeared. In January 1978, Sutcliffe murdered nineteen year-old Helen Rytka, who had only been involved in street soliciting for a matter of days (Kinnell 2008), in a warehouse yard after he picked her up in Huddersfield's red-light district. For fear of repercussions from the police for soliciting, Helen's twin sister Rita waited over 24 hours before reporting her sister's disappearance. The delay in reporting Helen's disappearance meant that the police missed a vital window when Sutcliffe's car could have been identified and picked up while he was still in the area. Referring to the murder of Helen Rytka and Yvonne Pearson, Kinnell (2008) condemns the criminalization of street soliciting at the time for intensifying the vulnerability of sex workers and hindering the murder investigation. Relatedly, the investigation itself also placed women at greater risk due to heightened surveillance and the use of women as live bait within the Bradford and Leeds red-light districts (Yallop 1993; Kinnell 2008). As Yallop (1993) notes, the police's use of women on the streets to bait the killer 'created a situation where they were virtually conspiring with the killer, inviting him, tempting him, to walk along Church Street and pick his next victim' (p. 209).

The remaining attacks and murders all took place out with red-light districts, reflecting Sutcliffe's response to covert police surveillance across the North of England. Reflecting on the surveillance operations and the creation of 'tolerance' zones during the murders, Kinnell makes the following points:

> From that time onwards, Sutcliffe attacked only non-sex workers, outside red-light districts. The implications of this are chilling, not so much because, as Yallop asserted, the amnesty in Bradford was intended as a trap to lure the Ripper into another attack, or because the strategy of covert observations failed to catch the killer, but because the strategy of amnesty and intense monitoring of the movements of sex workers and clients succeeded in deterring the killer from these areas and these potential victims, whereupon 'innocent' women were targeted. (Kinnell 2008: 13)

In May 1978 Vera Millward was murdered in hospital grounds in Manchester—Vera was the last sex worker to be murdered by Sutcliffe (Kinnell 2008). Remaining victims were Josephine Whitaker, a building society clerk who was murdered in April 1979 on parkland in Halifax on the way home from visiting her grandmother. Student Barbara Leach was murdered in Bradford on the way home from a night out with friends in September 1980. In August 1980, Marguerite Walls, a civil servant, was murdered in Pudsey between Leeds and Bradford on her way home from work, but was originally not included in the 'Ripper' investigation. In November 1980, student Jacqueline Hill was attacked and killed in Headingley, the student area of Leeds, on her way home from a seminar in Leeds city centre. The murders of Barbara Leach and Jacqueline Hill in particular, provoked fear and outrage amongst the public and prompted activist responses from feminists in regard to the murders themselves and the police and media constructions of 'innocent' and 'non-innocent' victims. Uphanda Bandaya survived an attack in Leeds in September 1980, as did Teresa Sykes in Huddersfield in November 1980.

The majority of Sutcliffe's attacks took place in the red-light areas of the cities of Leeds and Bradford in the North of England, but also in Manchester and several smaller towns in the county of West Yorkshire. Victims were approached from behind and hit over the head with a hammer; they were often then slashed across the breasts and abdomen with clothing rearranged to reveal mutilated bodies. The location of the attacks and early victims' connections to sex work led to assumptions early on in the case that the murderer was a 'prostitute-killer' given seven of the women killed were engaged in selling sex on a regular basis or more sporadically. More ambiguously, police working on the case would often refer to Sutcliffe's victims as 'good-time girls' (Yallop 1993; Peace 2001). They applied this label to women who may not have been prostitutes but were viewed pejoratively due to their lifestyle (Smith 2013). This is expressed in the following statement from Detective Superintendent Dennis Hoban following the murder of Emily Jackson in January 1976: 'We are quite certain the man we are looking for hates prostitution … I am quite certain this stretches to women of rather loose morals who go into public houses and clubs, who are not necessarily prostitutes' (cited in Kinnell 2008: 5). Kinnell (2008) notes that the assumption that Sutcliffe was a prototypical 'prostitute killer' who only attacked prostitutes, or those he mistook for prostitutes, has been sustained within both academic and true crime narratives on the case. This is in spite of the fact that nine women were unmistakably not selling sex. Indeed, it is often assumed when sex-workers are murdered they are targeted specifically; however, as Kinnell (2008) further notes, they may merely represent available and vulnerable female victims for men who want to kill women. Sutcliffe's early attacks and his progressive, indiscriminate murder of women outside of red-light areas would suggest a more general motivation to murder women rather than the claimed hatred of prostitutes.

The police investigation is infamous for its failings (Yallop 1993; Byford 1981). During the course of the murders, police failed to follow up on a series of vital clues, which could have led them to catch Sutcliffe earlier. For instance, they interviewed Sutcliffe a total of nine times and failed to look into his previous convictions for violence (Yallop 1993). They also ruled out surviving victims who did not fit the profile of a killer targeting prostitutes and 'good-time girls', but who unfortunately provided remarkably accurate descriptions of their attacker. Arguably, the greatest failing of the investigation was the unquestioning acceptance of three hoax letters and a tape recording claiming to be the Ripper and signing off as 'Jack' which were sent to the police in 1979. The regional accent of the voice on the tape originated from the North East of England rather than West Yorkshire and this led police to believe the murderer came from out of area. On one occasion when Peter Sutcliffe was interviewed he was ruled out because of he had the wrong accent. The tape and letters formed the basis of a massive publicity campaign launched in the latter half of 1979, involving posters, television test cards and the widespread broadcasting of the hoax tape in pubs, nightclubs, youth clubs and football matches. It was estimated that 40,000 people a day rang up to hear the voice on the tape (Caputi 1987).

The publicity campaign took place during the summer and autumn of 1979, almost four years after the first murder of Wilma McCann in 1975 and around the time of the murders of building society clerk Josephine Whitacker in April 1979 and student Barbara Leach in September 1979. Initial media and public apathy towards victims who were prostitutes was replaced by a climate of fear fuelled by the increasing realization that all women were now at risk. The police were overwhelmed by public response to the tape but the publicity machine ceased in February 1980, producing as one senior officer at the time commented, '100% rubbish' (Yallop 1993). Sutcliffe went on to murder two more women and attack two women who survived before he was caught in Sheffield in January 1981 by two uniformed officers carrying out a random check on the false license plates on his car. A hammer and screwdriver were found by officers who returned to the scene of the arrest and after two days of questioning, Sutcliffe confessed to the murders.

At the trial Sutcliffe pleaded guilty to manslaughter based on diminished responsibility. He claimed he was suffering from paranoid schizophrenia and had heard voices from God sending him on a divine mission to rid the streets of prostitutes. Initially, both prosecution and defence were prepared to accept a guilty plea of manslaughter on the grounds of diminished responsibility due to schizophrenia. The judge however, rejected this and insisted on a trial by jury which found Sutcliffe guilty of murder with the defence of insanity dismissed. During the trial the defence claimed the murders were not motivated by sexual sadism and Sutcliffe was driven by a hatred of prostitutes. Notwithstanding, the trial heard from the prosecution how Sutcliffe slashed the majority of his victims across the breasts and abdomen, raped Helen Rytka while she was dying, inserted a wooden plank into Emily Jackson's vagina and stabbed Josephine Whitaker repeatedly in the vagina with a screwdriver. Indeed, feminist commentators have questioned the distinction that the male dominated legal and medical professions made at the time between a delusional 'divine mission' to kill women and the sadistic murder of women (Hollway 1981; Cameron and Frazer 1987) as arguably both can be identified as femicide located within a culture of misogyny (Radford and Russell 1992). Such misogyny extends to the male-dominated legal process which perpetuated the denial of victimhood of 'non-respectable' victims and the more general lack of value afforded to the lives of thirteen murdered women, as well those who survived attacks (Bland 1992; Hollway 1981; Smith 2013; Yallop 1993). This is evident in the construction of the murder of prostitutes by the prosecution as rational and the insinuation that the actions of Sutcliffe's wife and mother may have provoked his motivation to murder women (Smith 2013).

Methodological Considerations

The nature of these murders and their representation form a key feature of our recent criminal history and as such, provide the opportunity for reflection and comparative analysis to set against contemporaneous crime experiences and criminological analyses (D'Cruze et al. 2005). Moreover, this involves analyses which go beyond academic criminology and embrace the study of crime as inevitably interdisciplinary and intertextual (Brown 2003; Carrabine 2008; Downing 2013). With this in mind, the chapters include discussions from history, cultural studies, and popular criminology. The project is further inspired by calls to embrace creativity and expand the criminological imagination (Young 2011; Walklate and Jacobsen 2017; Jacobsen 2014). In light of the above, it is accurate to locate this book and the wider project which informs it, within the field of cultural criminology, defined by O'Neill and Seal (2012) in the following way:

> [t]he everyday meanings of crime and crime control – as they emerge in the media, city and urban spaces, and as part of globalization (Ferrell et al. 2004). Methodologically, historical, archival, ethnographic, textual and visual analyses are most commonly used. (O'Neill and Seal 2012: 9)

The emphasis within cultural criminology on interrogating the meaning and construction of crime from across a number of cultural and empirical sources resonates with this project which consists of an oral history project exploring memories of the murders, complemented by interrogation of the portrayal of the murders in true crime and crime fiction. Combining texts produced by academic research with those from cultural production offers a fuller sense of how both individuals responded to and remembered these murders and their place in the collective memory/social imaginary.

THE ORAL HISTORY PROJECT

The project used oral history interviews with a 'topical' and 'autobiographical' focus (Roberts 2002) in order to explore individuals' memories of the murders. The project aimed to explore women's fears from the time—given the dominant narrative about the murders portrayed women's fears as intense and all encompassing. More generally, the project sought to gain some sense of how the murders and the discourses surrounding them pervaded daily life in material and embodied ways, and shaped the 'structure of feeling' for those living closest to them.

Ten women and two men, who were living in Leeds at the time of the murders were interviewed for the project, along with interviews and informal discussions with four key informants. The sample included a feminist activist and two women working as sex-workers in the Leeds red-light district during the murders. Given the nature of the research, ages of interviewees ranged from mid-50s to early 60s. In addition, email correspondence, which confirms women's fears and men's experiences as potential suspects are also included as supporting data. Oral history interviews share the same methodological problems found more generally in qualitative research, but as research extends further into the past, questions of 'truth' within research accounts become more salient due to the fallibility and selectivity of memory (Lummis 1998; Samuel and Thompson 1990; Passerini 1992; Thompson 1993). Recalling the past does not therefore produce a literal reproduction, it involves rewriting and revising past events (Samuel and Thompson 1990) from the vantage point of the present as a response to actual events (Polkinghorne 2007). However, accessing an exact account of the past is not the point. Rather, oral testimonies provide the opportunity for individuals to interrogate events for themselves and to imbue them with meaning (Portelli 1998; Polkinghorne 2007; Presser 2009).

Analysis of research findings from the oral history project included both categorical and narrative approaches. As Alleyne (2015) notes, combining the two approaches is commonplace in social science research. To clarify, categorical or thematic analysis involves looking across a number of texts to highlight common themes and 'isolate elements of narrative and realign these to fit into nodes on a classificatory scheme' (Alleyne 2015: 41). Such approaches are an established way of handling qualitative data in the social sciences (Glaser and Strauss 1967). In contrast, analysis of narrative involves working within texts to explore connections and work with the story/ies in the individual text. Riessman provides a useful distinction between the two approaches, noting that 'narrative keeps the story together for analytical purposes, while grounded theory approaches tend to pull the text apart into discrete, coded segments' (Riessman 2008, cited in Alleyne 2015: 45). Themes from research findings are explored in chapters four and five which deploy both categorical and narrative approaches: chapter four examines the complexities and ambiguities evident in women's accounts of their fears during the murders and chapter five offers alternative representations of victims derived from the research findings.

ANALYSING POPULAR CRIMINOLOGY

In her reading of crime and law in film and crime fiction, Sheila Brown (2003) eschews the analysis of the minutiae of texts in terms of semiotic/linguistic or literary analysis in favour of a 'fully sociological treatment' of crime representations (p. 81). Taking her cue from Alison Young's (1996) examination of detective fiction, which by focusing on the evolution of the genre, reveals historical transformation and the onset of modernity, she argues that detective or crime fiction:

> [a]llows us to see the story as telling the story of the culture from which it emanates, and it does so free of the complexities of either literary-critical or cultural textual analysis. It is essentially a sociology of the fictive text. (Brown 2003: 81)

Crime fiction and indeed popular criminological texts more widely, thus have the potential to be considered sociological and historical documents which can contribute to academic epistemologies on crime and culture (Carrabine 2008; Wakeman 2014; Rafter 2007; Jacobsen 2014), as well as speaking to debates about criminology's relationship with the social and political sphere (Loader and Sparks 2011; Brown and Rafter 2013). Rafter (2007) was one of the first criminologists to explicitly identify 'popular criminology'—defined as assorted textual and visual popular representations of crime which have the potential to be an epistemological resource for academic criminology. Focusing specifically on films concerning crime and the law, Rafter (2007) highlights their potential to foster fresh intellectual, ethical and emotional responses to offending, violence and victimization. Likewise, Wakeman (2013) views popular criminological texts as both challenging and shoring up the ideological status quo with the means to rethink crime epistemologies and criminal justice policy. Moreover, the salience of representational forms for understanding crime and the social, becomes more evident with the realization that cultural forms are not only texts to be studied but are sites of meaning making in and of themselves given that boundaries between the real and the mediated are increasingly blurred in late modern culture (Sparks 1992; Brown 2003; Wakeman 2014). Embracing popular criminology in this way fits with Jacobsen's notion of a 'criminology of the possible' whereby a fuller set of methodologies helps further expand the criminological imagination beyond more conventional approaches.

Hence, the discussions included herein resonate with Jacobsen's call for 'cultural, critical and creative criminology' (p. 19) and the recognition that popular cultural texts have much to tell the academic criminologist about how both academics and various publics think through all aspects of crime. This is both in sociological/criminological terms, as well as performing affective work which can transform our emotional and intellectual engagement with crime. With this in mind, the chapters to follow embrace the importance of history for studying crime and the pivotal nature of narrative in understanding both individual stories, but also the narratives produced by intellectual and political movements. More specifically, a number of popular criminological texts portraying the Sutcliffe case are examined in the latter part of the book. This is in order to explore the way in which fictive and true crime texts contribute to both popular and academic understandings of the case, which go beyond the stock representations from news media. These additional representational layers pose further questions for both popular and criminological understandings of this case.

A FEMINIST PERSPECTIVE

Feminist perspectives within criminology introduced gendered understandings to experiences of offending, victimization and punishment, and in so doing, rendered masculinity and femininity visible to the criminological gaze (Smart 1976; Naffine 1997; Miller 2010). The work presented here falls within the field of critical cultural criminology, but is also underpinned by feminist analyses, which identify social life as shaped by gender identities and power inequities between men and women. Acknowledging feminism's variety and breadth, Heidensohn and Gelsthorpe (2007) identify feminism's common ground in identifying 'men's material interest in the domination of women and the different ways in which men construct a variety of institutional arrangements to sustain this domination' (p. 382). More specifically, radical feminist analyses identify male violence against women as systemic and structural: the means by which men secure and demonstrate power and control over women as part of patriarchy (Brownmiller 1975; Kelly 1987; Hanmer and Saunders 1984; Stanko 1987; Mackay 2015).

This type of analysis however, mistakenly assumes a coherence and instrumentality to gender relations, which often cannot account for complexity and the intersections with other aspects of inequality and identity (Smart 1989; McCall 2005), as well as the fluidity of masculinity and the role of class and locality in determining masculine violence (Hall et al. 2008; Dorling 2004; Winlow 2001; Treadwell and Garland 2011; Ellis 2015). That said, the consistency of men's violence against women in varying forms, across social space/s and at the level of the global (Walby and Allen 2004; Department of Health 2005; Mackay 2015; Sen 1990; Reilly 2008), is sufficiently systemic that it can be linked to gender, power and masculinity which thus requires a structural analysis of violence and power based on gender relations.

Indeed, the Sutcliffe case which is the focus of this book arguably demands such a framework. Not only is the case an example of femicide (Radford 1992), which should be located in the wider context of patriarchal violence and misogynist cultures, but the representation of women and the delineation of victims based on respectability and sexual propriety bring into sharp focus the necessity of adopting a feminist position. Indeed, this case demonstrates in the starkest terms, how gender determines relationships to crime, victimisation and justice. Here was a man murdering and attacking women, pursued by the West Yorkshire Police, an institution populated primarily by men who made no bones of their contempt for the prostitutes who were murdered. Street prostitution of course, is itself also highly gendered, made up as it was/is by marginalized women who are vilified by sexual double standards embedded in policy and the wider culture. Victims not connected to prostitution, but who were also perceived by police as transgressing the rules of feminine respectability, whose transgressions included going to the pub, mental illness and having more than one partner (Smith 2013), were also renounced as victims and described as 'good-time girls'. Furthermore, a wide range of research reveals the inherence of gender to fear of crime and the negotiation of violence. A large body of work from both within and out with feminism evidences the qualitative and quantitative differences in the way that men and women negotiate the prospect of violent victimization (Painter 1992; Stanko 1997; Valentine 1989, 1992) with feminist work revealing fear of male violence and sexual violence as informing women's fears. The Sutcliffe case, exemplifying the threat of the stranger occupying public space, presents as an especially extreme example of the way in which women's fear of male violence and attendant social and spatial restrictions operate within patriarchal culture.

Recognition of the consistency of patriarchy and masculinity in accounting for violence against women and its framing underpins the discussions to follow. At the same time however, the discussions also recognize the fluidity of gender relations and identities and the tensions and contradictions across feminist knowledges. To this end, I draw on Janice Haaken's (2010) work on the myths and counter-myths generated by the feminist movement and specifically the 'battered women's movement' in its attempt to construct an analysis of women's oppression founded on shared experience and an attendant collective story. Haaken's aim is not to reject the feminist project. She maintains that 'the critique of gender domination that is at the heart of feminist analysis' must not be lost (p. 44). Rather, highlighting the importance of storytelling—within popular culture, individual narratives, as well as the stories generated from academic and political positions, Haaken works with 'myths and counter-myths' to 'open up a creative space between two opposing claims' (p. 13). In essence, Haaken is committed to feminism, but is uneasy with claims to grand narratives, which claim to speak for all women simultaneously, but where voices and experiences of different groups of women such as working—class women and women of colour are often lost if they deviate from the stock script.

Haaken's concerns regarding divergent voices and stories from within feminism are brought cogently to the fore in debates regarding women's involvement in the sex industry. The approach adopted by radical feminism defines the selling of sex as prostitution and as intrinsically violent and exploitative (Jeffreys 2008, 2009; Barry 1996; Raymond 2013). In contrast, those who adopt the sex work position—often referred to as 'sex positive' feminists (Cameron 2018), argue that often, women's participation in the sex industry is a matter of agency and deserving of rights and recognition (Scoular 2004; Agustin 2007; O'Neill 2010; Sanders 2016; Armstrong 2015). These ideological battles over the meaning of prostitution now appear to be embedded and intractable and often come to the fore in debates regarding the most appropriate and effective way to regulate the sex industry (Kinnell 2008).

I mention these opposing positions at this point because they are pivotal to the Sutcliffe case and the history of feminism from that time. It has been argued that the murders and the activism they inspired were something of catalyst in the 'politicisation of sexuality' around prostitution and the shoring up of opposing positions (Walkowitz 1992; Ferris 2015). To be sure, the figure of the 'prostitute' features heavily in this case given the number of victims linked to prostitution and assumptions regarding Sutcliffe's motivations as a 'prostitute-killer'. This occurred alongside the indifference, wholesale misogyny and denial of victimhood directed at victims linked to prostitution by police, media and the wider culture. All of which are part of a longer history of repression and stigmatization of women involved in prostitution (Walkowitz 1982, 1992; O'Neill 2010). Many of these themes feature within the discussions to follow, which acknowledge these tensions, whilst also attempting to give voice to both sides of the debate, underpinned by the conviction that for both sides, the welfare and well-being of women is paramount. Moreover, the significance of terminology and the loaded nature of the terms used in the context of sex work are also recognized. Accordingly, references to sex work, sex worker, prostitution and prostitute and 'Ripper' will be applied sensitively and where appropriate and relevant to the discussions that follow.

OUTLINE OF CHAPTERS

The discussion in the introduction and the subsequent chapters in this volume focus on the Sutcliffe murder case, but use this focus on one specific criminal event/s to expand analysis of a range of criminological concerns. In doing so, the chapters in this volume contribute to a 'cultural, creative, critical criminology' which goes beyond the disciplinary parameters of academic criminology, taking in history and cultural studies. This current chapter offers an overview and background to the Sutcliffe case and details of the police investigation. It also outlines the methodology, which informs the book and the wider project, highlighting the use of oral history and locating the project within the field of cultural criminology, as well as emphasising the value of popular criminology for developing the academic criminological imagination. Lastly, the chapter positions the project within a feminist framework, highlighting the importance of feminism for analysing this case. Chapter 2 focuses explicitly on history and place, examining the socio-historical context in which the murders took place and assessing the extent to which this case can be conceived of as a crime specific to time and place. The chapter also deals with the manner in which crime and violence become associated with specific places and serve to transform and define place identity in the wake of violence. Chapter 3 explores socio-structural and cultural approaches to serial murder, which eschew individual and psychological approaches in favour of explanations which highlight social and economic factors as fostering serial murder. The chapter also addresses the cultural life and progress of the serial killer and the serial killer as object of captivation and ubiquity within popular culture. Drawing upon the Sutcliffe case, the chapter also addresses the gendered nature of the serial killer and the role of masculinity and misogyny in shaping the actuality and representation of serial murder. The chapter concludes by arguing for greater integration of approaches which focus on class and the political economy alongside feminist perspectives. Chapter 4 explores how the history of feminism is bound up with Sutcliffe case. It charts the history of radical feminism in the 1970s and how feminist activism was galvanised by the murders and the cultures of misogyny and victim-blaming which surrounded them. The chapter also includes discussion of divergent narratives, which criticise the movement on the grounds of insensitivity to race and the exclusion of the voices of sex workers from activism and dialogue at the time of the murders. The chapter also engages with the opposing debates on sex work/prostitution, which as stated earlier, form a crucial element of the history of this case and were arguably forged amidst feminist activism and debate around the Sutcliffe case. Relatedly, Chapter 4 also examines the dominant fear narratives from the time and drawing upon research findings from the oral history project, presents a more complex picture of women's fear experiences based around class, locality and the voices of sex workers.

Chapters 5 and 6 deal with representation of victims as they emerged within this project with Chapter 5 specifically exploring how victims were remembered and referred to by respondents who took part in the oral history project. The chapter acknowledges the fallibility of memory and the fragmented nature of respondents' recollections of victims, highlighting that although some respondents engaged in processes of Othering victims, others took up alternative positions, which challenge dominant and simplistic representations of the female victims of male violence. Following on from this, Chapter 6 focuses on related themes, exploring how these murders have been portrayed within crime fiction and true crime: Gordon Burn's Somebody's Husband, Somebody's Son; David Yallop's Deliver Us from Evil; David Peace's Nineteen Seventy Seven and Nineteen Eighty; Pat Barker's Blow Your House Down. In doing so, the chapter returns to the theme of the framing of victims in the Sutcliffe case, but also focuses on misogyny, masculinity and violence against women within these texts. In addition, I also highlight how some of the texts offer alternative and more sympathetic representations of sex workers linked to class. The chapter ends by acknowledging the ethical issues and tensions, which representations of graphic violence against women often provoke: Do portrayals of misogyny and the brutalized female body ever possess progressive potential or do they by default perpetuate women's objectification and subordination?

References

Agustin, L. (2007). *Sex Work at the Margins: Migration, Labour Markets and the Rescue Industry*. London: Zed Books.

Alleyne, B. (2015). *Narrative Networks: Storied Approaches in a Digital Age*. London: Sage.

Armstrong, L. (2015). From Law Enforcement to Protection? Interactions Between Sex Workers and Police in a Decriminalized Street-Based Sex Industry. *British Journal of Criminology, 57*(3), 570–588.

Barry, K. (1996). *The Prostitution of Sexuality: The Global Exploitation of Women*. New York: New York University Press.

Bilton, M. (2006). *Wicked Beyond Belief: The Hunt for the Yorkshire Ripper* (Rev. ed.). London: Harper Perennial.

Bland, L. (1992). The Case of the Yorkshire Ripper: Mad, Bad, Beast or Male? In J. Radford & D. E. H. Russell (Eds.), *Femicide: The Politics of Women Killing*. Buckingham: Open University Press.

Brown, M., & Rafter, N. (2013). Genocide Films, Public Criminology, Collective Memory. *British Journal of Criminology, 53,* 1017–1032.

Brown, S. (2003). *Crime and Law in Media Culture*. Buckingham: Open University Press.

Brownmiller, S. (1975). *Against Our Will: Men, Women and Rape*. Harmondsworth: Penguin.

Burn, G. (2004). *Somebody's Husband, Somebody's Son*. London: Viking.

Byford, L. (1981). *The Yorkshire Ripper Case: Review of the Police Investigation of the Case by Lawrence Byford, Esq., C.B.E., Q.P.M., Her Majesty's Inspectorate of Constabulary*. London: Home Office.

Cameron, D., & Frazer, E. (1987). *The Lust to Kill*. Cambridge: Polity.

Cameron, J. J. (2018). *Reconsidering Radical Feminism: Affect and the Politics of Heterosexuality*. Washington: University of Washington Press.

Caputi, J. (1987). *The Age of the Sex Crime*. Bowling Green: Bowling Green State University Popular Press.

Carrabine, E. (2008). *Crime, Culture and the Media*. Cambridge: Polity.

D'Cruze, S., Jackson, L. A., & Rowbotham, J. (2005). Gender, Crime and Culture in the Twentieth-First Century: Conversations Between Academics and Professionals. *History Workshop Journal, 60,* 139–151.

Department of Health. (2005). *Responding to Domestic Abuse*. London: HMSO.

Dorling, D. (2004). Prime Suspect: Murder in Britain. In C. Pantazis, S. Tombs, & D. Gordon (Eds.), *Beyond Criminology: Taking Harm Seriously*. London: Pluto Press.

Downing, L. (2013). *The Subject of Murder*. Chicago: University of Chicago Press.

Ellis, A. (2015). *Men, Masculinities and Violence: An Ethnographic Approach*. London: Routledge.

Ferrell, J., Hayward, K., Morrison, W., & Presdee, M. (2004). *Cultural Criminology Unleashed*. New York: Routledge.

Ferris, S. (2015). *Street Sex Work and Canadian Cities: Resisting a Dangerous Order*. Alberta: University of Alberta Press.

Gilman Srebnick, A., & Levy, R. (2005). *Crime and Culture: An Historical Perspective*. Aldershot: Ashgate.

Glaser, B., & Strauss, A. (1967). *The Discovery of Grounded Theory: Strategies for Qualitative Research*. Hawthorne, NY: Aldine de Gruyter.

Greer, C. (2007). News, Media, Victims and Crime. In P. Davies, P. Francis, & C. Greer (Eds.), *Victims, Crime and Society*. London: Sage.

Haaken, J. (2010). *Hard knocks: Domestic Violence and the Psychology of Storytelling*. London: Routledge.

Hall, S., Winlow, S., & Ancrum, C. (2008). *Criminal Identities and Consumer Culture: Crime, Exclusion and the Culture of Narcissism*. Cullompton: Willan.

Hanmer, J., & Saunders, S. (1984). *Well Founded Fear: A Community Study of Violence to Women*. Leeds: Hutchinson.

Heidensohn, F., & Gelsthorpe, L. (2007). Gender and Crime. In M. Maguire, R. Morgan, & R. Reiner (Eds.), *The Oxford Handbook of Criminology* (4th ed.). Oxford: Oxford Press.

Hollway, W. (1981, October). 'I Just Wanted to Kill a Woman' Why? The Ripper and Male Sexuality. *Feminist Review, 9*, 33–40.

Jacobsen Hviid, M. (2014). *The Poetics of Crime: Understanding and Researching Crime and Deviance Through Creative Sources*. New York: Routledge.

Jeffreys, S. (2008). *The Idea of Prostitution*. Melbourne: Spinifex Press.

Jeffreys, S. (2009). *The Industrial Vagina: The Political Economy of the Global Sex Trade*. London: Routledge.

Kelly, L. (1987). The Continuum of Sexual Violence. In J. Hanmer & M. Maynard (Eds.), *Women, Violence and Social Control*. London: Macmillan.

Kinnell, H. (2008). *Violence and Sex Work in Britain*. Cullompton: Willan.

Loader, I., & Sparks, R. (2011). *Public Criminology*. London: Routledge.

Lummis, T. (1998). Structure and Validity in Oral Evidence. In R. Perks & A. Thomson (Eds.), *The Oral History Reader*. London: Routledge.

Mackay, F. (2015). *Radical Feminism: Feminist Activism in Movement*. London: Palgrave Macmillan.

McCall, L. (2005). The Complexity of Intersectionality. *Signs, 30*, 1771–1800.

Miller, J. (2010). Commentary on Heidensohn's 'The Deviance of Women': Continuity and Change over Four Decades of Gender, Crime and Social Control. *British Journal of Sociology, 61*, 134–139.

Naffine, N. (1997). *Feminism and Criminology*. Cambridge: Polity.

O'Neill, M. (2010). Cultural Criminology and Sex Work: Resisting Regulation Through Radical Democracy and Participatory Action Research (PAR). *Journal of Law and Society, 37*(1), 210–232.

O'Neill, M., & Seal, L. (2012). *Transgressive Imaginations: Crime, Deviance and Culture*. Basingstoke: Palgrave Macmillan.

Painter, K. (1992). Different Worlds: The Spatial, Temporal and Social Dimensions of Female Victimisation. In D. Evans, N. Fyfe, & D. Herbert (Eds.), *Crime, Policing and Place: Essays in Environmental Criminology*. London: Routledge.

Passerini, L. (1992). *Memory and Totalitarianism*. Oxford: Oxford University Press.

Peace, D. (2001). *Nineteen Eighty*. London: Serpents Tail.

Polkinghorne, D. (2007). Validity Issues in Narrative Research. *Qualitative Inquiry, 13*(4), 471–486.

Portelli, A. (1998). What Makes Oral History Different? In R. Perks & A. Thomson (Eds.), *The Oral History Reader*. London: Routledge.

Presser, L. (2009). The Narratives of Offenders. *Theoretical Criminology, 13*, 177–200.

Radford, J. (1992). Introduction. In J. Radford & D. Russell (Eds.), *Femicide: The Politics of Woman Killing*. New York, NY: Twayne.

Radford, J., & Russell, D. (1992). *Femicide: The Politics of Woman Killing*. New York, NY: Twayne.

Rafter, N. (2007). Crime, Film and Criminology: Recent Sex Crime Movies. *Theoretical Criminology, 11*(3), 403–420.

Raymond, J. G. (2013). *Not a Choice, Not a Job: Exposing the Myths of the Global Sex Trade*. Virginia Dulles: Potomac Books.

Reilly, N. (2008). *Women's Human Rights: Seeking Gender Justice in a Globalising Age*. Cambridge: Polity.

Roberts, B. (2002). *Biographical Research*. Buckingham: Open University Press.

Samuel, R., & Thompson, P. (1990). *The Myths We Live By*. London: Routledge.

Sanders, T. (2016). Inevitably Violent? Dynamics of Space, Governance and Stigma. *Special Issue: Problematizing Prostitution: Critical Research and Scholarship, Studies in Law, Politics and Society, 71*, 93–114.

Scoular, J. (2004). The 'Subject' of Prostitution: Interpreting the Discursive, Symbolic and Material Position of Sex/Work Within Feminist Theory. *Feminist Theory, 5*(3), 343–355.

Sen, A. (1990). *More Than 100 Million Women Are Missing*. http://www.nybooks.com/articles/archives/1990/dec/20/more-than-100-million-women-are-missing/. Accessed 1 April 2014.

Smart, C. (1976). *Women, Crime and Criminology*. London: Routledge and Kegan Paul.

Smart, C. (1989). *Feminism and the Power of the Law*. London: Routledge.

Smith, J. (2013). *Misogynies: Reflections on Myth and Malice*. New York: Fawcett Columbine.

Sparks, R. (1992). Reason and Unreason in 'Left Realism': Some Problems in the Constitution of the Fear of Crime. In R. Matthews & J. Young (Eds.), *Issues in Realist Criminology*. London: Sage.

Stanko, E. (1987). Typical Violence, Normal Precaution: Men, Women and Interpersonal Violence in England, Wales, Scotland and the USA. In J. Hanmer & M. Maynard (Eds.), *Women, Violence and Social Control*. London: Macmillan.

Stanko, E. (1997). Safety Talk: Conceptualising Women's Risk Assessment as a Technology of the Soul. *Theoretical Criminology, 1*(4), 479–499.

Thompson, P. (1993). Family Myth, Models and Denials in the Shaping of Individual Life Paths. In D. Bertaux & P. Thompson (Eds.), *Between Generations*. Oxford: Oxford University Press.

Treadwell, J., & Garland, J. (2011). Masculinity, Marginalisation and Violence: A Case Study of the English Defence League. *British Journal of Criminology, 11*(5), 1171–1193.

Valentine, G. (1989). The Geography of Women's Fear. *Area, 21*, 385–390.

Valentine, G. (1992). Images of Danger: Women's Sources of Information About the Spatial Distribution of Male Violence. *Area, 24*, 22–29.

Wakeman, S. (2013). 'No One Wins. One Side Just Loses More Slowly': The Wire and Drug Policy. *Theoretical Criminology, 18*, 224–239.

Wakeman, S. (2014). Fieldwork, Biography and Emotion: Doing Criminological Auto-Ethnography. *British Journal of Criminology, 54*, 705–721.

Walby, S., & Allen, J. (2004). *Domestic Violence, Sexual Assault and Stalking: Findings from the British Crime Survey*. London: Home Office Research, Development and Statistics Directorate.

Walklate, S., & Jacobsen Hviid, M. (Eds.). (2017). *Liquid Criminology: Doing Imaginative Criminological Research*. London: Routledge.

Walkowitz, J. (1982). Jack the Ripper and Myth of Male Violence. *Feminist Studies, 8*(3), 542–574.

Walkowitz, J. (1992). *City of Dreadful Delight: Narratives of Sexual Danger in Victorian London*. Chicago: University of Chicago Press.

Wilson, D. (2007). *Serial Killers: Hunting Britons and Their Victims 1966–2006*. Hampshire Hook: Waterside Press.

Winlow, S. (2001). *Badfellas*. Oxford: Berg.

Yallop, D. (1993). *Deliver Us From Evil*. Reading: Cox and Wyman.

Young, A. (1996). *Imagining Crime: Textual Outlaws and Criminal Conversations*. London: Sage.

Young, J. (2011). *The Criminological Imagination*. Cambridge: Polity.

CHAPTER 2

Locating the 'Yorkshire Ripper': A Crime of Time and Place?

Abstract This chapter explores the social and historical context of the Sutcliffe case, identifying how narratives of political and economic crisis in 1970s Britain combine with cultural conditions associated with northern England such as economic decline, deindustrialisation and working-class masculinity to form the backdrop to these murders and the police investigation. The chapter also draws on the concept of hauntology to highlight how space and place are transformed by violent events. In conclusion, the chapter argues that although misogyny and violence against women may demonstrate culturally-specific features linked to class and locality, patriarchal violence nevertheless transcends the local. Having said that, it is argued that locally and historically-specific conditions can expand understandings of the social and situational nature of violence and murder.

Keywords History · Culture · Masculinity · Place · Hauntology

INTRODUCTION

Psychological and individual-orientated explanatory frameworks dominate the research literature on serial murder (Bartol and Bartol 2008; Purcell and Arrigo 2006; Hickey 2013; Holmes and Holmes 1996; Webber 2010). Given the rarity of serial murder and the emphasis on

© The Author(s) 2018
L. Wattis, *Revisiting the Yorkshire Ripper Murders*,
Palgrave Studies in Victims and Victimology,
https://doi.org/10.1007/978-3-030-01385-1_2

psychopathology within the academic and popular imagination, the privileging of these approaches appears self-evident. Peter Sutcliffe's plea of diminished responsibility on the grounds of schizophrenia and hearing voices from God instructing him to murder women linked to prostitution certainly aligns to this type of approach. However, as Grover and Soothill (1999) have pointed out, we ignore the social, historical and cultural conditions of serial murder 'at our peril' for 'without a focus upon wider social factors in causing offender behaviour, any understanding of crime cannot be complete' (p. 1477). Compelling evidence for the role of the social in engendering serial murder is highlighted by the spike in murders in the troubled Weimar Germany in the interwar period. The rise in serial murder in Germany at this time has been linked to social and economic, which also contributed to the rise of fascism (Tatar 1995; Soothill 1996). Indeed, structural conditions have now been embraced by a number of academics who connect etiologies of violence and homicide and the situation of victims, many of whom are marginalized and disregarded, to social structure and culture, and to history and place (Leyton 1986; Soothill 1996; Grover and Soothill 1999; Haggerty 2009; Hall and Maclean 2009; Wilson 2007, 2012; Hall and Wilson 2014; Wilson et al. 2016). And of course, feminism's take on structure and the serial murder of women names it as femicide and connects it to patriarchy, masculinity and misogyny (Cameron and Frazer 1987; Hollway 1981; Caputi 1987; Smith 2013; Bland 1992).

Notwithstanding the fact that there is evidence of serial type murders across different historical periods and societies (Soothill 1996), the following two chapters will address the wider socio-historical factors which may have some bearing on the historical and geographical proliferation of serial murder. Chapter 3 explores in more detail the role of structure and culture in engendering serial killing, alongside the veneration and fascination with serial killers within cultural production and popular culture (Jenkins 1994; Seltzer 1998; Schmid 2005). This current chapter focuses more explicitly on the Yorkshire Ripper murders and their connection to place, history and culture, considering both national and local historical/cultural contexts. In an examination of the Victorian serial killer Mary Ann Cotton, David Wilson (2013) places 'Cotton into the social, economic and cultural context that dominated her life' to provide 'the backdrop against which Cotton's story has to be told and understood' (p. 23). I aim to do something of the same with regard the Sutcliffe case.

Subsequent discussions in this chapter combine commentaries from academic criminology, crime fiction and cultural studies to explore the real and imagined landscapes of crime and place as they relate to the Yorkshire Ripper murders. It is argued that drawing upon popular criminological texts—true crime and crime fiction, alongside academic criminology, contributes to a more creative criminology which embraces both the figurative and the real in attempts to enhance criminological epistemologies and understandings of crime, violence and culture (Wakeman 2013; Jacobsen 2014; Wender 2015).

A SERIAL KILLER IN YORKSHIRE

Crime happens in specific times and places for specific reasons: you have to ask for example why was Jamie Bulger taken from a shopping centre in Liverpool and not in Leeds? Why was Stephen Lawrence killed in south London? These things don't happen by chance. It wasn't the Cornwall Ripper, it was the Yorkshire Ripper; it happened here for a variety of very specific reasons that we don't want to look at any more. (David Peace, quoted in Upson 2001: 41)

After carrying out four attacks on women in the late 1960s and the summer of 1975, Peter Sutcliffe murdered Wilma McCann in November 1975 in the Chapeltown area of Leeds. He would murder twelve more women and attack a further five across West Yorkshire and Manchester before his arrest in January 1981. This was mid-point in a decade which as Shaw (2011) notes, 'was pushed to the brink of social disintegration' (p. 5), and which has come to be characterized by violence, industrial conflict, financial crises and the collapse in legitimacy of the political class (Beckett 2010; Runciman 2013). Moreover, the decade also witnessed rising racial tensions and racist violence as a result of the 'expansion and consolidation of organisations of the neo-fascist right' (Gilroy 2002: 152). Conservative Edward Heath was elected prime minister in 1970 and presided over rising inflation and escalating tensions in industrial relations. The miners' strike of 1974 led to blackouts and the three-day week: Edward Heath's 'inability to manage a rapidly deteriorating industrial and economic climate' culminated in defeat and humiliation in the dispute with the miners, followed by marginal electoral defeat in 1974 (Maguire 2011: 12). For Runciman, this lack of political efficacy is situated within the wider political decline of the West and the failure of Western democratic states to govern effectively. Likewise, Hobsbawn (1995) stresses economic and political decline at the global level as the 'Golden Age' of Western capitalism's growth between 1947–1973 receded into a world post-1973 which 'lost its bearings and slid into instability and crisis' (p. 403). Subsequent Labour administrations in the latter half of the 1970s faced economic crises, rising unemployment, inflation and volatile and unstable industrial relations. As Beckett (2010) reflects, something 'profound and unsettling did happen to Britain in the seventies, and Britons have been living with the consequences ever since' (cited in Shaw 2011, p. 5). Indeed, Beckett (2010) views the decade in terms of decline, anxiety and a sense of the apocalyptic. Likewise, Runciman (2013) refers to the 'dark days of the 1970s' where 'parts of Britain appeared practically ungovernable'.

The epigraph at the beginning of this section comes from the crime writer David Peace. As a writer, Peace is renowned for the use of history within his fiction, combining quasi-fictional worlds with key events from recent British history as a means of interrogating social, political and cultural conditions (Shaw 2011). His Red Riding quartet of novels (1999, 2000, 2001, and 2002) deploy the Yorkshire Ripper murders and the police investigation as a backdrop for the mapping of a fictional narrative of crime and violence mainly perpetrated by the police themselves. Peace grew up in West Yorkshire close to where the Sutcliffe murders were taking place and it is clear from interviews with the writer and the presence of the 'Ripper' within his narrative that the case was affecting, both for him and the wider local community. Moreover, as the above quote makes clear, he is resolute that history, culture and place create what Haggerty (2009) identifies as the 'necessary conditions' for serial murder. Peace and his commentators (Maguire 2011; Keyes 2011; Shaw 2010, 2011; Brown 2012) acknowledge the national historical context of the 1970s as a wider vantage point from which to consider a number of key events, which feature in his fiction: amongst them is the figure of the Yorkshire Ripper. This national context is then transposed to look specifically at the state of the North at this time or, as Shaw puts it, positioning 'Yorkshire against a wider (dis) United Kingdom' (p. 25). For instance, Maguire (2011) uses the wider context of 1970s Britain in crisis to discuss localized instances of police corruption in West Yorkshire dating back to the 1950s, as well as the endemic financial malpractice connected to housing and regeneration in local authority 'single party municipal fiefdoms of the North' in the 1970s and 1980s (p. 16). Likewise, Keyes (2011) notes that 'the state of Yorkshire forms the backdrop to Peace's ongoing examination of the social, ideological, physical and economic costs of deindustrialization in the 1970s and 80s' (p. 20). Katy Shaw (2011), who has written extensively about Peace's canon, sums up these links in the following way:

> As a microcosm of the UK during the 1970s, Yorkshire is presented as a county founded on criminality ... The Red Riding Quartet provides a damning analysis of the conditions that conspire to produce specific crimes ... the four novels offer a stark portrait of crime as a product of late twentieth-century British society. (Shaw 2011: 67)

In this way, the Red Riding quartet of novels (*1974, 1977, 1980, and 1983*), and the critical responses they inspire, represent a complex appreciation of the socio-historical and spatial context of crime, identifying the Sutcliffe case as a crime of its time. In doing so, this work demonstrates the criminological and sociological utility of fictional narratives for excavating history and culture (Brown 2003; Gilman Srebnick and Levy 2005) where often, 'fiction can illuminate a time and a place more clearly than fact' (Peace, cited in Shaw 2011: 5).

CLASS, MASCULINITY AND VIOLENCE

Economic and industrial decline feature prominently in the 1970s crisis narratives which have come to define the decade. As Maguire (2011) observes, social and economic crisis was geographically concentrated and was felt especially 'in the old, pre-eminently Victorian, industrial heartlands of Britain' (p. 10). Moreover, as the effects of economic and industrial transformation were fully realized and established in the 1990s and 2000s, academic commentaries have continued to document the impact of the loss of traditional working-class industries on communities and the working-class male subject in terms of crime and violence (Winlow 2001; Hall et al. 2008; Treadwell and Garland 2011; Ellis 2015).

Large scale de-industrialisation of the Northern regions did not fully take hold until the late 1970s and into the 1980s as part of the Thatcher government's dismantling of manufacturing in the United Kingdom (Lewis and Townsend 1989; Bailoni 2014). Having said that, as Maguire (2011) observes, traditional industries across the North were in decline long before Thatcherite closures and selloffs, as the post-war boom faded, replaced by industrial conflict and economic crises (see also Bailoni 2014). For instance, the Northern textile industry, which dominated the cities of Leeds and Bradford and the mill towns of West Yorkshire, had been in long-term decline following the Second World War, but became part of the 'devastation of manufacturing' in the North in the 1980s (Webster 2006; Leeds City Council 2016). Moreover, the marked economic and cultural distinctions between the North and South of the United Kingdom were established long before the acceleration of deindustrialization in the late 1970s and 1980s as industrial specialisms developed in the nineteenth Century. Regional disparities were nevertheless ossified in the 1970s and 1980s as the consequences of Thatcherite economic policy gave rise to increasing social inequality concentrated in former industrial heartlands in the North of England (Bailoni 2014).

The consequences of deindustrialization in the former hubs of manufacturing are well-documented in terms of economic decline and marginalization, the dereliction of physical space and the breakdown of working class culture and community (MacDonald and Marsh 2005; MacDonald et al. 2005; Dorling 2004; Winlow 2001; Hall et al. 2008; Ellis 2015). Much of this body of work concentrates on the implications for the working-class male subject and the proliferation of intra-male violence in these locations (Winlow 2001; Hall et al. 2008; Treadwell and Garland 2011; Ellis 2015)—what Maguire (2011) refers to as 'communal emasculation' within the former industrial regions. As Winlow (2001) points out, '[w]orking-class men have been denied the possibility of expressing a measure of their masculinity through hard manual labour and a considerable number have had their image and self-image further attacked by an absolute rise in unemployment' (p. 64). This has led to the concentration and elevation of violence and criminality in former industrial locales as violence and criminal markets have become a central means of identity formation and economic opportunity for men living in these areas (Winlow 2001; Hall et al. 2008; Treadwell and Garland 2011).

The timeline of deindustrialization, crises of masculinity and the Sutcliffe murders is however, chronologically out of kilter as a means for understanding Sutcliffe's motivations in terms of a 'crisis of masculinity' (Jefferson 1998) brought about deindustrialization. The degeneration of the North was underway in the mid-1970s, but with many men still employed in traditional manufacturing (Sutcliffe himself was a lorry driver for an engineering form), the effects of mass unemployment were not fully realized until the early 1980s (Dorling 2004; Bailoni 2014). Although the dynamics of masculinity in these two historical contexts do share commonalities; we are nevertheless, looking at distinct phases in the history of industrialization, class and masculinity. Notwithstanding, from within this body of work, Treadwell and Garland (2011) stress the importance of adopting a historical perspective on the transformation of working-class masculinity:

> If it is disproportionately those men who face the loss of traditionally stable opportunities that figure most highly in the connection between crime and masculinity (Winlow 2001; Hall 2002), then we must undoubtedly understand the longer historical trajectories and socio-economic, political and cultural forces that shape such masculinities. (p. 624)

Thinking through gender, masculinity and the Sutcliffe murders demands more focus on how Northern working-class masculinity and gender relations during this earlier 1970s period played out in communities such as the one in which Peter Sutcliffe grew up as well as in the wider culture of the North of England in the 1970s and beyond.

Gender relations in the 1970s are characterised in terms of sexual ambivalence relating to the myth of sexual liberation alongside entrenched masculinist ideologies about women's sexual conduct (Roberts 2015), with women still denied basic economic rights such as being able to take out a mortgage or buy a car in their own name (Kimpton Nye, n.d.). O'Hagan (2012) explores child abuse amongst media and institutional figures in the 1960s and 1970s, identifying the seedy and exploitative culture within light entertainment during this period as fostering the conditions for the cult of predatory 'celebrity masculinity' (Boyle 2017) and the sexualisation and abuse of children and young people. This is embodied in the systematic abuse perpetrated by Jimmy Saville and other male celebrities at the time (O'Hagan 2012; Davies 2016). For O'Hagan (2012) the seedy tone and ambivalence towards abuse within the entertainment industry formed part of the 1970s cultural consciousness more generally.

More specifically, Shaw (2011) notes that David Peace's work reflects the 'tightly masculine structure' of Yorkshire and the North of England' where 'violence against women seems to operate at every level of society' (Shaw 2011: 26–31). Peace himself refers to the North, 'with its "violent bloody times" and [h]ard towns for hard men' (Peace 1999: 23, cited in Keyes 2011: 21). Moreover, additional commentaries on the murders from true crime also highlight the 1970s night-time economy in the pubs and clubs in the red-light districts of Leeds and Bradford as sleazy, sexist and pornographic where the objectification and disempowerment of women was commonplace (Yallop 1993; Burn 2004). This is what Shaw (2011), reflecting on Peace's work, refers to as the 'periodicised construction of sexuality' (p. 26).

The links between masculinity and the murders have also been explored in feminist analyses and true crime writing. Feminists situate Sutcliffe's actions within the wider context of masculinity, misogyny and patriarchy (these themes will be explored in greater depth in subsequent chapters); however, feminist analyses have also addressed the fragility of Sutcliffe's masculinity at the individual level (Ward Jouve 1988; Hollway 1981; Smith 2013).

The links between masculine culture and Sutcliffe's biography are also explored extensively in the literary true crime text *Somebody's Husband, Somebody's Son* (Burn 2004). Gordon Burn is a highly regarded writer of true crime and fiction whose body of work has applied literary sensibilities to the nature of crime, violence and celebrity (Myers 2009). Burn was also an influential forerunner to David Peace. Both writers share a preoccupation with interrogating history and culture in order to understand events, and both writers offer alternative criminological epistemologies by way of fictional and true crime narratives (Brown 2003; Wakeman 2013). In *Somebody's Husband, Somebody's Son*, Burn proffers no sociological analysis of his own, but the sociological work is done via his close attention to the 'facts' of the story (Highsmith 1984; Cooke 2016), providing detailed description of Sutcliffe's biography and relationships. In doing so, he presents a 'psycho-social' examination of Sutcliffe and working-class masculinity (Jefferson 1998; Gadd 2000; Treadwell and Garland 2011), positioning Sutcliffe's fragile personal masculinity within a culture of overt masculinity and misogyny amongst his friends and family. Burn identifies aggression, physical prowess, alongside violence against women and 'latent aggression towards women' (Colebrook 2012: 49) as acceptable masculine traits within this small-town Northern community, alluding to a localized and exaggerated version of misogyny (see also Ward Jouve 1988). I explore these themes in more depth in Chapter 6.

These masculine traits extend beyond Sutcliffe and his peer group and are manifest in the police and the wider local culture. For instance, Leeds United football fans chanted Police 0, Ripper 13 and 'Ripper' badges declaring *Leeds United, More Feared than the Ripper*, were sold outside

Leeds United football ground. In terms of the police, sexist attitudes relating to feminine respectability and sexual propriety have been noted as impacting on the course of the investigation (Bland 1992; Smith 2013). Referring to a police dossier on the murders which detailed the characteristics of Sutcliffe's victims, Joan Smith (2013) reveals how the police categorized women as 'innocent' and 'non-innocent' based on class and lifestyle such as drinking, cohabiting and mental 'instability'. Smith (2013) further argues that the police's misogyny led to significant investigative failings because genuine victims were excluded if they did not fit the assumed victim profile of prostitutes and 'good-time girls' pursued by a criminal Other akin to the shadowy and unidentified Victorian Jack the Ripper figure. Moreover, during the murders, West Yorkshire vice squads continued to aggressively pursue and prosecute women engaged in soliciting in the red-light areas of Leeds and Bradford, as well as deploying women as live bait to try and catch the killer (Kinnell 2008).

CRIME, VIOLENCE, SPACE AND PLACE

The links between crime and place are a key focus within criminology. Criminologists explore the links between place, offending, victimisation and fear of crime (Evans et al. 1992; Bottoms and Wiles 1997; Hale 1996). The Chicago School, and later work adopting a similar approach, emphasises the situated and highly localised nature of crime and urban problems in Western cities (Davis 1990; Wacquant 2008). However, as Downes and Rock (2007) point out, the focus on crime and place does not merely relate to the concentration of rates of offending, victimization and the number of offenders living in particular neighbourhoods, but also to crime meanings which attach themselves to particular locales, and which circulate within the social imaginary (Bottoms et al. 1987; Wattis et al. 2011). And this is a twofold process, relating to the interplay between criminogenic urban topographies and the transformation of space/place by acts of crime and violence (Jenks 2003; Linnemann 2015). So for instance, writing about the Kray twins, Jenks (2003) observes how '[t]he twins' tale is and always will be inextricably bound to the signs, symbols, rituals and folklore of London's East End' (p. 114). However, in the case of the Krays, Jenks also highlights the material conditions which led to the emergence of criminal cultures and organized crime in the East End, identifying the physical division of London and the concentration of poor and immigrant populations in East End ghettoes. In this way, social and material forces combined to produce crime realities alongside representations where '[o]utstanding and exaggerated cultural motifs have become lodged in history and folklore' (pp. 122–123). Likewise, Walkowitz (1982) has shown how the White Chapel murders involving the murder of five women linked to prostitution in 1888 in London's East End, which invoked the figure of Jack the Ripper, became synonymous with poverty and crime in the East End, forming the locus for middle-class fears about the dangerous classes and 'urban degeneracy'. Walkowitz (1982) argues that 'Whitechapel thus provided a stark and sensational backdrop for the Ripper murders: a moral landscape of light and darkness, a nether region of illicit sex and crime, both exciting and dangerous' (p. 547).

In the same way, the 'Yorkshire Ripper' has become associated with the social and economic decline of Northern England in the 1970s, which manifests not just socially and culturally, but within the deterioration of urban and industrial space (Maguire 2011; Keyes 2011; Shaw 2010; Ward Jouve 1988). For instance, Langstraat (2006) observes how the collapse of the textile industry in Leeds left in its wake the abandonment and depreciation of former industrial spaces around the Leeds core periphery. Ward Jouve (1988) makes links between the murders and their physical backdrop, reflecting on 'what connections there were between the socio-economic dereliction which much of the geography expressed, and the type of violence which was at work in the nooks and crannies of those landscapes' (p. 18). Burn (2004) also explores the cultural and physical backdrop of the murders, describing how the grand houses of Chapeltown, which were the legacy of the Victorian textile industry in West Yorkshire, were now a 'picture of 'inner-city' dereliction and decay'. Burn (2004) depicts the topography of Chapeltown in the 1970s as characterised by bedsits and boarding houses, down market pubs and illegal drinking clubs.

As Shaw (2011) notes, 'The Yorkshire Ripper operates alone, usually at night, within the sites created by post-industrial fallout (p. 67). Indeed, many of Peter Sutcliffe's victims were attacked and abandoned in maze-like alleyways—an characteristic feature of the terraced streets of the North of England: spaces between places—waste ground between allotments, cemeteries and industrial sites, playing fields, playgrounds, parklands, factory and railway yards. This is what Biressi (2001) refers to as 'the cartographies of murder' (p. 171). An example of this is Burn's description of Huddersfield's red-light district, Great Northern Street, where 19 year-old Helen Rytka was murdered and left in a timber yard: '[i]ts railway arches and its abattoir … its general air of rankness and dereliction' (Burn, p. 197).

Hall and Wilson (2014) identify the macro roots of serial murder in social instability, inequality and cultures of competitive individualism which characterize the neo-liberal economic order (see also Grover and Soothill 1999; Haggerty 2009; Wilson 2007, 2012; Harrison and Wilson 2008). But Hall and Wilson (2014) insert an additional level to their analysis of serial murder by focusing on the meso—the intermediate setting between the micro and the macro, to draw attention to the spatiality of serial killing. Namely, the fact that offenders often target victims in depreciated, empty, liminal spaces created by industrialization and deindustrialization which are imbued with situational risk. These spaces emerged during industrialisation and are a staple feature of urban industrial and post-industrial landscapes. A 'former part of the urban social body' (p. 647), they have ceased to function in a positive way and are no longer subject to civic and state regulation (Atkinson and Parker 2011; Hayward 2012). As such, these are the spaces which provide the situational conditions for violence and homicide because they offer 'both victims and prolonged concealment' (Hall and Wilson 2014: 646).

The urban spaces of industrial and post-industrial dereliction outlined by Hall and Wilson frequently overlap as the liminal spaces of street-prostitution/sex work (Ellison and Weitzer 2015; Harrison and Wilson 2008). Historically, the regulation of sex work in public space has related to its spatiality and attempts by vested interests to remove prostitution/sex work from public space (Lowman 1992; Kinnell 2008; Sanders 2016). The criminalization and regulation of street-sex workers forces them to work in these liminal spaces, which as many commentators highlight, exacerbate their vulnerability to violence and serial murder due to situational factors and contact with other criminal markets (Sanders and Campbell 2007; Sanders 2016). As Sanders (2016) observes, '[t]he very physicality of the "red light district" suggests vulnerability' (p. 100). Global, technological and economic forces have transformed the 'geographies of sex work' in late capitalism and street prostitution represents one small part of the sex industry (Hubbard and Whowell 2008; Sanders 2016). These liminal spaces and their anti-social nature, nonetheless continue to define prostitution in the public and policy imagination (Sanders 2016). In this way, the social and spatial organization of prostitution, its governance via the criminal justice system which has resulted in the criminalisation and stigmatisation of sex workers, has normalized violence against sex workers and rendered it socially and situationally possible (Lowman 1992; Kinnell 2008; Ferris 2015; Sanders 2016).

Feminist work on space, gender and fear has also highlighted how the structural factors which account for women's greater fearfulness become realized specifically as spatial experiences (Valentine 1989, 1992; Stanko 1990, 1997; Pain 1991; Koskela 1997). In this way, although not all of Peter Sutcliffe's victims were linked to prostitution/sex work and not all were attacked in the types of spaces described above, all of his victims were attacked at times and in places which women are encouraged to fear as part of the gendered spatialisation of fear.

VIOLENCE, HAUNTOLOGY AND PLACE

Despite the attempt s made to exorcise them, the spaces we travel through are alive with ghosts of the dead. Attached to homes, towns and people, the ghosts conjured by cultural production continue to make themselves known. So, if we are to 'learn to live' we must confront these ghosts of past violence and reckon the force of haunting as a social phenomenon (Derrida 2006). (Linnemann 2015: 530)

I don't like that road … I've just been looking for accommodation for my daughter and one of the, as soon as they said Alma Road, I, I knew where it was and I thought "urrgh", But it was on the list and it looks like it was quite nice flats. You know perfectly and it looks well-lit and that now. But you have to drive past. It's on, you know, it's just further up on the left hand side and I just, even though it's totally irrational, I did, I just checked that off the list sort of "no". It's the right price range … a nice flat and everything but no. You know that's a totally irrational fear of that street and there's nothing wrong with that street now. It's not, it's no different, and it's probably safer than ten of the other streets that I've looked at. But in my mind that's not a possibility to get accommodation on that street.

Extract from interview with Anna who grew up in Headingley where Jacqueline Hill was murdered in November 1980.

The discussion thus far has centred on history and place, as both backdrop and potential catalyst for the Sutcliffe murders. Interrogating the locations of crime should not just be concerned with criminogenic contexts as they foreground criminal events, but should also focus on the transformation of place in the wake of crime and violence, and the interplay between the two. As Sparks et al. (2001) observe:

When people talk about crime they are often also talking about places...
We may not for the most part have understood very clearly how powerfully
those metaphors and meanings are relayed through the representation of
places and the creation of 'place myths' (Lash and Urry 1994; Shields 1991).
(Sparks et al. 2001: 887, their emphasis)

Relatedly, Jenks (2003) notes how past events become 'striking images'
that are projected onto particular geographies' (p. 114). To return to
the Sutcliffe case, Leeds-based artist Emma Bolland explored the lasting presence of the Sutcliffe murders using visual images, text and
audio, noting that it is the anonymity of the spaces of violence and the
attempts to erase the horror of past events which intensifies their violent history: 'It is the ordinary which heightens and defines the extraor-
dinary' (Bolland n.d.). In this way place and crime become irrevocably
linked. So for instance, Gordon Burn maintains that in the ten years
following the murders, Bradford 'remains the city of the Ripper'
(p. 349). This is evidenced by the fact that the house in Bradford where
Peter Sutcliffe lived with his wife Sonia has become a site of 'dark tour-
ism' for those who want to experience 'the frisson of 'the Ripper's
house' (Burn 2004: 349). The murder of three women involved in
prostitution in Bradford's 'red-light district' by Stephen Griffiths in
2009 reinvigorates the connection between murder and liminality in
these locations (Ward Jouve 2010). Moreover, allusions to cannibalism and the media's reference to Griffiths as the 'Crossbow Cannibal'
reflect and reinforce macabre fascination with the 'Ripper' figure which
began with the White Chapel murders and has persisted thereafter
(Caputi 1987; Downing 2013).

The interview quote which begins this section comes from the
oral history project. In the extract Anna discusses the location where
Jacqueline Hill, Sutcliffe's last victim, was murdered in Headingley in
November 1980. Headingley was a leafy suburb of Leeds where many
students lived, Anna had grown up in the area and at the time she was
interviewed had recently returned to Leeds to look for student accommodation for her daughter. As the extract highlights, returning to the
area had provoked a strong emotional response which can be understood in terms haunting and spectrality (Derrida 1994; Gordon 2008;
Pilar Blanco and Pereen 2013). These concepts have been deployed
by a number of writers to make sense of 'haunting's attachment to

place' (Pilar Blanco and Pereen 2013: 395) and the way in which past events—often involving violence and atrocity, continue to 'haunt' social space. Linnemann (2015) refers to this as the 'phenomenology of place' Linnemann (p. 517), arguing that acts of violence and the cultural texts they inspire 'animate social space with spectral power (Bell 1997; Gordon 2008; Armstrong 2010)' (Linnemann 2015: 517). Shaw (2010) also draws attention to spectrality and haunting as devices in David Peace's work where 'intertextual haunts' (p. 53), serve to emphasise the 'intrinsically haunted nature of the contemporary world' (p. 48).

Linnemann (2015) draws upon 'haunting' in his interrogation of the murder of a Kansas farming in 1959, which inspired Trueman Capote's literary true crime text In Cold Blood—lauded as a pioneering work of the true crime genre, in which 'Capote reported on real crimes with the artistic detail and aesthetic beauty of lyrical fiction' (Linnemann 2015: 515). Linnemann (2015) argues that 'tracing the figures brought into being by Capote' highlights 'the ways in which the ghosts attached to people, places and things, linger in the social imaginary' (p. 517). In this way, acts of violence become inscribed onto spaces which are irrevocably transformed as sites of commemoration and macabre fascination:

> For decades, these ghosts have lured 'dark tourists' to a non-descript cross-roads in Dallas to relive the assassination of a young President (Foley and Lennon 1996), somber travelers to grey fields in Poland to remember the savagery of the Holocaust (Brown 2009) and this writer, to a lonesome farmhouse far 'out there' on the Kansas plains to contemplate the murder of an entire family … It is here in this haunted cultural ether that the assassin still stands armed with his rifle, cattle cars remain stacked with emaciated, tortured bodies and four shotgun blasts perpetually claim six human lives. (Linneman 2015: 518)

For Linnemann it is 'the spectacularisation' inherent to true crime which establishes and calls forth violent events in space and time: 'the scenes of their violent creations haunt the pages of In Cold Blood, its readers, the homes and lonely landscapes of western Kansas (Linnemann 2015: 530). Certainly, Yallop's (1993) vivid descriptions of the 1970s night-time economy in the 'red-light' areas of Leeds and Bradford, and his commentary on the policing of street soliciting during the murders and Burn's (2004) study of Sutcliffe via the presentation of the minutiae of small town working-class life perform this function in the context of the Sutcliffe case. Equally, fictional representations 'animate' the situated nature of past violence and play to the inherent emotionality of place (Smith et al. 2005). David Peace's work has been discussed at length in this respect, but Pat Barker's novel *Blow Your House Down*, which presents a fictional depiction of working-class women involved in street prostitution in an unnamed Northern city where a serial killer is targeting women, does similar creative criminological work in calling forth images of urban liminality overlaid with violence. Chapter 6 will explore in more depth the importance of popular criminological texts for addressing sociological and criminological concerns.

The relationship between crime, place and history appears on the one hand as self-evident. For instance, there are clear links between social inequality, economic marginalization and the geographical concentration of violence in late capitalist societies (Currie 2009; Dorling 2004; Brookman 2005; Hall and MacLean 2009; Winlow 2001; Hall et al. 2008). Equally, the historically and geographically situated nature of serial murder would suggest that time, place and other macro-level factors can offer enhanced understandings of such violence (Soothill 1996; Haggerty 2009; Wilson 2007; Hickey 2013). Moreover, a closer examination of specific cases often go a step further, scrutinizing the role of culturally and historically specific factors as the contexts for such violence (Downing 2013; Wilson 2013; Hall and Wilson 2014). In the case of the Yorkshire Ripper, the concentration of economic and industrial crisis in the North of England, physical/industrial dereliction, and gender structures and cultures which determine the social, legal and material conditions of prostitution and the position and worth of women more generally are recognized as the backdrop to these murders. All of the above characterize the North of England in the 1970s and have led to claims that the case was a crime of its time and place when both macro and meso levels of explanations are taken into account (Burn 2004; Upson 2001; Shaw 2010, 2011). This chapter has sought to deal with this local and historical specificity, as well as considering how place meanings are altered in the wake of criminal events. That said, the extract below from an article written for the feminist magazine *Spare Rib* in 1981, shortly after Peter Sutcliffe was arrested, puts forth a different view, critiquing how the media at the time drew upon the trope of the culture and physicality of North to understand the murders:

Another technique might be termed the Argument from Geography. The murders, several 'background' pieces suggested, were the product of a particular environment: tough, northern, working-class, patriarchal, sordid and commercial – a place where sex could be described as 'business'. Elsewhere in England's green and pleasant land, apparently sex is wholly unrelated to money, there is no industry or pollution, and men do not attack women. (Merck 1981: 17)

Merck's comments illustrate how violence against women transcends the local and how this Northern-centred, localized framing of the murders runs the risk of viewing this violence solely in terms of Northern working-class masculinity, which detracts from male violence against women and femicide as systemic in the context of patriarchy (Caputi 1987; Hollway 1981; Radford 1992; Mackay 2015). So in this respect, David Peace's claim regarding the possibility of a 'Cornwall Ripper, which featured earlier in the chapter, is altogether possible even if situational and cultural circumstances may differ. Moreover, recent revelations regarding sexual harassment and abuse in the film industry, the charity sector and other institutions further highlights that misogyny, harassment and sexual violence are not bounded by place and history and are therefore not an exclusive characteristic of 1970s gender relations. Having said that, as demonstrated in this chapter, locally and historically-specific conditions can nonetheless expand our understandings of the social and situational nature of violence and murder, institutional responses to it and their representation.

References

Atkinson, R., & Parker, S. (2011, July 7–9). *The Autotomic City: The Strategic Ejection of Unruly Urban Space*. International RC21 Conference on Urban Order, Crime and Citizenship, Amsterdam.

Bailoni, M. (2014). *The Effects of Thatcherism in the Urban North of England*. Metropolitics.eu. www.metropolitiques.eu/The-effects=of-Thatcherism-in-the-html.

Bartol, C. R., & Bartol, A. M. (2008). *Criminal Behaviour a Psychosocial Approach* (8th ed.). New York: Pearson.

Beckett, A. (2010). *When the Lights Went Out: What Really Happened to Britain in the Seventies*. London: Faber and Faber.

Biressi, A. (2001). *Crime, Fear and the Law in True Crime Stories*. New York: Palgrave Macmillan.

Bland, L. (1992). The Case of the Yorkshire Ripper: Mad, Bad, Beast or Male? In J. Radford & D. E. H. Russell (Eds.), *Femicide: The Politics of Women Killing*. Buckingham: Open University Press.

Bolland, E. (n.d.). Emma Bolland: (Short Paper For Occursus 'Post-traumatic Landscapes Symposium'). *Every Place a Palimpsest* (Part Two).

Bottoms, A. E., & Wiles, P. (1997). Environmental Criminology. In M. Maguire, R. Moran, & R. Reiner (Eds.), *Oxford Handbook of Criminology*. Oxford: Clarendon Press.

Bottoms, A. E., Mawby, R. I., & Walker, M. A. (1987). A Localised Crime Survey in Contrasting Areas of a City. *British Journal of Criminology, 27*, 125–154.

Boyle, K. (2017). Hiding in Plain Sight. *Journalism Studies, 19*(11), 1562–1578.

Brookman, F. (2005). *Understanding Homicide*. London: Sage.

Brown, R. (2012). 'Armageddon Was Yesterday—Today We Have a Serious Problem': Pre and Postmillennial Tropes for Crime and Criminality by David Peace and Stieg Larsson. In C. Gregoriou (Ed.), *Constructing Crime: Discourse and Cultural Representations of Crime and 'Deviance'*. Basingstoke: Palgrave Macmillan.

Brown, S. (2003). *Crime and Law in Media Culture*. Buckingham: Open University Press.

Burn, G. (2004). *Somebody's Husband, Somebody's Son*. London: Viking.

Cameron, D., & Frazer, E. (1987). *The Lust to Kill*. Cambridge: Polity.

Caputi, J. (1987). *The Age of the Sex Crime*. Bowling Green: Bowling Green State University Popular Press.

Colebrook, M. (2012). The Edgier Waters of the Era: Gordon Burn's Somebody's Husband, Somebody's Son. In C. Gregoriou (Ed.), *Constructing Crime: Discourse and Cultural Representations of Crime and 'Deviance'*. Basingstoke: Palgrave Macmillan.

Cooke, R. (2016, July 16). Somebody's Husband, Somebody's Son: An Unflinching Look at the Yorkshire Ripper. *The Guardian*.

Currie, E. (2009). *The Roots of Danger: Violent Crime in Global Perspective*. Upper Saddle River, NJ: Prentice Hall.

Davies, D. (2016). *In Plain Sight: The Life and Lies of Jimmy Saville*. London: Quercus.

Davis, M. (1990). *City of Quartz: Excavating the Future in Los Angeles*. New York: Verso.

Derrida, J. (1994). *Specters of Marx: The State of the Debt, the Work of Mourning and the New International*. New York and London: Routledge.

Dorling, D. (2004). Prime Suspect: Murder in Britain. In C. Pantazis, S. Tombs, & D. Gordon (Eds.), *Beyond Criminology: Taking Harm Seriously*. London: Pluto Press.

Downes, D., & Rock, P. (2007). *Understanding Deviance: A Guide to the Sociology of Crime and Rule Breaking*. Oxford: Oxford University Press.

Downing, L. (2013). *The Subject of Murder*. Chicago: University of Chicago Press.

Ellis, A. (2015). *Men, Masculinities and Violence: An Ethnographic Approach*. London: Routledge.

Ellison, G., & Weitzer, R. (2015). The Dynamics of Male and Female Street Prostitution in Manchester, England. *Men and Masculinities, 20*(2), 181–203.

Evans, D., Fyfe, N., & Herbert, D. (Eds.). (1992). *Crime, Policing and Place: Essays in Environmental Criminology.* London: Routledge.

Ferris, S. (2015). *Street Sex Work and Canadian Cities: Resisting a Dangerous Order.* Alberta: University of Alberta Press.

Gadd, D. (2000). Masculinities, Violence and Defended Psychosocial Subjects. *Theoretical Criminology, 4*(4), 429–449.

Gilman Srebnick, A., & Levy, R. (2005). *Crime and Culture: An Historical Perspective.* Aldershot: Ashgate.

Gilroy, P. (2002). *There Ain't No Black in the Union Jack: The Cultural Politics of Race and Nation.* London: Routledge.

Gordon, A. (2008). *Ghostly Matters: Haunting and the Sociological Imagination.* University of Minnesota Press.

Grover, L., & Soothill, K. (1999). British Serial Killing: Towards a Structural Explanation. *The British Criminology Conferences: Selected Proceedings,* Volume 2. Papers from the British Criminology Conference, Queens University, Belfast, 15–19 July 1997. This volume published March 1999. Editor: Mike Brogden.

Haggerty, K. (2009). Modern Serial Killers. *Crime, Media, Culture, 5,* 168.

Hale, C. (1996). Fear of Crime: A Review of the Literature. *International Review of Victimology, 4*(2), 79–150.

Hall, S., & MacLean, C. (2009). A Tale of Two Capitalisms: Preliminary Spatial and Historical Comparisons of Homicide rates in Western Europe and the USA. *Theoretical Criminology, 13,* 303–319.

Hall, S., & Wilson, D. (2014). New Foundations: Pseudo-Pacification and Special Liberty as Potential Cornerstones for a Multi-level Theory of Homicide and Serial Murder. *European Journal of Criminology, 11*(5), 635–655.

Hall, S., Winlow, S., & Ancrum, C. (2008). *Criminal Identities and Consumer Culture: Crime, Exclusion and the Culture of Narcissism.* Cullompton: Willan.

Harrison, P., & Wilson, D. (2008). *Hunting Evil: Inside the Ipswich Serial Murders.* London: Sphere.

Hayward, K. (2012). Cultural Geography, Space and Crime. In S. Hall & S. Winlow (Eds.), *New Directions in Criminological Theory.* London: Routledge.

Hickey, E. W. (2013). *Serial Murders and Their Victims* (6th ed.). Wadsworth: Cengage Learning.

Highsmith, P. (1984). Fallen Women. *London Review of Books, 6*(11), 20–22.

Hobsbawn, E. (1995). *Age of Extremes: The Short Twentieth Century 1914–1991.* London: Abacus.

Hollway, W. (1981, October). 'I Just Wanted to Kill a Woman' Why? The Ripper and Male Sexuality. *Feminist Review, 9,* 33–40.

Holmes, R. M., & Holmes, S. T. (1996). *Profiling Violent Crimes: An Investigative Tool*. Thousand Oaks: Sage.

Hubbard, P., & Whowell, M. (2008). Revisiting the Red Light District: Still Neglected, Immoral and Marginal? *Geoforum, 39*(5), 1743–1755.

Jacobsen Hviid, M. (2014). *The Poetics of Crime: Understanding and Researching Crime and Deviance Through Creative Sources*. New York: Routledge.

Jefferson, T. (1998). "Muscle", "Hard Men" and "Iron" Mike Tyson: Reflections on Desire, Anxiety and the Embodiment of Masculinity. *Body and Society, 4*(1), 77–98.

Jenkins, P. (1994). *Using Murder: The Social Construction of Serial Homicide*. New York: Routledge.

Jenks, C. (2003). *Transgression*. London: Routledge.

Keyes, J. (2011). "No Redemption": The Death of the City in the Work of David Peace. In K. Shaw (Ed.), *Analysing David Peace*. Cambridge: Cambridge Scholars.

Kinnell, H. (2008). *Violence and Sex Work in Britain*. Cullompton: Willan.

Koskela, H. (1997). 'Bold Walk and Breakings': Women's Spatial Confidence Versus Fear of Violence. *Gender, Place and Culture, 4*, 301–319.

Langstraat, J. W. (2006). The Urban Regeneration Industry in Leeds: Measuring Sustainable Urban Regeneration Performance. *Earth & Environment, 2*, 167–210.

Leeds City Council. (2016). *Leeds Economy Handbook*.

Leyton, E. (1986). *Hunting Humans: The Rise of the Modern Multiple Murderer*. Toronto: McClelland and Stewart.

Lewis, J., & Townsend, A. (1989). *The North-South Divide: Regional Change in Britain in the 1980s*. London: Paul Chapman.

Linnemann, T. (2015). Capote's Ghosts: Violence, Murder and the Spectre of Suspicion. *British Journal of Criminology, 55*, 514–533.

Lowman, J. (1992). Street Prostitution Control: Some Canadian Reflections on the Finsbury Park Experience. *The British Journal of Criminology, 32*(1), 1–17.

MacDonald, R., & Marsh, J. (2005). *Disconnected Youth: Growing Up in Britain's Poorest Neighbourhoods*. Basingstoke: Palgrave Macmillan.

MacDonald, R., Shildrick, T., Webster, C., & Simpson, D. (2005). Growing Up in Poor Neighbourhoods: The Significance of Class and Place in the Extended Transitions of Socially Excluded Young Adults. *Sociology, 39*(5), 873–891.

Mackay, F. (2015). *Radical Feminism: Feminist Activism in Movement*. London: Palgrave Macmillan.

Maguire, P. (2011). Politics and Class in the 1970s/80s. In K. Shaw (Ed.), *Analysing David Peace*. Cambridge: Cambridge Scholars.

Merck, M. (1981, July). Sutcliffe: What the Papers Say. *Spare Rib, 10*.

Myers, B. (2009, July 22). Gordon Burn Was One of the Greatest Writers of His Age. *The Guardian.*

O'Hagan, A. (2012, November 8). Light Entertainment: Andrew O'Hagan Writes About Child Abuse and the British Public. *London Review of Books.* https://www.lrb.co.uk/v34/n21/andrew-ohagan/light-entertainment.

Pain, R. (1991). Space, Sexual Violence and Social Control: Integrating Geographical and Feminist Analyses of Women's Fear of Crime. *Progress in Human Geography, 15,* 415–431.

Peace, D. (1999). *Nineteen Seventy Four.* London: Serpents Tail.

Pilar Blanco, M. D., & Pereen, E. (2013). Possessions: Spectral Places/ Introduction. In M. D. Pilar Blanco & E. Pereen (Eds.), *The Spectralities Reader.* London: Bloomsbury.

Purcell, C., & Arrigo, B. (2006). *The Psychology of Lust Murder.* Burlington, MA: Elsevier.

Radford, J. (1992). Introduction. In J. Radford & D. Russell (Eds.), *Femicide: The Politics of Woman Killing.* New York, NY: Twayne.

Roberts, Y. (2015, April 15). 'Ooh You Were Awful': Why I Can't Look Back on the Sexist Seventies With Kindness. *The Observer.*

Runciman, D. (2013). The Crisis of British Democracy: Back to the '70s or Stuck in the Present? *Institute for Public Policy Research.* https://www.ippr/juncture/the-crisis-of-british-democracy-back-to-70s-or-stuck-in-the-present.

Sanders, T. (2016). Inevitably Violent? Dynamics of Space, Governance and Stigma. *Special Issue: Problematizing Prostitution: Critical Research and Scholarship, Studies in Law, Politics and Society, 71,* 93–114.

Sanders, T., & Campbell, R. (2007). Designing Out Vulnerability, Building in Respect: Violence Safety and Sex Work Policy. *The British Journal of Sociology, 58*(1), 1–19.

Schmid, D. (2005). *Natural Born Celebrities: Serial Killers in American Culture.* London: University of Chicago Press.

Seltzer, M. (1998). *Serial Killers: Death and Life in America's Wound Culture.* London: Sage.

Shaw, K. (2010). *David Peace: Texts and Contexts.* Brighton: Sussex Academic Press.

Shaw, K. (Ed.). (2011). *Analysing David Peace.* Cambridge: Cambridge Scholars.

Smith, J. (2013). *Misogynies: Reflections on Myth and Malice.* New York: Fawcett Columbine.

Smith, M., Bondi, L., & Davidson, J. (Eds.). (2005). *Emotional Geographies.* Aldershot: Ashgate.

Soothill, K. (1996). Murder: The Importance of the Structural and Cultural Conditions. *Journal of Forensic Medicine, 3,* 161–165.

Sparks, R., Girling, E., & Loader, I. (2001). Fear and Everyday Urban Lives. *Urban Studies, 38*(5–6), 885–898.

Stanko, E. (1990). *Everyday Violence: How Women and Men Experience Physical and Sexual Danger.* Pandora Press.

Stanko, E. (1997). Safety Talk: Conceptualising Women's Risk Assessment as a Technology of the Soul. *Theoretical Criminology, 1*(4), 479–499.

Tatar, M. (1995). *Lustmord: Sexual Murder in Weimar Germany.* Princeton: Princeton University Press.

Treadwell, J., & Garland, J. (2011). Masculinity, Marginalisation and Violence: A Case Study of the English Defence League. *British Journal of Criminology, 11*(5), 1171–1193.

Upson, N. (2001, August 20). Hunting the Yorkshire Ripper. *New Statesman.*

Valentine, G. (1989). The Geography of Women's Fear. *Area, 21,* 385–390.

Valentine, G. (1992). Images of Danger: Women's Sources of Information About the Spatial Distribution of Male Violence. *Area, 24,* 22–29.

Wacquant, L. (2008). *Urban Outcasts: A Comparative Sociology of Advanced Marginality.* Cambridge: Polity.

Wakeman, S. (2013). 'No One Wins. One Side Just Loses More Slowly': The Wire and Drug Policy. *Theoretical Criminology, 18,* 224–239.

Walkowitz, J. (1982). Jack the Ripper and Myth of Male Violence. *Feminist Studies, 8*(3), 542–574.

Ward Jouve, N. (1988). *The Street Cleaner.* New York: Marion Boyars.

Ward Jouve, N. (2010, May 29). Bradford Murders Show Area Still Beset by Death, 30 Years After Ripper Case. *The Guardian.*

Wattis, L., Green, E., & Radford, J. (2011). Women Students' Perceptions of Crime and Safety: Negotiating Fear and Risk in an English Post-industrial Landscape. *Gender, Place and Culture, 18*(6), 749–767.

Webber, C. (2010). *Psychology and Crime.* London: Sage.

Webster, C. (2006). Race, Space and Fear: Imagined Geographies of Racism, Crime, Violence and Disorder in Northern England. *Capitalism and Class, 80,* 95–122.

Wender, J. (2015). The Phenomenology of Arrest: A Case Study in Poetics of Police-Citizen Encounters. In M. H. Jacobsen (Ed.), *The Poetics of Crime: Understanding and Researching Crime and Deviance Through Creative Sources.* London: Ashgate.

Wilson, D. (2007). *Serial Killers: Hunting Britons and Their Victims 1966–2006.* Hampshire Hook: Waterside Press.

Wilson, D. (2012). Late Capitalism, Vulnerable Populations and Violent Predatory Crime. In S. Hall & S. Winlow (Eds.), *New Directions in Criminological Theory.* London: Routledge.

Wilson, D. (2013). *Mary Ann Cotton: Britain's First Female Serial Killer.* Hook Hants: Waterside Press.

Wilson, D., Yardley, R., & Pemberton, S. (2016). The 'Dunblane Massacre' as a 'Photosensitive Plate'. *Crime, Media, Culture, 13,* 1–14.

Winlow, S. (2001). *Badfellas.* Oxford: Berg.

Yallop, D. (1993). *Deliver Us from Evil.* Reading: Cox and Wyman.

CHAPTER 3

Structural and Cultural Perspectives on Serial Murder

Abstract This chapter analyses serial murder on a number of levels. Firstly, it acknowledges the dominance of psychologically-informed perspectives on serial killing in both the academic and popular imagination. The discussion then moves on to explore approaches which stress the importance of history, social structure and culture in explaining the proliferation of serial murder and the growing ubiquity and fascination with the figure of the serial killer in US and British culture in late modernity. The latter part of the chapter then examines feminist structural and cultural analyses of femicide and serial murder. The chapter concludes by arguing for greater integration between feminist approaches and social structural approaches which privilege class and the political economy as a means of theorising and accounting for the proliferation of serial murder in late capitalist societies.

Keywords Psychological explanations of serial murder · Structural and cultural approaches to serial murder · Modernity · Neo-liberalism · Serial murderer and popular culture · Masculinity · Feminism · Femicide

© The Author(s) 2018
L. Wattis, *Revisiting the Yorkshire Ripper Murders*,
Palgrave Studies in Victims and Victimology,
https://doi.org/10.1007/978-3-030-01385-1_3

INTRODUCTION

Psychological explanations which focus on individualised psychogical disorders dominate theorising and research on serial murder (Soothill 1993; Fox and Levin 2005; Purcell and Arrigo 2006; Webber 2010). The privileging of psychopathology means that the broader socio-cultural context of serial killing is often overlooked. However, work on serial killing has developed to include a growing body of work which analyses the role of structure and culture in etiology. This chapter explores differing perspectives on serial murder, focusing primarily on socio-structural explanations (Leyton 1986; Soothill 1996; Grover and Soothill 1999; Haggerty 2009; Wilson 2012) which identify the proliferation of serial killing in the context of modernity, late modernity and the neo-liberal social and economic order. In brief, key elements from this argument identify how interconnected features of modernity, capitalism and the free market economy, such as enhanced individualism, means-end rationality, widening inequality and a reduction in state protection, validates the mindset of the serial killer in late capitalism and fosters greater victim vulnerability.

Furthermore, the serial killer as popular cultural invention in modernity and late modenity eclipses the 'reality' of serial killing. Indeed, in the representational sphere, serial murder assumes a reality all of its own, which shapes popular and academic misconceptions about incidence and motivation (Jenkins 1994; Soothill 1996; Schmid 2005; Seltzer 1998; Downing 2013; Linnemann 2015). With this in mind, I also explore how the serial murderer emerged within popular culture, tracing this back to the 1888 White Chapel murders and the emergence of the Jack the Ripper figure, whose cultural presence went far beyond the reality of the murders themselves. Fueled by cultural production, the popularity and fascination with this type of murderer continued throughout the Twentieth Century to become a cultural mainstay.

The latter part of the chapter explores feminist structural and cultural perspectives on serial murder. Feminist work in this field identifies serial murder as an example of femicide and violence against women in the context of patriarchy, misogyny and masculinity. In addition, feminist analyses on reveal how the cultural default is to the celebrate the male killer and objectify, blame or deny the female victim any cultural presence.

To conclude the chapter, I assess feminist analyses alongside class-based, economic approaches, identifying feminism's strength in positioning serial murder in the wider context of patriarchy, but conceding that feminist analyses falter when we go beyond male offenders and female victims. In contrast, approaches favouring the political economy present a broader sense of structural and cultural conditions which shape offending and victimhhood (Hall and Wilson 2014; Jenkins 1994; Schmid 2005). To generate fresh insight and understandings of violence, and serial killing specifically, these distinct approaches would benefit from additional amalgamation.

The Psychology of Serial Murder

Definitions of serial murder vary in terms of number of victims, but there is consensus that this type of homicide involves two, three or more victims separated by time and location (Jenkins 1994; Egger 1984; Wilson 2007; Salfati et al. 2008). There is also some debate in the literature relating to motive where many writers maintain serial killing is not instrumental violence (Holmes and Holmes 1996; Hickey 2013). What this means is serial murder is killing for its own sake—for psychological/emotional gratification, as opposed to 'rational' or instrumental motivation. Indeed, both the academic and popular imaginary share a preoccupation with the serial killer as a solitary and psychologically pathological figure motivated by sexual gratification (Soothill 1993; Fox and Levin 2005; Purcell and Arrigo 2006; Webber 2010). As such, the quest to understand the serial killer at the level of the psychological has been dominated by the identification of a 'configuration of causes' (Wiest 2011: 82), linked to troubled biographies, personality disorders, participation in inappropriate leisure activities and so forth (Vronsky 2004). As Hinch and Hepburn (1998) note:

> '[t]he stereotype of a sexually sadistic killer has become paradigmatic in scholarly efforts to understand serial killers' and reflects the inclination to cluster psychological characteristics which render the serial killer psychologically and socially distinct in order to serve 'sensational interests'.

So for instance, Hickey (2013) identifies a range of psychological 'disorders' such as psychosis, neurosis and dissociative disorders, which are often linked to violent motivations; however, he further argues that the connections between psychological deficit and serial murder are often empirically weak. That said, despite discrediting clear connections, Hickey (2013) maintains that the majority of serial killers demonstrate some constellation of 'anti-social qualities but not in the same manner' (p. 79). Moreover, both popular and academic approaches often assume motivation relates to power and sexual gratification (Keppel and Walter 1999; Salfati and Bateman 2005). Again, Hickey (2013) both refutes and accepts these links, arguing that even where there is no explicit connection supporting sexual gratification as a motive, there is nonetheless the possibility that 'latent sexual motivations exist unknown even to the offender' (p. 79).

The drive to understand the etiology of the serial killer has its origins in offender profiling or 'personality typing' adopted by the U.S. Federal Bureau of Investigation (FBI) whose work sought to isolate and understand the 'criminal personality' by 'identifying the gross psychological characteristics of an individual based upon an analysis of the crimes he or she committed and providing a general description of the person utilizing those traits' (Ressler et al. 1988, cited in Canter et al. 2004). This resulted in the categorization of killers as either organized or disorganized (Douglas et al. 1986, 1992; Ressler et al. 1988). What this means is that the nature of the murder and the features of the crime scene are used to glean aspects of biography and 'read' the perpetrator's personality. Organized killers are thus presumed to be intelligent and sociable individuals who plan their crimes and target strangers; whereas disorganized killers are constructed as socially isolated loners in low status occupations who murder spontaneously. Other typologies have since been developed based upon the organized/disorganized framework which seek to further isolate motivational drivers and personality types (Holmes and DeBurger 1988; Keppel and Walter 1999; Holmes and Holmes 1996). However, this and other similar typologies have been criticised on methodological and empirical grounds (Blackburn 1993; Webber 2010; Canter et al. 2004; Bennell et al. 2013). Refutations of these dominant taxonomies have led Bennell et al. (2013) to question 'whether any model is likely to be found that can accurately capture the distinguishing features of serial murder/murderers' (p. 19). At the same time, Canter et al. (2004), whilst disabusing the organized/disorganised paradigm, have concluded that 'rather than being one sub-type of the serial killer, being organized is typical of serial killers as a whole' (p. 312). The UK psychological approach espoused by Canter and colleagues (Canter 2001; Canter and Wentinck 2004; Canter et al. 2004) circumvents some of these issues as it is primarily concerned with the situational characteristics of serial murder as opposed to the formulation of psychological taxonomies. This involves 'reading' crime scenes and/or crime scene behaviour across settings for patterns of behavior and is explicitly concerned with investigation and detection, thus avoiding what Grover and Soothill (1999) refer to as the subtle shift from the 'discourse of detection' to the 'discourse of causation'.

Webber (2010) contends that classifications used in profiling represent ideal types which ossify the behaviour and subjectivity of the offender and do not reflect potential changes in behaviour and motivation (see also Cresswell and Hollin 1994; Grover and Soothill 1999). Others note that psychological profiling is not scientifically rigorous, relying on conjecture and intuition, and drawing heavily on the popular mythologies and fictive representations of serial killing and its investigation which have proliferated in the latter part of the Twentieth Century (Canter et al. 2004; Webber 2010. It is worth noting that psychological profiling has never solved a case in isolation (Holmes and Holmes 1996), but is more commonly used in post hoc analyses of apprehended offenders (Webber 2010). Wiest (2011) also points out that psychological paradigms fail to account for the preponderance of male serial killers or why the majority of individuals presenting with psychological disorders or experiences of childhood trauma do not go onto become serial killers. Indeed, this body of work demonstrates a general lack of consideration for the role of social structure and culture in its analysis of etiology (Gadd and Jefferson 2007; Haggerty 2009; Wilson 2007; Grover and Soothill 1999), removing the violent individual from the historical, structural and cultural conditions which delineate and engender crime.

THE SOCIAL AND CULTURAL DIMENSIONS OF SERIAL KILLING

A number of writers challenge dominant assumptions which explain serial murder solely in terms of the psychologically defective individual, to think more broadly about historical, social and cultural conditions which 'foreground the social' in understandings of serial murder (Grover and Soothill 1999). Writers keen to stress that serial killing transcends historical and cultural context provide evidence of mass and serial murder involving sadism and cannibalism which predates modernity (Ramsland 2005; Miller 2014). Having said that, Grover and Soothill (1999) draw upon Durkheim's sociological study of suicide, conceived as the ultimate act of individual violence, to emphasise how relatively infrequent acts of extreme violence connect to social structure. Moreover, increases in serial killing in the last 200 years suggests that historical and cultural transformation also have some bearing on increases in serial murder. For instance, Hickey (2013) charts the 'rise' of serial murder in the US between 1795 and 1989, highlighting a marked increase in cases after 1950. Hickey (2013) identifies 367 cases of serial murder in the US between 1800 and 2004 with the majority (187) occurring between 1975 and 1995. Fox and Levin (2005) also note increases in serial murder in the latter half of the Twentieth Century with a significant spike in the 1980s. This is alongside the presence of the serial killer in culture where the ubiquity and extremity of real and mediated violence, greeted at once with indifference and fascination, has rendered the serial killer a beguiling celebrity figure which has spawned a culture industry in its own right (Schmid 2005; Wiest 2011; Seltzer 1998; Holmes and De Burger 1988; Jenkins 1994; Haggerty 2009).

Leyton's (1986) pioneeringwork began a focus on structure and serial murder, identifying class configurations during pre-industrial, industrial and postmodern periods as producing offender-perpetrator relationships specific to historical periods. Leyton's framework posits that within the pre-industrial period aristocratic killers murdered peasants and during the industrial period middle-class professionals murdered the marginalized and poorest members of the working-class. Finally, Leyton argues that in the modern period, working-class men murdered middle-class victims as an act of protest in response to class inequality and a lack of social mobility. A number of writers have adopted Leyton's focus on structure and serial killing, whilst analysing victim-perpetrator relationships differently. For instance, Grover and Soothill (1999) also identify perpetrators in the modern period as predominantly working-class men, but argue that serial murder as a form of 'homicidal protest' against middle-class victims, who fare better within the modern capitalist system, lacks currency within the modern British context. This is because victims are largely low status, powerless and marginalised and 'may be victimized because they are perceived as living outside the moral order of competitive capitalist economy' (Grover and Soothill 1999: 645).

Focusing on modernity, Haggerty (2009) builds on this approach, arguing persuasively that a set of 'necessary conditions' (p. 177) endemic to the modern period have caused serial murder to proliferate. Haggerty (2009) does not dispute the existence of 'sequential killing' prior to the modern period and concedes the shortcomings of his argument given that historical records are limited and that modernity cannot be conceived of as a monolithic event 'that arrived fully formed in different locations' (p. 170). That said, he locates serial killing 'in the context of modernizing processes' and draws upon Foucault's notion of historical ontology to argue that specific 'types' of individual are a product of 'historical and cultural specificity' (p. 171). This leads him to conclude that: 'In the absence of modern contexts, institutions and classifications, serial killers did not exist' (p. 171). Haggerty goes on to identify six 'distinctively modern' pre-conditions which engender serial killing: mass media and celebrity culture; the society of strangers; value-free means/end rationality; the vilification and marginalization of specific social groupings; emergence of enhanced opportunities for victimization; and the notion of 'social engineering'. So for instance, the mass media as a means of identity formation provides the cultural outlet and locus of subjectivity for the serial killer. The 'society of strangers' and the privatization of space—another corollary of capitalist development and urbanization, create the context of anonymity, which enables killers to 'prey on strangers' (p. 176).

Haggerty also discusses how 'opportunity structures' brought about by modernity facilitate easier access to victims, while the categorization of populations as part of the modernist project has resulted in the 'denigration' of specific social groups set against the benchmark of 'idealised citizenry' (p. 182). For Haggerty, antipathy, revulsion and the mission of 'progressive' eradication are values, which are shared by modernity and 'visionary serial killers': 'Through a distorted mirror, serial killers reflect back and act upon, modernity's distinctive valuations' (Haggerty 2009: 181). This view is further reinforced by the failure of formal agencies to protect and secure justice for marginal groups who appear 'beyond the law' (p. 179). Thus, greater accessibility, coupled with marginalization and inequality represent the 'mutually reinforcing operation of modernist frameworks of denigration and victimization opportunity structures' (Haggerty 2009: 182).

Likewise, Wilson (2007, 2012; Harrison and Wilson 2008) explores how the free market economies of neo-liberal late modernity have created widening social inequalities, individualism and a decline in collective social life which have brought about margin- ality, vulnerability and increases in violence (Dorling 2004; Hall and Maclean 2009; Hall 2012). Indeed, this echoes broader commentar- ies on the proliferation and concentration of violence and the rela- tionship between masculinity and violence in the context of deepening inequalities and social and economic marginalization in late capital- ist societies (Winlow 2001; Dorling 2004; Currie 2009; Hall et al. 2008). Wilson (2007, 2012) draws attention to social inequality and corresponding increases in serial murder specifically, noting that 'as late capitalism has begun to widen the gap between the 'haves' and the 'have nots', the numbers of serial killers and their victims has grown accordingly ... when the social structure in which they oper- ate allows them to do so' (Wilson 2012: 22–24). In this way, Wilson adopts a more explicit concern with the state's culpability in rendering victims vulnerable.

THE CULTURAL PROGRESS OF THE SERIAL KILLER

Cultural production around serial murder has proliferated within late modern cultures of violence where fetishized cultural incarnations eclipse the actuality of serial killing, assuming a reality all of their own (Seltzer 1998; Schmid 2005; Wiest 2011; Haggerty 2009). It was the White Chapel Murders of 1888 and the media response to them, which invoked the earliest cultural archetype of the sex killer or lust murderer (Downing 2013; Linnemann 2015). The murder and mutilation of five impoverished women with links to prostitution by the still unknown killer in the East End of London occurred in the midst of Victorian society's burgeoning fascination with violence and murder. This was fuelled by the emergence of a range of representational forms, from the basic single sheeted broadside to theatrical productions and most significantly, the rise of the mass newspaper print media—a central pil- lar of modernist progress (Flanders 2011). As Brown (2003) notes, it is during this period that media and culture become 'indivisible' (p. 25) with the media becoming a key producer of popular cultural products, which both provoked and satiated the Victorian fascination with horror and violence amidst anxieties relating to mass urbanization and social and technological change. Sensationalist media reporting of the White Chapel murders was pivotal in invoking the mythos of the killer, with representation far exceeding the actuality of the violence (Walkowitz 1982; Flanders 2011). Letters written to the police and the central news agency by an individual who claimed he was the murderer played a further role in invoking the Ripper myth. In addition, Flanders (2011) discusses how the print media at the time (and latterly fictive and the-atrical representations) revelled in reporting and depicting the murders, summoning up gothic imagery and the figure/s of Jekyll and Hyde to emphasise the murderer's beast-like quality, also employing humour and gratuitous detail. For Flanders (2011) this represents the invention of murder as 'entertainment' and 'spectacle' (p. 466).

According to Cyriax (1993) the figure of 'Jack the Ripper', as the first embodiment of this type of murderer within culture, 'stands at the gateway of the modern age' (Cyriax 1993, cited in Biressi 2001: 66). Echoing this point, Downing identifies the sexually-motivated killer as a modernist creation, congruent with the development of scientific clas-sification as part of the project of modernity. Downing highlights how the sex murderer or 'lust murderer' was identified within the German pseudoscience of sexology. This analysis of aggressive masculine sexuality was constructed as the flipside of the rational masculine subject and is misogynist in its depiction of a passive female sexuality constructed as the provocation for such violence. As such, this creation, as realized across a range of modernist discourses, exemplifies links between modernity, serial killing and misogyny, revealing modernity as highly gendered in its projection of masculinity and femininity, as well as the offender and the victim of crime (Morrison 1995). Downing (2013) further argues that Jack the Ripper 'has remained a cultural figure of folklore through which the contemporary serial sex killer can be read and understood' (Downing 2013: 89). The legacy of which can be seen in later twentieth Century representations of sex murderers—both fictive and actual (Caputi 1987; Downing 2013). Indeed, the figure of the Ripper—both the Victorian version and later cases, have become staples for cultural production as 'Ripperama' (ranging from novels, short stories, film, television, plays, songs and poems) and pseudo-criminological 'Ripperology' (Caputi 1987; Jenkins 1994; Schmid 2005).

The Cultural Life of the Serial Killer
in the Twentieth Century

> The serial killer has become a dominant cultural representation since the
> 1960s. The killer emerged in a moment of historical rupture when an
> alternative cultural framework was crystallizing. (King 2006: 113)

As highlighted in the previous section, violence as entertainment has a
long history (Brown 2003; Flanders 2011). That said, the availability and consumption of representational violence has intensified
and proliferated in late modern globalised cultures (Seltzer 1998;
Schmid 2005; Jewkes 2013; Castells 1996; Brown 2003; Carrabine
2008; Ray 2011). As Ray (2011) observes, 'images of war, death and
suffering are consumed as representations of everyday life' (Ray 2011:
60). For Brown (2003), it is via 'representational texts' that we connect
to violence. Noting the ambivalence at the heart of this engagement,
Brown observes how the 'simultaneous censure' of criminals, occurs as
'we devour voraciously as many media images of violence as we can get
our hands on' (pp. 125–126). Mark Seltzer (1998) deploys the notion
of wound culture to comprehend America's pathological public sphere
'in which addictive violence has become a collective spectacle' and
symptomatic of a wider cultural malaise (p. 253). The late modern fascination with the figure of the serial killer can be understood within this
wider context of cultural violence.

The serial killer's cultural ubiquity was established in the 1970s and
1980s as the 'serial killer industry' took off via widespread cultural production and academic interest (Soothill 1993; Jenkins 1994; Seltzer 1998;
Wilson 2007). Jenkins (1994) notes the key cultural moment as when the
US Federal Bureau of Investigation's (FBI) took ownership of the 'serial
killer problem' in the late 1970s. In his cultural history of serial killing,
Jenkin's (1994) notes spikes in serial murder in the US from the mid-1960s
onwards, identifying five cases of particular notoriety: Son of Sam; John
Wayne Gacy; The Hillside Strangler; Atlanta Child Murders and Ted Bundy.
These 'newsworthy' cases garnered inordinate media attention which
stretched well beyond trial, as well as being kept alive for decades by popular criminology. For Jenkins, the media's ongoing coverage of high-profile cases was instrumental in inserting serial murder into the US popular
imagination and providing the FBI with a further "enemy within" to validate the organisation's existence and expansion (see also Schmid 2005).

As Jenkins observes, federal law enforcement, which had previously not considered murder as a federal matter, positioned itself as the only effective means of addressing what was popularly perceived as the burgeoning serial killer problem. Moreover, although serial murder as a term/concept has a longer history predating the FBI, the Bureau's repeated reference to the term meant that it became synonymous with the organization (Jenkins 1994; Schmid 2005). Positive representations of the FBI proliferated within popular cultural work from the 1980s and into the 1990s. As Schmid notes, the serial killer myth was propagated by 'the overwhelming laudatory tone of popular cultural representations of the FBI' (p. 87). The highpoint was Thomas Harris' novel *Silence of the Lambs* and its film adaptation. According to Jenkins (1994), the film was pivotal in popularizing offender profiling and the FBI via the 'myth of the mindhunter'—the assumption that key individuals within the organization possessed some exceptional ability to understand the psyche of such offenders and apprehend them.

Jenkins observes that serial killers have featured within film since the 1930s initially inspired by the Ripper figure but then progressing to draw upon other high profile cases during the course of the decade. Jenkins identifies the interaction between several genre defining cultural moments such as Alfred Hitchcock's Psycho and the 'Slasher' genre as fuelling and responding to growing cultural interest in violence of this type. Likewise, Schmid (2005) argues that murder has featured since the earliest days of film, but it was the slasher genre which ushered in the age of extreme violence on-screen. Furthermore, as Jarvis (2007) notes, it is within film, that serial killers maintain their most 'conspicuous presence'. Extending upon Jenkins' audit of cultural production from the early 1990s, Jarvis (2007) notes the number of films involving serial killers proliferated after 1990 and at the time of writing in 2007, the IMDB database listed over 1000 titles. Jarvis goes on to identify 'seminal' filmic and fictional representations from post-1990: Thomas Harris' Hannibal Lecter novels and film adaptations; the novel and film American Psycho; and the film Se7en. Arguably, these genre-defining texts have been central in delineating the serial killer in the cultural imagination, defined by a range of attributes: intellectual, charismatic, supernatural and superhuman, sexually-motivated and sadistic with the ability to hide in plain sight (Jenkins 1994; Biressi 2001). Indeed, the Thomas Harris novels and the subsequent film adaptations depicting the 'intelligent and articulate' offender (Jenkins 1994: 89), offer us a murder who is attractive, and relatable (Clover 1992; Jenkins 1994; Schmid 2005).

In addition to popular cultural production, the serial killer has also inspired an industry around artefacts or murderabilia (Schmid 2005; Wiest 2011; Jarvis 2007). Below, Wiest (2011) presents an exhaustive list of what she defines as first type murderabilia of 'branded' serial killer products. These are differentiated from 'second' type artefacts whose provenance derives from the killers themselves:

> Murderabilia items of the first type are widely available on the Internet and in novelty stores. One of the largest Web sites specializing in such sales (serialkillercalendar.com) offers a huge array of "macabre merchandise" featuring serial murderers and other killers, including T-shirts; calendars; DVD sets; three series of trading cards; wall posters; wall clocks; throw pillows; action figures; postcards; mugs and steins; wooden keepsake boxes; notebooks; artwork; tote and messenger bags; aprons featuring cannibal killers; eight issues of the Serial Killer Magazine; energy drinks; and recordings of news footage, interviews, and confessions. Similar Web sites offer additional clothing and household items, apparel for children and pets, skateboards, and even computer fonts resembling serial murderers' handwriting. One site, CafePress (cafepress.com) allows users to create their own items with images and words of their choosing, and this has produced T-shirts, stickers, magnets, buttons, travel cups, and mouse pads with creepy slogans and quoted words of serial murderers. (Wiest 2011: 96)

Schmid (2005) extends the analysis of the serial killer in culture by naming the serial killer as 'exemplary modern celebrity' (p. 4) brought forth by a combination of the proliferation of the visual image, the cult of celebrity and the fascination and enjoyment of violence as key features of late/postmodern culture. So for instance, to return to *The Silence of the Lambs*, the popularity of the film reconfirmed the continuing status of the psycho killer as superstar (Rubin 1998, in Schmid 2005: 115). Echoing Brown (2003), Schmid identifies the contradiction at the heart of our relationship with cultural violence which is exemplified in the figure of the serial killer where 'tensions between horrified expulsion and ambivalent fascination with the criminal are likely to be particularly intense because of the extremity of the serial killer's actions' (p. 115).

The arrival of the Islamic terrorist embodying the violent Other and object of fear following 9/11 necessitates further re-evaluation of the cultural status of the serial killer. In the epilogue to Natural Born Celebrities, Schmid (2005) reassesses the cultural appeal of the serial killer when set against the figure of the terrorist arguing that the serial killer retains a place within the culture, whereas the terrorist is always the violent Other, residing out with the community. Moreover, Schmid (2005) claims that the serial killer performs a reassuring function as a 'familiar' evil with an accepted place in culture: 'Whether a film is based on Ted Bundy, Jeffrey Dahmer or Aileen Wuornos, the pantheon of familiar names allows the viewer to return to pre-9/11 days when evil had a comfortably American face' (p. 254). For Schmid, this additional function is further evidence of the 'multi-accentuality' of the serial killer and reinforce his insider status in US and Western culture. Moreover, Schmid (2005) further argues that the terrorist Other enables the disavowal of violence as intrinsic to US and Western culture more widely.

THE SERIAL KILLER IN BRITISH CULTURE

Soothill (1993) argues that the dominance of North American culture has been pivotal in defining broader cultural understandings of serial murder in Western culture (see also Jenkins 1994; Seltzer 1998; Soothill 1993; Schmid 2005; Wiest 2011). Writing in 1988, Jenkins notes that In the British context, serial killers account for only a small proportion of murders—perhaps one or two percent in any given year, noting twelve serial murderers between 1940 and 1980, with a total of 107 victims, but with a notable spike from the 1960s onwards. Wilson's (2007) more recent analysis lists 19 serial killers and 326 victims between 1960 and 2006, linking increases to widening inequality and declining social protections. Despite its rarity, the serial murderer has been a compelling figure in British culture with a number of British cases from the 1960s onwards remaining vivid within collective memory due to their disturbing nature.

A crude review of internet search results for some of the names on David Wilson's (2007) list and more widely, gives some indication of the notoriety of specific offenders. So for instance, the Moors Murderers, Peter Sutcliffe, Dennis Nielsen, Fred and Rosemary West and Steve Wright have attracted significant media attention and cultural longevity. Often the long shadow cast by these cases is explained by virtue of their macabre nature (D'Cruze et al. 2006) alongside persistent cultural production which animates and sustains the figure of the 'British serial killer' in the collective memory (Linnemann 2015). As Fuss (1993) observes, '[t]ales of serial killers in our newspapers have become our new serial literature, with regular instalments, stock characters, behavioural profiles, and a fascinated loyal readership' (Fuss 1993, in Biressi 2001: 165).

The focus on specific offenders also offers an opportunity to read the culture at a specific historical moment (Brown 2003; Gilman Srebnick and Levy 2005; Shaw 2010, 2011). So for instance, to take the case of Ian Brady and Myra Hindley who became known as the Moors Murderers. The couple murdered and tortured four children and a seventeen year-old boy in Oldham, Greater Manchester between 1963 and 1965, before burying victims on moorland. Biressi (2001) argues that this case offers a 'contemporary inflection' to sexually-motivated murder, typifying the 'modern British sex crime', as well as being the 'case against which many subsequent cases were to be measured' (pp. 67–70). The murders embody a sense of British identity given how the case was understood in terms of class and region. As Downing (2013) notes, class was integral 'in defining subjectivity, social agency and criminal transgression' (p. 101) in the context of this case. The working-class couple from the North West of England were depicted as pursuing the 'dream of exceptionality', seeking to transcend the banality of early 1960s working-class life via the consumption of explicit literature chronicling torture and sadism and committing acts of spectacular sexual violence and murder against children. Commenting on Emlyn Williams (1967) *Beyond Belief*, which interrogates the case, Downing further highlights how the working-class murderess was viewed by the author as something of an anachronism given assumptions regarding the murdering subject as embodying masculine exceptionality. Moreover, Downing also points to the way in which the case was deployed as a means to denounce 1960s social mobility and permissiveness by conservative commentators, thus challenging the mythology of the 1960s as a decade of optimism and social progress. The claim being that the murders were a consequence of allowing sexually transgressive and violent literary material to fall into hands of working-class men such as Brady, who had neither the culture nor the education to deal with it.

As referred to above, the case inspired Emlyn William's (1967) *Beyond Belief*, regarded as a literary classic of the true crime genre, setting the template for true crime's preoccupation with the biography of the offender and further establishing the genre of high-end true crime pioneered by Trueman Capote's *In Cold Blood*. Biressi also acknowledges how other high profile cases inspired a specific type of British cultural production around serial murder which she identifies as 'a sub-genre of true crime, a sub-genre of the crime novel and a specialist field of reportage in which the weekend press in particular will serialise books devoted to particularly notorious criminals' (p. 165). Moreover, the persistent cultural interest and activity around Myra Hindley is further evidence of the fetishisation of the serial killer—this time in British culture (Schmid 2005). This has included her notorious mug shot being used in a photographic portrait which was exhibited at the Royal Academy and Stephen Morrissey (of the seminal 1980s indie band The Smiths) composing a song about Hindley. That said, the persistent fixation on Hindley is also propelled by the additional vilification of violent women, and especially those involved in the murder of children, who are viewed as 'doubly deviant' in the face of broader social norms but also those relating to femininity, maternity, violence and transgression (Jewkes 2013; Seal 2010; Barlow 2015; Downing 2013).

Drawing upon a number of literary and journalistic think pieces from the 1980s and 1990s (Hobsbawn 1995; Winder 1991; Jenkins 1994), Biressi draws attention to how perceived increases in random acts of violence and homicide and its representation in true crime were viewed as symptomatic of social decline during this period. These commentaries connect the proliferation of violence and the consumption of serial murder as imported from the US and can be read as an expression of wider anxieties about the Americanisation of culture. Biressi goes onto identify Peter Sutcliffe and Dennis Nilsen as encouraging 'the public appetite for true crime and fictional crime stories' at this time (p. 169), further embedding the serial killer within British culture and also inscribing atrocity onto specific locations.

Denis Nilsen murdered at least 15 young men in his North London flat between 1978 and 1983. After murdering his victims, Nilsen would often keep the bodies in the flat for great lengths of time before disposing of them. For Downing (2013) Nilsen 'is one of the most represented faces of serial killing in a contemporary British culture fascinated by the figure of the murderer' (p. 126). Additionally, the tableau of domestic horror—pornography, rape, abuse, voyeurism prostitution (Amis 2000; Ferguson 2004) surrounding the murders of at least ten young women by Fred and Rosemary West at their family home in Gloucester, which came to light in 1995, guaranteed their notoriety in 'British criminal history' (Burnside 1998). Gordon Burn, who applied the conventions of new journalism (Rossmanith 2014; Alleyne 2015) to the Sutcliffe case, applied similar attention to detail and literary/fictive sensibility to the West case, combining mundane details of the everyday with accounts of depravity and atrocity to produce a further work of high-end true crime as social history (Myers 2009). Moreover, the crimes of Fred and Rose West extends notions of what the sex crime represents in modern British culture (Biressi 2001), invoking a macabre sense of British identity, small town life and warped domesticity. Likewise, the Sutcliffe murders occupy a similarly prominent position in recent British history. The duration of the murders and attacks, the related fear they provoked and the apparent inability of the police to catch the killer can at least in part explain their impact on culture. Additionally, as illustrated in the previous chapter, the case spoke to a specific time and place (Upson 2001; Brown 2012; Shaw 2010, 2011), as well as leaving its mark upon the culture of the late 1970s, further establishing the figure of the serial killer onto the British popular imaginary.

In an appraisal of the cultural status of the serial murderer following the death of the 'Moors Murderer' Ian Brady in 2017, Bennett (2018) touches on the main themes covered in this chapter relating to the fetish-isation of the serial killer in a culture captivated by violence and the allu-sion to exceptionality, often perpetuated by self-promotion on the part of offenders. She notes that the 'serial killer industry' shows no sign of abating as a tenth film about Ted Bundy, the murderer of an estimated 30 women in the US in the 1970s, was about to be commissioned. And to return to our cultural starting point, the recent opening of the Ripper Museum in the East End of London is the latest enterprise concerned with the earliest carnation of 'Ripper' (Orr 2015), reflecting the endur-ing celebration of the male murderer and the persistent disregard for murdered women. Indeed, many of the broader social and cultural com-mentaries on serial murder fail to acknowledge the male killer explicitly. It is within feminist approaches that the gender dynamics of serial killing is explored more fully.

Naming the Killer as Male: Feminist Analyses of Serial Murder

Some consideration of gender is evident in existing studies of serial kill-ing, which privilege class and the socio-economic order. For instance, both Grover and Soothill (1999) and Wilson (2007) highlight how patriarchal power and control feature when men kill women and chil-dren. Looking specifically at the Yorkshire Ripper case, Wilson (2007) also highlights how masculine cop culture within the police shaped

misogynist attitudes and lack of regard for victims which led to investigative failings and lack of protection for women involved in prostitution. Gender is not so explicit in other analyses. Haggerty's (2009)
examination of modernity and the serial killer does not consider how
the constitution of the killer's subjectivity and value system may go
beyond the means end rationality associated with modernity and may
also relate to the murdering subject as masculine (Cameron and Frazer
1987; Downing 2013). Moreover, this approach does not acknowledge
modernity itself as gendered (Morrison 1995). Indeed, it is fair to say
that in general, structural explanations ultimately privilege the political economy and the impact of the current economic order in shaping motivation and victim vulnerability (Wilson 2007, 2012; Hall and
Wilson 2014). Equally, key work focusing on the serial killer in culture—from Jack the Ripper through to those offenders who occupy
the cultural landscape of the Twentieth Century (real and fictional),
often do not name the fetishized and celebrated killer in culture as male
(Seltzer 1998; Schmid 2005).

But murder is not 'gender-neutral' (Corradi et al. 2016), with gender determining social and situational characteristics and relationships
between victims and perpetrators (Brookman 2005; Dorling 2004; ONS
2016). Violence, homicide and serial murder are committed overwhelm-
ingly by men (Newburn and Stanko 1994; Polk 1998; Jefferson 2002;
Ray 2011; Kelleher and Kelleher 1998; Miller 2014). Hickey's (2013)
study of serial murder in the U.S. between 2004 and 2011 highlights
86% of offenders as male with similar ratios evident amongst homicide
perpetrators: men comprise around two thirds of homicide victims and
90% of perpetrators (Chan 2001; Brookman 2005; Smith et al. 2011;
ONS 2016). Given men's higher rates of victimisation, feminism's politicization of the murder of women requires some clarification. Men kill
women and men kill men; however, what feminist commentators draw
attention to is the fact that men kill women because they are women and
this is rooted in masculinity and misogyny as traits of patriarchy (Ingala
Smith 2013; Radford and Russell 1992). Furthermore, although men
do figure significantly as victims of serial killers, the majority of victims
are women who are most frequently linked to sex work/prostitution
(Godwin 2008; Hickey 2013; Quinet 2011). When men are victims of
serial killers, power dynamics still figure in the relationship between victim and perpetrator (Cameron and Frazer 1987; Downing 2013).

The murder of women by men was politicized and 'named' as gynocide by Daly (1973) and latterly as femicide (Rivera 2005) as part of second wave feminist mobilization and academic analysis of gender, power and violence in the 1970s. Moreover, this radical perspective identifies violence and murder as systemic and global, encompassing an array of male-perpetrated abuses against women. This is illustrated in Dworkin's commentary on gynocide as 'the systematic crippling, raping, and/or killing of women by men ... the relentless violence perpetrated by the gender class men on the gender class women' (Dworkin 1981, cited in Caputi 1987: 3). Radford (1992) echoes these sentiments, defining femicide as the murder of women by virtue of the fact that they are women: a conscious action emanating from misogyny, control, propriety and disregard for women's humanity (see also Jeffries 2013; Schmidt-Camacho 2010; Ingala Smith 2013).

With regards serial murder specifically, feminist analyses take issue with the depoliticisation of the sex or lust murderer in both popular and academic understandings, whose masculinity is obscured by individual and pathological explanations of deviance and the veneration of the masculine murdering subject (Caputi 1987; Cameron and Frazer 1987; Hollway 1981; Downing 2013; Warkentin 2010). In a survey of 'the established canon of sexually motivated serial murders' (p. 19), Cameron and Frazer (1987) note women's virtual absence from the history of perpetrators who are almost exclusively male. That said, the authors concede that this analysis only goes so far and does not account for male victims. Given the preponderance of male perpetrators, they nevertheless identify misogyny and sadistic sexuality 'under the banner of masculinity' (p. 166), but add the quest for transcendence as making up the defining features of the masculine murderer. Likewise, Downing's more recent meditation on the murdering subject in culture, identifies the drive to be exceptional, to transcend the ordinariness of self and existence as inherent to masculinity. Moreover, Downing's analysis highlights how the captivation with violence and the serial killer (Seltzer 1998; Schmid 2005) is gendered—evident in the commission, representation and regard for violence across modernity and late modernity. This leads Downing to argue that ultimately, '[a] murderer-worshipping culture is a misogynistic one' (Downing 2013: 92).

Indeed, the representation of the sexually-motivated murderer of women and his victims brings into sharp relief how gender operates in the sphere of representation, which thus calls for 'gender aware' readings of culture (Downing 2013; Warkentin 2010). This pattern of representation is consistent across media and criminal justice framings of female victims of sexual violence in terms of gratuity and victim blaming (Benedict 1992; Lees 1997; Wykes and Welsh 2009; Jewkes 2013). Frequently, the discourses speak for themselves in terms of their unambiguous misogyny or the wholesale erasure of victims alongside the elevation of the killer in reportage which date back to the media's reporting of the White Chapel murders (Walkowitz 1982; Caputi 1987; Cameron and Frazer 1987; Warkentin 2010). Drawing on Caputi's work, Downing (2013) notes the ubiquity of the gendered sex crime in popular culture: 'As Caputi has relentlessly catalogued, sex crime is everywhere. It is the titillating subject matter of crime fiction, television, film, men's magazines; naturalized and banalised in our culture as "entertainment"' (p. 95). For Warkentin (2010), the recurrence of the 'Ripper' in cultural production illustrates the contemporary relevance of the Nineteenth Century murders in regard to gender, power, violence and representation. To return to the Sutcliffe murders, the case features in a number of feminist analyses of sexually-motivated serial murder or lust murder, which focus on the connections between masculinity, sexuality and misogyny where the actions of the killer are explained as an exaggerated manifestation of the wider culture which normalizes violence against women and encourages aggressive male sexuality (Bland 1992; Hollway 1981; Caputi 1987; Cameron and Frazer 1987). The murders also lay bare extreme and embedded cultures of misogyny, reflected in attitudes towards prostitutes, condemnatory discourses regarding women's respectability and sexuality, and subsequent victim blaming (Caputi 1987; Hollway 1981; Smith 2013). The misogynist framing of Sutcliffe's victims will be explored in more depth in chapter five.

The value of broader structural and cultural readings of serial killing is beyond question. Relating motivation, opportunity and the status and availability of victims to social transformation and contemporary structures and cultures has advanced academic understandings of serial murder considerably. And, as with more recent perspectives on violence and harm (Hall 2012; Hall and Winlow 2015), the related work on serial murder brings into sharp focus the consequences of the current political economy and the erosion of the social in engendering violence, exacerbating marginality and removing state protection. This is alongside the fostering of a collective mind-set which has absorbed the classification of citizens based on economic value amidst the selfishness and amorality intrinsic to late capitalism (Haggerty 2009; Wilson 2012; Harrison and Wilson 2008; Hall and Wilson 2014).

Feminist analyses of violence against women and the murder and serial murder of women has something of a longer history, originating from second wave feminism's concern with male violence and sexual violence as the key facets of patriarchy (Kelly 1987; Brownmiller 1975; Mackay 2015). Within feminist analyses, it is the male outlook derived from patriarchy and misogyny, which accounts for violence and the way in which it is represented. Indeed, when it comes to 'Ripper-style' sexually motivated murders, such unambiguous examples of misogynist violence work very well with a feminist analysis. Even if patriarchy and misogyny cannot fully account for all manifestations of serial murder, such violence is for the most part circumscribed by relations of masculinity and power (Cameron and Frazer 1987; Downing 2013). That said, feminist analyses often fail to account for violence beyond the male perpetrator and female victim, which go against the grain of explanations rooted in masculinity and misogyny such as those involving female violence and sadism. Indeed, Morrissey (2003) argues that criminological and feminist approaches have failed to analyse violent women adequately, relying mostly on cultural interrogations of the violent woman in discourse. Moreover, as Brown (2003) argues, mostly on sweeping references to misogyny within many feminist commentaries do not capture fully the complexity of textual 'violence inscribed in the female body for spectacle' often presenting as tautological, 'defining of and defined by, violence' (Brown 2003: 134).

These distinct explanatory frameworks (cultural, structural, feminist) are more often than not sequestered from one another as they carry out their theoretical work on violence and serial killing, calling forth the figure of offender and victim in different ways. Greater integration of structural frameworks on serial murder would expand understandings and address some of the complexities of etiology and representation. My aim has thus been to privilege a feminist analysis, but one which acknowledges the value of these broader frameworks and takes on board Miller and Mullins's (2006) recommendation that feminist scholarship should engage with 'broader criminological thought' in order to 'both challenge and enrich the broader enterprise of criminological theory-building'.

REFERENCES

Alleyne, B. (2015). *Narrative Networks: Storied Approaches in a Digital Age*. London: Sage.

Amis, M. (2000). *Experience*. London: Jonathan Cape.

Barlow, C. (2015). Silencing the Other: Gendered Representations of Co-accused Women Offenders. *The Howard Journal of Criminal Justice, 54*(5), 469–488.

Benedict, H. (1992). *Virgin or Vamp: How the Press Covers Sex Crimes*. Oxford: Oxford University Press.

Bennell, C., Bloomfield, S., Emeno, K., & Mussolino, E. (2013). Classifying Serial Sexual Murderers: An Attempt to Validate Keppel and Walter's 1999 Model. *Criminal Justice and Behaviour, 40*(11), 5–23.

Bennett, C. (2018, May 21). We Learn Nothing from Ian Brady's Murder: We're Just Fetishising Him. *The Guardian*.

Biressi, A. (2001). *Crime, Fear and the Law in True Crime Stories*. New York: Palgrave Macmillan.

Blackburn, R. (1993). *The Psychology of Criminal Conduct: Theory, Research and Practice*. Chichester: Wiley.

Bland, L. (1992). The Case of the Yorkshire Ripper: Mad, Bad, Beast or Male? In J. Radford & D. E. H. Russell (Eds.), *Femicide: The Politics of Women Killing*. Buckingham: Open University Press.

Brookman, F. (2005). *Understanding Homocide*. London: Sage.

Brown, S. (2003). *Crime and Law in Media Culture*. Buckingham: Open University Press.

Brown, R. (2012). 'Armageddon Was Yesterday—Today We Have a Serious Problem': Pre and Postmillennial Tropes for Crime and Criminality by David Peace and Stieg Larsson. In C. Gregoriou (Ed.), *Constructing Crime: Discourse and Cultural Representations of Crime and 'Deviance'*. Basingstoke: Palgrave Macmillan.

Brownmiller, S. (1975). *Against Our Will: Men, Women and Rape*. Harmondsworth: Penguin Books.

Burnside, J. (1998, September). Lustmord. *London Review of Books*.

Cameron, D., & Frazer, E. (1987). *The Lust to Kill*. Cambridge: Polity.

Canter, D. (2001). *Criminal Shadows: The Inner Narratives of Evil*. Irving, TX: Authorlink Press.

Canter, D. V., & Wentink, N. (2004). An Empirical Test of Holmes and Holmes's Serial Murder Typology. *Criminal Justice and Behavior, 31*, 489–515.

Canter, D. V., Laurence, J. A., Alison, E., & Wentink, N. (2004). The Organized/Disorganized Typology of Serial Murder: Myth or Model? *Psychology, Public Policy and Law, 10*(3), 293–320.

Caputi, J. (1987). *The Age of the Sex Crime*. Bowling Green: Bowling Green State University Popular Press.

Carrabine, E. (2008). *Crime, Culture and the Media*. Cambridge: Polity.

Castells, M. (1996). *The Rise of the Network Society*. Oxford: Blackwell.

Chan, W. (2001). *Women, Murder and Justice*. Basingstoke: Palgrave Macmillan.

Clover, C. (1992). *Men, Women and Chainsaws*. Princeton: Princeton University Press.

Corradi, C., Marcuello Servos, M., & Boira, S. (2016). Theories of Femicide and Their Significance for Social Research. *Current Sociology, 64*(7), 975–995.

Cresswell, D. M., & Hollin, C. R. (1994). Multiple Murder: A Review. *British Journal Criminology, Delinquency and Deviant Social Behaviour, 22*, 395–414.

Currie, E. (2009). *The Roots of Danger: Violent Crime in Global Perspective*. Upper Saddle River, NJ: Prentice Hall.

Daly, M. (1973). *Beyond God the Father: Towards a Philosophy of Women's Liberation*. Boston: Beacon Press.

D'Cruze, S., Walklate, S., & Pegg, S. (2006). *Murder: Social and Historical Approaches to Understanding Murder and Murderers*. Cullompton: Willan.

Dorling, D. (2004). Prime Suspect: Murder in Britain. In C. Pantazis, S. Tombs, & D. Gordon (Eds.), *Beyond Criminology: Taking Harm Seriously*. London: Pluto Press.

Douglas, J. E., Burgess, A. W., & Ressler, R. K. (1992). *Crime Classification Manual: A Standard System for Investigating and Classifying Violent Crime*. New York: Simon and Schuster.

Douglas, J. E., Ressler, R. K., Burgess, A. W., & Hartman, C. R. (1986). Criminal Profiling from Crime Scene Analysis. *Behavioural Sciences and Law, 4*, 401–421.

Downing, L. (2013). *The Subject of Murder*. Chicago: University of Chicago Press.

Dworkin, A. (1981). *Pornography: Men Possessing Women*. New York: Perigee.

Egger, S. A. (1984). A Working Definition of Serial Murder and the Reduction of Linkage Blindness. *Journal of Police Science and Administration, 12*(3), 348–357.

Ferguson, E. (2004, February 15). There's Nobody Home. *The Guardian*.

Flanders, J. (2011). *The Invention of Murder*. London: Harper Press.

Fox, J. A., & Levin, J. (2005). *Extreme Killing: Understanding Serial and Mass Murder*. London: Sage.

Gadd, D., & Jefferson, T. (2007). *Psychosocial Criminology: An Introduction*. Los Angeles, CA: Sage.

Gilman Srebnick, A., & Levy, R. (2005). *Crime and Culture: An Historical Perspective*. Aldershot: Ashgate.

Godwin, G. M. (2008). *Hunting Serial Predators*. Sudbury, MA: Jones & Bartlett.

Grover, L., & Soothill, K. (1999). British Serial Killing: Towards a Structural Explanation. *The British Criminology Conferences: Selected Proceedings* (Vol. 2). Papers from the British Criminology Conference, Queens University, Belfast, 15–19 July 1997. This volume published March 1999. Editor: Mike Brogden.

Haggerty, K. (2009). Modern Serial Killers. *Crime Media, Culture, 5*, 168.

Hall, S. (2012). *Theorising Crime and Deviance: A New Perspective.* London: Sage.

Hall, S., & MacLean, C. (2009). A Tale of Two Capitalisms: Preliminary Spatial and Historical Comparisons of Homicide rates in Western Europe and the USA. *Theoretical Criminology, 13*, 303–319.

Hall, S., & Wilson, D. (2014). New Foundations: Pseudo-Pacification and Special Liberty as Potential Cornerstones for a Multi-Level Theory of Homicide and Serial Murder. *European Journal of Criminology, 11*(5), 635–655.

Hall, S., & Winlow, S. (2015). *Revitalising Criminological Theory: Towards a New Ultra-Realism.* London: Routledge.

Hall, S., Winlow, S., & Ancrum, C. (2008). *Criminal Identities and Consumer Culture: Crime, Exclusion and the Culture of Narcissism.* Cullompton: Willan.

Harrison, P., & Wilson, D. (2008). *Hunting Evil: Inside the Ipswich Serial Murders.* London: Sphere.

Hickey, E. W. (2013). *Serial Murders and Their Victims* (6th ed.). Wadsworth: Cengage Learning.

Hinch, R., & Hepburn C. (1998). Researching Serial Murder: Methodological and Definitional Problems. *Electronic Journal of Sociology, 3*(2), 1–11.

Hobsbawn, E. (1995). *Age of Extremes: The Short Twentieth Century 1914–1991.* London: Abacus.

Hollway, W. (1981, October). 'I Just Wanted to Kill a Woman' Why? The Ripper and Male Sexuality. *Feminist Review, 9*, 33–40.

Holmes, R. M., & Deburger, J. (1988). *Serial Murder.* London: Sage.

Holmes, R. M., & Holmes, S. T. (1996). *Profiling Violent Crimes: An Investigative Tool.* Thousand Oaks: Sage.

Ingala Smith, K. (2013). *This Thing About Male Victims.* https://kareninga-lasmith.com/2013/04/29/this-thing-about-male-victims.

Jarvis, B. (2007). Monsters Inc.: Serial Killers and Consumer Culture. *Crime, Media Culture, 3*(2), 326–344.

Jefferson, T. (2002). Subordinating Hegemonic Masculinity. *Theoretical Criminology, 6*, 63–88.

Jeffries, F. (2013). Documentary Noir in the City of Fear: Feminicide, Impunity and Grass Roots Communication in Ciudad Juarez. *Crime Media Culture, 9*(3), 301–317.

Jenkins, P. (1994). *Using Murder: The Social Construction of Serial Homicide.* New York: Routledge.

Jewkes, Y. (2013). *Media and Crime* (2nd ed.). London: Sage.

Kelleher, M. D., & Kelleher, C. L. (1998). *Murder Most Rare: The Female Serial Killer*. Westport, CT: Praeger.

Kelly, L. (1987). The Continuum of Sexual Violence. In J. Hanmer & M. Maynard (Eds.), *Women, Violence and Social Control*. London: Macmillan.

Keppel, R. D., & Walter, R. (1999). Profiling Killers: A Revised Classification Model for Understanding Sexual Murder. *International Journal of Offender Therapy and Comparative Criminology, 43*, 417–437.

King, A. (2006). The Serial Killer and the Postmodern Self. *History of Human Sciences, 19*(3), 109–125.

Lees, S. (1997). *Carnal Knowledge: Rape on Trial*. Harmondsworth: Penguin.

Leyton, E. (1986). *Hunting Humans: The Rise of the Modern Multiple Murderer*. Toronto: McClelland and Stewart.

Linnemann, T. (2015). Capote's Ghosts: Violence, Murder and the Spectre of Suspicion. *British Journal of Criminology, 55*, 514–533.

Mackay, F. (2015). *Radical Feminism: Feminist Activism in Movement*. London: Palgrave Macmillan.

Miller, L. (2014). Serial Killers: I. Subtypes, Patterns, and Motives. *Aggression and Violent Behavior, 19*, 1–11.

Morrison, W. (1995). *Theoretical Criminology: From Modernity to Post-modernism*. London: Cavendish.

Morrissey, B. (2003). *When Women Kill: Questions of Agency and Subjectivity*. New York: Routledge.

Myers, B. (2009, July 22). Gordon Burn Was One of the Greatest Writers of His Age. *The Guardian*.

Newburn, T., & Stanko, E. (1994). *Just Boys Doing Business: Men, Masculinities and Crime*. London: Routledge.

Office for National Statistics. (2016). *Homicide: Findings from Analyses Based on the Homicide Index Recorded by the Home Office Covering Differing Aspects of Homicide*. London: Office for National Statistics.

Orr, D. (2015, August 15). Jack the Ripper Is an Invented Villain but His Victims Were Real: A Museum to These Crimes Is a Disgrace. *The Guardian*.

Polk, K. (1998). *When Men Kill*. Cambridge: Cambridge University Press.

Purcell, C., & Arrigo, B. (2006). *The Psychology of Lust Murder*. Burlington, MA: Elsevier.

Quinet, K. (2011). Prostitutes as Victims of Serial Homicide: Trends and Case Characteristics, 1970–2009. *Homicide Studies, 15*, 74–100.

Radford, J. (1992). Introduction. In J. Radford & D. Russell (Eds.), *Femicide: The Politics of Woman Killing*. New York, NY: Twayne.

Radford, J., & Russell, D. (1992). *Femicide: The Politics of Woman Killing*. New York, NY: Twayne.

Ramsland, K. (2005). *The Human Predator: A Historical Chronicle of Serial Murder and Forensic Investigation*. New York, NY: The Berkley Publishing Group.

Ray, L. (2011). *Violence and Society*. London: Sage.

Ressler, R. K., Burgess, A. W., & Douglas, J. E. (1988). *Sexual Homicides: Patterns and Motives*. Lexington, MA: Lexington Books.

Rivera, M. (2005). La historia de las mujeres que nombran el mundo en femenino [The History of Women Who Name the World by Using the Female Gender]. *Acta Historica et Archaeologica Mediaevalia, 26*, 1155–1164.

Rossmanith, K. (2014). Plots and Artefacts: Courts and Criminal Evidence in the Production of True Crime Writing. *Australian Feminist Law Journal, 40*(1), 97–111.

Salfati, C. G., & Bateman, A. L. (2005). Serial Homicide: An Investigation of Behaviourial Consistency. *Journal of Investigative Psychology and Offender Profiling, 2*, 121–144.

Salfati, C. G., James, A. R., & Ferguson, L. (2008). Prostitute Homicides: A Descriptive Study. *Journal of Interpersonal Violence, 23*, 505–543.

Schmid, D. (2005). *Natural Born Celebrities: Serial Killers in American Culture*. London: University of Chicago Press.

Schmidt-Camacho, A. S. (2010). Ciudadana X: Gender Violence and the Denationalisation of Women's Rights in Ciudad Juarez, Mexico. In R. L. Fregoso & C. Bejarano (Eds.), *Terrorising Women: Feminicide in the Americas*. Washington: Duke University Press.

Seal, L. (2010). *Women, Murder and Femininity: Gender Representations of Women Who Kill*. Basingstoke: Palgrave Macmillan.

Seltzer, M. (1998). *Serial Killers: Death and Life in America's Wound Culture*. London: Sage.

Shaw, K. (2010). *David Peace: Texts and Contexts*. Brighton: Sussex Academic Press.

Shaw, K. (Ed.). (2011). *Analysing David Peace*. Cambridge: Cambridge Scholars.

Smith, J. (2013). *Misogynies: Reflections on Myth and Malice*. New York: Fawcett Columbine.

Smith, K., Coleman, K., Eder, S., & Hall, P. (2011). *Homicides, Firearm Offences and Intimate Violence*. London: Home Office HMSO.

Soothill, K. (1993). The Serial Killer Industry. *Journal of Forensic Psychiatry, 4*(2), 342–354.

Soothill, K. (1996). Murder: The Importance of the Structural and Cultural Conditions. *Journal of Forensic Medicine, 3*, 161–165.

Upson, N. (2001, August 20). Hunting the Yorkshire Ripper. *New Statesman*.

Vronsky, P. (2004). *Serial Killers: The Method and Madness of Monsters*. New York: Berkley.

Walkowitz, J. (1982). Jack the Ripper and Myth of Male Violence. *Feminist Studies, 8*(3), 542–574.

Warkentin, E. (2010). "Jack the Ripper" Strikes Again: The "Ipswich Ripper" and the "Vice Girls He Killed". *Feminist Media Studies, 10*, 35–49.

Webber, C. (2010). *Psychology and Crime.* London: Sage.

Wiest, J. B. (2011). *Creating Cultural Monsters: Serial Murder in America.* Boca Raton, FL: CRC Press.

Williams, E. (1967). *Beyond Belief.* London: Pan.

Wilson, D. (2007). *Serial Killers: Hunting Britons and Their Victims 1966–2006.* Hampshire Hook: Waterside Press.

Wilson, D. (2012). Late Capitalism, Vulnerable Populations and Violent Predatory Crime. In S. Hall & S. Winlow (Eds.), *New Directions in Criminological Theory.* London: Routledge.

Winder, R. (1991, April 27). When Murder Is Not Enough. *The Independent.*

Winlow, S. (2001). *Badfellas.* Oxford: Berg.

Wykes, M., & Welsh, K. (2009). *Violence, Gender and Justice.* London: Sage.

CHAPTER 4

Feminist Histories and the Sutcliffe Murders: Interrogating Fear, Race and the 'Sex Wars'

Abstract This chapter explores how the history of feminist activism and the development of feminist theory and research coincided with the Sutcliffe murders. It highlights how the murders galvanised local feminist activism in West Yorkshire in response to the murders and police and media treatment of many of the victims. The chapter analyses alternative histories from the time which critique feminist activism as insensitive to race whilst other commentators claim that sex workers and their advocates were denied any voice within feminist debates at the time. The latter section of the chapter draws upon research findings to unpack the dominant fear narrative surrounding the murders, revealing the complexity and ambiguity of fear experiences both in the context of this case and beyond.

Keywords Radical feminism · Revolutionary feminism · Reclaim the Night · Feminist history · Race · Sex wars · Women's fear of crime

INTRODUCTION

Chronologically, the Yorkshire Ripper case occurred in the midst of the growth of academic feminism and feminist activism as part of the emergence of radical feminism and the Women's Liberation Movement (WLM) from the late 1960s onwards. It can be argued that these murders became a key event in the history of radical feminism. With this

© The Author(s) 2018   69
L. Wattis, *Revisiting the Yorkshire Ripper Murders*,
Palgrave Studies in Victims and Victimology,
https://doi.org/10.1007/978-3-030-01385-1_4

mind, this chapter will explore how feminist activism and academic scholarship developed against the backdrop of the Sutcliffe murders. It will explore how feminist academics and activists were galvanised by the murders which became a means to envisage the linkages between fear, violence against women and social and spatial restriction in the context of patriarchy.

The chapter then progresses to interrogate the overarching story presented by feminism from this time. In doing so, it considers criticisms from those who accuse the movement of insensitivity to issues of race in the routing of activist marches through Black communities which resonates with broader criticisms of second wave feminism as ethnocentric (hooks 1982; Hill Collins 1990). This discussion also explores alternative accounts of feminism and sex work from this period, highlighting the dominance and legacy of the radical feminist analysis of prostitution and the tensions within feminism over prostitution and sex work perspectives, which became established in the United Kingdom at around the time of the murders and continue to reverberate in contemporary academic and policy debates. Alternative counter narratives are also explored by way of my own research findings, which both corroborate the story of women's fear and the threat of the 'Ripper', whilst also offering up alternative experiences of fear, resistance and fearlessness which attest to the complexity and ambiguity of fear experiences both in the context of this case and beyond.

THE HISTORY OF FEMINISM AND THE SUTCLIFFE MURDERS

Mackay (2015) charts the development of second wave feminism and the establishment of the WLM in the UK, influenced by feminist activism in the US, which emerged in response to the side lining and denigration of women and women's issues within the revolutionary movements of the Left in the United States in the late 1960s. During this period feminism's political and academic development analysed the root causes of women's oppression in patriarchy and formulated responses to engender change. As Mackay (2015) observes, amidst the differing strands of feminism from this time, radical feminism and its related off-shoot revolutionary feminism, arguably formulated the most compelling and wide-ranging theoretical framework, locating male violence against women at the heart of their analysis of patriarchal social relations. Moreover, feminist academic analysis combined with activist responses to male violence via the formation of grassroots responses to domestic and sexual violence via the creation of rape crisis centres and the founding of the refuge movement (Lupton 1994; Morgan and Jenkins 2005; Jones and Cook 2008).

Indeed, the emergence of radical feminism as part of second wave feminism ushered in a focus on the gendered nature of violence, revealing the extent of hidden violence against women perpetrated by men. Key texts from the 1970s and 1980s revealed how rape and sexual violence, domestic violence and sexual harassment were sufficiently widespread to be considered structural in the context of patriarchy and central to the control and subordination of women via fear of men's violence (Brownmiller 1975; Riger and Gordon 1981; Hanmer and Saunders 1984; Kelly 1987; Mackinnon 1987, 1989). A large body of work thereafter identified women's fear of crime as higher and distinct from men's. This was explained via a number of connected factors: the construction of public risk emanating from the threat of the male stranger, fear of sexual violence, actual experiences of harassment and violence and the construction of feminine vulnerability (Hanmer and Saunders 1984; Kelly 1987; Pain 1991; Painter 1992; Valentine 1989, 1992). Moreover, radical feminism also took on pornography and prostitution (and continues to do so) within a wider analysis of what constitutes violence against women (Mackay 2015), locating the sex industry within frameworks of exploitation and sexual objectification (Lederer 1980; Dworkin 1981; Mackinnon 1987; Barry 1996). So for instance, radical feminism views prostitution as a reflection of male heterosexual, patriarchal power and as violence against women in and of itself (Pateman 1983; Jeffreys 2008; Barry 1996). As a number of writers have noted (Walkowitz 1992; Kinnell 2008; Sanders 2016; Ferris 2015), the 'sex wars' debate (Sanders 2016), which refers to the opposing ideological and policy positions on prostitution as violence set against the sex as work perspective, advocated by many working in the sex industry, became established within this period.

The majority of Peter Sutcliffe's victims were attacked in Leeds and Bradford between 1975 and 1980. The Sutcliffe murders occurred at a time when radical feminist activism was taking off nationally and internationally. At the local level, West Yorkshire became a locus for burgeoning activism. The controversial Revolutionary Feminist Group, which advocated feminists' political and sexual separatism, viewing feminist women's involvement in heterosexual relationships and political collaboration with men as antithetical to the feminist cause, was formed in Leeds in 1977. The radical feminist critique of heterosexuality as oppressive and based upon women's submission and objectification (Rich 1980; Mackinnon 1987; Dworkin 1976; Leeds Revolutionary Feminist Group 1981) informs this position which occurred in response to the perceived growing influence of liberal feminism within the wider feminist movement (Jeffreys 1977; Guest 2006; Mackay 2015). The Leeds Revolutionary Feminists (LRF) were also clearly galvanised by the serial murder of women on their doorstep. Indeed, feminist activism, both nationally and locally, reacted against the actual murders, as well as police and media attitudes towards certain victims viewed as culpable due to a perceived lack of respectability. As Walkowitz (1992) notes in relation to the case, 'feminists were most coherent in their denunciation of the police and press treatment of victims' (p. 236). At the time the murders were taking place, the Radical and Revolutionary Feminist message regarding male violence against women as a structural force central to women's subordination was crystallising amidst local activism, which itself formed part of the development of the wider national and international second wave feminist movement. For feminists at the time, the murders themselves, police and media indifference towards many victims and the folk hero status bestowed upon the murderer were clear evidence of how violence against women and misogyny operates in the context of patriarchy.

Mackay (2015) identifies Revolutionary Feminism's activism in West Yorkshire and their analysis of male violence as informing the ethos and structure of the Reclaim the Night (RTN) marches, which formed a central element of the activist response to the Sutcliffe murders. Finn Mackay (2015) is a central figure in the contemporary resurgence of the feminist movement in the 2000s. She is also responsible for the revival of the current RTN marches and has explored the origins of RTN as part of the wider history of second wave feminism. She notes how marches in European cities in 1976 captured the imagination of British feminists based in Leeds, who were taken with the notion of 'physically taking back the streets against male violence' (p. 75). As Mackay further notes, the Sutcliffe murders inspired Leeds-based feminists to organize two marches on 12th November 1977 to protest against the murders and male violence against women more generally, as well as to remember victims. The event was advertised in *Spare Rib* in the following way:

12 November: Torchlit women only midnight demonstration in the Chapeltown area of Leeds, organized by the local Revolutionary Feminist Group on the themes every woman has the right to walk alone at night without fear, and fight rape. They hope that other towns will do the same on that night in order to attract publicity. (*Spare Rib* 64, 1977, cited in Mackay 2014: 81)

Two years later, following the murder of student Barbara Leach in September 1979, feminists reacted with positive action to protect women students at Bradford University, organizing self-defence classes, escorts and women-only mini-buses. In addition, 400 women marched through the streets of the city railing against the demands for curfews to be placed upon women by police, media and more widely. For instance, following Barbara's murder, the Vice Chancellor of the University of Bradford called for women students not to go out alone after dark (Yallop 1993).

Walkowitz (1992) notes how the activist surge amongst West Yorkshire feminists 'spearheaded' national activism with the formation of WAVAW (Women against Violence against Women) and the hosting of the WLM Violence against Women Conference in Leeds in November 1980. She refers to 'a coincidence of events' (p. 234) whereby the conference in Leeds took place shortly after the murder of student Jacqueline Hill by Peter Sutcliffe in November 1980. This provoked further anger and engagement in 'direct action against "men" and the "media", who were viewed as responsible for violence against women by way of the circulation of misogynist material. This involved local and national demonstrations by feminists campaigning against the sale of pornography and the picketing of sex shops and cinemas showing films glorifying sexual violence and the sexual murder of women (Yallop 1993; *Spare Rib* 1980; Kinnell 2008).

FEMINISM AND THE SUTCLIFFE MURDERS: EXPLORING ALTERNATIVE HISTORIES

The late 1970s was arguably a key historical moment for emergent radical and revolutionary feminist politics and these murders became a central component of this story. Feminists were inspired to mobilise women to take back the night in the context of the wider systemic threat of male violence, as well as railing against police indifference and victim blaming towards victims not deemed respectable and therefore culpable. As the journalist and activist Kinnell (2008) reflects, 'The Yorkshire Ripper case was my reason for becoming a campaigner against sexual violence. I was angry, like many others, that the police only really seemed to step up the investigation when the first "non-prostitute" was killed' (Bindel 2005, cited in Kinnell 2008: 18).

However, local feminist activism at the time of the murders has been accused of racism, as well as failing to engage with sex workers and their advocates. For instance, Mackay highlights how following the two marches in Leeds, the organisers were publicly accused of racism because one of the marches was routed through Chapeltown. The area is ethnically diverse with a long history of immigrant settlement—in particular a large Black Afro-Caribbean community has settled there (Farrar 1996, 2012). Historically, there have been longstanding tensions between police and the Black community in Chapeltown, culminating in riots in 1975, 1981, and 2001. Chapeltown is also notorious as the former Leeds red-light district and the location of four murders and two attacks by Peter Sutcliffe.

In a balanced commentary on these events, Mackay (2015) draws attention to letters sent to the feminist newsletter WIRES condemning the organisers for racism and insensitivity by marching through an over-policed Black area. Mackay acknowledges subsequent academic criticisms of the Leeds RTN marches and RTN more generally on the grounds of racism or at best, failing to consider fully the position of Black communities. In brief, marching through a Black community may have reinforced assumptions regarding Black men's criminality and sexuality, and drawn police attention to an already over-policed and harassed community. The following extract cited by Mackay reflects these sentiments:

> The 'Reclaim the Night marches in the late 1970s demanded amongst other things, greater police protection for 'women' (read: white women). Many of these marches were routed through the hearts of black communities. Not only was this interpreted as an invitation to exert greater control over these areas, but it reinforced the association of Afro-Caribbean youth with crime. This played into racist notions of the 'coloured' male rapist and white female victim. (Cox 1990, cited in Mackay 2015: 95)

Mackay (2015) defends the decision to march through Chapeltown because it was where four women had been murdered and many of the march organisers lived in the area. She also points out that there was no collusion between activists and police: organisers did not seek police permission, nor did they demand an increased police presence. They were, she argues, 'working outside of the state' (p. 92). In addition, as Mackay states, residents were informed and consulted prior to the march taking place and march organisers were aware of the ramifications of marching through Chapeltown's Black community. Mackay further argues that concerns about racism need to be understood in the wider context of race relations in Great Britain in the 1970s. Racial conflict and the criminalisation of Black men was highlighted in Hall et al.'s (1978) *Policing the Crisis* which identified how the 1970s tabloid media constructed a popular discourse of disproportionate Black criminality and the racialisation of street crime. Extending on these themes, Gilroy (2002) argues that the criminalisation of Black men coincided with racist and nationalist agendas in the 1970s, with racist calls to law and order justified as the necessary means to deal with excessive Black criminality. The critics of RTN clearly take issue with what they view as yet another instance where Black communities are criminalised—this time via feminist activists' mishandling of race in their response to the Sutcliffe murders.

Moreover, at the level of the local, Farrar's (1996) historical exploration of immigrant settlement in Chapeltown, written from the dual perspective of academic and long term Chapeltown resident, highlights additional levels of complexity with regard the relationship between race and the Sutcliffe case. Farrar identifies how pejorative framings of Chapeltown by media and politicians began as early as the 1950s when Black Caribbean immigrants began to settle there. Farrar (1996) argues that Chapeltown's identity as a 'mecca of vice' was fully realised by the mid-1970s amidst political and media concerns about relationships between Black men and White women linked to street prostitution in the area. He further argues that the combination of physical dereliction, actual crime rates and the criminalisation of the Afro-Caribbean community led to the construction of a stigmatised place identity, which was intensified when the area became associated with the Sutcliffe murders. In this way, the timing of the murders and their association with an already stigmatised and criminalised local Black community may have in some way reinforced racist assumptions about Black deviance even before the RTN marches took place.

Farrar illustrates the complexity and contradiction of this imagining of place stigma based as it was around notions of Black men's criminality and White women's deviant sexuality, arguing that "the power of the 'Ripper' saga in enforcing Chapeltown's reputation lies in the silence 'Ripper' narratives have about race" (p. 11). The Sutcliffe murders intensified place stigma. Initially this was via racist assumptions, but the killer turned out to be a White man and this is not named explicitly.

In conclusion, to return to the issue of racism and the RTN marches, there does appear to be some conflation between racism and a lack of sensitivity to race on the part of feminist activists. Mackay's balanced history of these events is at pains to present both sides of the argument, conceding concerns about racism and recognising (but ultimately refuting) charges of racism against feminist activists. Mackay concludes that these concerns need to be understood within the wider context of 1970s race relations and broader debates within the feminist movement. Mackay is not specific here, but she is likely referring to Black feminist critiques of feminism's ethnocentrism and the failure to grasp Black women's differential experiences of oppression and violence in a racist and patriarchal society (hooks 1982; Hill Collins 1990; Anthias and Yuval Davis 1993; Haaken 2010). For instance, it is clear that patriarchal violence and gender were privileged in this context, whereas for Black women, racist violence may supersede patriarchal violence (hooks 1982; Yeatman 1994). In the context of the Sutcliffe murders, race is overshadowed by gender as the 'master oppression' (Yeatman 1994) and alternative voices are to an extent, lost from this history.

FEMINISM, PROSTITUTION
AND THE SUTCLIFFE MURDERS

Further critiques relate to claims that radical feminists excluded sex workers and groups representing sex workers from the activist dialogue at the time. For Kinnell (2008) this is reflected in the fact that the 1977 RTN Marches and other protests only took place following the murders of women not linked to sex work: marches and protests followed the murder of Jayne MacDonald in July 1977 and students Barbara Leach and Jacqueline Hill in September 1979 and November 1980 respectively. Kinnell draws upon Yallop's observations to highlight this:

There had been ... no public marches through the streets after the murder of Wilma McCann, Emily Jackson, and Irene Richardson, all in Leeds. There was no female outcry after Tina Atkinson had been brutally murdered in Bradford, or Maureen Long attacked in the same city, or Yvonne Pearson also murdered in the same city. No feminists took to the streets after the murder of Jean Jordon. They were equally mute after Vera Millward had been hacked to death. There was no feminist public protest after what was left of Helen Rytka had been discovered. It is abundantly clear that it took the deaths of non-prostitutes, of Jayne MacDonald in Leeds, Josephine Whitaker in Halfifax and Barbara Leach in Bradford, to produce public action from women. (Yallop 1993, cited in Kinnell 2008: 19)

Kinnell further argues that prostitution/sex work was largely invisible from activist concerns at the time with no will to engage with groups representing the interests of sex workers to think through issues relating to aggressive policing and the criminalization of sex work. For instance, Kinnell notes that the campaign to abolish imprisonment for soliciting initiated by the Programme for the Reform of the Law on Soliciting (PROS) began in 1975 and 'culminated in the abolition of imprisonment for soliciting and loitering offences in 1982' is invisible from the feminist story from the time, which only really emphasizes the relationship between the murders and radical feminist activism (Kinnell 2008: 21).

Likewise, Walkowitz (1992) notes how feminist unity in response to police and media misogyny and indifference towards victims connected to sex work was ruptured as 'the uneasy consensus established by feminists in the face of Yorkshire Ripper soon began to unravel as feminists confronted the issue of pornography as well as the politics of prostitution' (p. 241). The development of radical feminism's 'joined up' analysis of the varied aspects of male violence to include prostitution and pornography and the emergence of powerful voices which positioned prostitution within patriarchy led to the entrenchment of polarised positions—prostitution as violence and sex as work, in what is commonly referred to as the 'sex wars' (Walkowitz 1992; Kinnell 2008; Ferris 2015). These opposing positions may well have existed prior to the growth in analysis and activism in the wake of the Sutcliffe murders, but this historical moment appears fundamental to the bedding in of divergent positions, which persist in academic dialogue, production and activism (Raymond 2013; Barry 1996; Jeffreys 2008, 2009; Scoular 2004; Sanders 2016; Phoenix 2009; O'Neill 2010; Agustin 2007; Kinnell

2008). As Ferris (2015) puts it, the case established 'feminism's deeply ambivalent relationship to the sex industry' (p. 34). Moreover, Kinnell (2008) argues that radical feminist responses to the Sutcliffe murders have played a significant role in shaping perceptions of violence against sex workers as inevitable, as well as exerting significant influence over the regulation of prostitution via criminalisation and criminal justice, informed by an abolitionist ideology. For Ferris (2015), the radical feminist stance on prostitution, which became fully realised following the Sutcliffe case, increased the marginalisation of sex workers and 'further damaged the already troubled relationship between sex workers and mainstream culture' (p. 34).

The radical feminist position on prostitution identifies it as 'inherently gendered' where for the most part, gender identity determines who prostitutes will be and who will purchase sex (Jeffreys 2009; Mackey 2015). Relatedly, this position views all forms of prostitution as intrinsically exploitative and violent, perpetuated by heterosexual relations in patriarchy, which promote women's sexual objectification and subordination (Raymond 2013; Barry 1996; Jeffreys 2008, 2009). Moreover, as Jeffreys (2009) asserts, prostitution and other sectors of the sex industry, such as strip clubs, perpetuate misogyny and reproduce and reinforce masculine privilege by way of the exclusion of women from 'male only' spaces where gender roles are circumscribed around women's objectification.

Jeffreys (2008) claims that the normalisation of prostitution, which occurred in the wake of the sexual revolution, promoted prostitution as a positive life choice for women. Indeed, for Jeffreys (2008), it is this normalisation of 'the idea of prostitution', which perpetuates its existence and acceptance. Relatedly, radical feminist perspectives refute that women can ever enter into prostitution voluntarily—the oppressive socio-economic conditions surrounding it mean women's agency/choice is simply not possible (Raymond 2013). Jeffreys' (2009) more recent analysis, which focuses on the intrinsic harms of prostitution, especially in light of global neo-liberalism and the growth and diversification of the sex industry, conveys the radical feminist position in the following way:

> All these systems create harms to the status of women and other social and political harms such as crime and corruption that are a regular part of prostitution industries ... Common to all these forms of prostitution is the idea that men have the right to access women for sexual use, an idea that is formed from cultures of misogyny and male dominance. (Jeffreys 2009: 128)

The opposing position, often taken up by those involved in the sex industry (ECP; Scarlett Alliance, UKNSWP) and academics who support them, demands the recognition of sex work as a legitimate profession and lobbies for the rights and recognition of sex workers and appropriate regulation of sex work to ensure the safety and welfare of sex workers (Scoular 2004; Brooks-Gordon 2008; Agustin 2007; Phoenix 2009; Kinnell 2008; O'Neill 2010; Armstrong 2015; Sanders 2016). Broadly, the sex work or 'sex-positive' approach takes issue with radical feminism on the grounds that its structural analysis does not recognise the complexities of the sex industry or the exploitative nature of paid labour more generally. Radical feminism has also been accused of conflating prostitution with a wider critique of heterosexuality and fails to include the voices and experiences of sex workers themselves.

So for instance, Walker (1999) argues that the fixation with structural exploitation within radical feminist analyis obfuscates the actuality of 'poverty, violence, criminalisation' which many women face (p. 168). Scoular (2004) notes that the overly simplistic analysis of the gender dynamics of prostitution fails to grasp what is actually a 'complex social interaction' (Scoular 2004: 134). Focusing on violence against sex workers, Sanders (2016) argues that constructing sex work or 'prostitution' as intrinsically violent 'has allowed structural factors to persist which have led to violence against sex workers as acceptable'. For Sanders this diverts from actual violence perpetrated against sex workers (Sanders 2016: 94). Moreover, Sanders further argues that despite high levels of violence across the globe, sex work should not be viewed as inevitably violent. In a study focusing on migration and the sex industry, Agustin (2007) rejects what she refers to as the perpetual victims label assigned to those involved in the sex industry by so called 'feminist fundamentalists', further arguing that feminism routinely conflates migrants who sell sex with trafficked women, when the reality is many have made an economic choice to make their living in the sex industry.

These opposing perspectives most frequently clash in the domain of policy and regulation. Radical feminists favour abolitionism and the use of the criminal justice system (more recently focusing on the criminalisation of male clients) to regulate and outlaw prostitution so that it cannot exist (Ekberg 2004; Farley 2004; Raymond 2004; Bindel 2017). The sex work position is critical of criminal justice regulation, pointing to a history of stigmatisation and oppression via the construction of the prostitute as deviant and Other within legal and criminal justice discourse (Kinnell 2008; O'Neill 2010; Sanders 2016; Vanwesenbeeck 2017). What is more, this position highlights how the current criminalisation of sex work and sex workers, even when dressed up within a welfare approach (Sanders 2009), exacerbates archetypal prostitute stigma (Lowman 2000; Hallsgrimdottir et al. 2008; Sanders 2016) which places sex workers at risk from violence as they seek to avoid prosecution and criminalisation (Sanders 2016; Kinnell 2008; Sanders 2009; Sanders and Campbell 2007). As Penfold et al. (2004) observe: 'The criminalization of soliciting and loitering also leads to a perception among street sex workers that they have no recourse to justice' (p. 367).

Radical feminist and sex positive positions appear to be intractable. Sex positive feminists view the radical feminist position as failing to grasp the complexity and nuance of sex workers' experiences, arguing that many sex workers do not view their involvement in the sex industry as violent or exploitative. Notwithstanding, one cannot disavow the power and gender dynamics which are inherent across much of the sex industry and the implications for women of sexual objectification and the perpetuation of misogyny (Jeffreys 2009; Dines 2012). That said, the contested terrain over women's sexual agency versus sexual objectification is fraught with ambiguity and contradiction. For instance, does agreement with radical feminism and the belief in the sex industry as largely exploitative mean that by default one must adopt outright condemnation of feminine sexual agency and expression in the context of heterosexual relations (see, Marks and Neville 2017 for an interesting discussion of these complex questions).

Both sides of this debate lay claim to research evidence to support their position via the presentation of the 'happy hooker' or the 'sex work survivor' (Chapkis 1997), which are then deployed to counter the opposing position. Notwithstanding, the argument that sex workers are unaware of the conditions of their own exploitation (Raymond 2013), the sale of sex will likely comprise both sets of experiences, providing powerful examples of the myths and counter-myths of feminism (Haaken 2010). In-depth ethnographic work on the experiences of sex workers illuminates the complexities and contradictions of agency, economic imperatives and the gendered contexts in which much of the sex industry operates (Aoyama 2008; Zheng 2009). For instance, Zheng's (2009) ethnography of hostesses in China highlights the patriarchal conditions in which women work in terms of harassment and the abusive behaviour of male clients. At the same time however, Zheng also reveals how hostess work is a means by which many poor Chinese women from rural areas can escape extreme poverty and achieve a much higher standard of living.

COUNTER-NARRATIVES ON FEAR AND THE 'RIPPER'

In the cities most vulnerable to the killer, there had been in the days that immediately followed Jacqueline's murder a fear that spread like the wind. It is difficult for any man to comprehend the depth of that fear, of how totally it affected every thought and deed of the women in those cities. (Yallop 1993: 330)

"I have lived five years of utter fear", declared a female correspondent residing in Yorkshire in a letter to the feminist journal *Spare Rib*, "having to think twice before taking a trip to the corner shop … I've had five years of looking hard at every man I know and fearing he could be the one. I've had five years of impotent fury at being chained in [at night] when I'd rather be out". (Extract from Spare Rib, cited in Walkowitz 1992: 231)

The above extracts reflect the dominant fear narrative surrounding the 'Yorkshire Ripper' and the way in which feminists linked this to a wider analysis of women's fear of men and male violence against women. However, my own research findings, whilst supporting much of this narrative, also reveal more ambiguous accounts. Indeed, this received account of fear did not emerge consistently across within my own research findings. Stories of extreme and pervasive fears were evident, but this was alongside less categorical accounts of how women engaged with threat of the 'Ripper'. The quote below from Laura supports the high-fear version of events. Laura was a student at Leeds University during the murders and recounts a set of intense fear-related emotions. She refers to obsession, hysteria, as well as the practice of private safety/security in the wake of the murder of fellow Leeds University student, Jacqueline Hill:

Laura: But I think it became quite…we were very scared I think. I think after Jacqueline, you know it…we became a bit obsessed I suppose by it.
Interviewer: Really?
Laura: Yes. I think so. We were very frightened and I suppose we were a lot more careful about what we did and the thing about security and whether your house felt you know was safe in terms of the kind of locks and making sure that you locked up and kept your windows closed and that has an effect as well. Normally, you might want to have your windows open at night. But that, we didn't do that. And I suppose, yeah that was the thing I remember most. It's the fear really and the kind of … Not hysteria but it did get a bit like that. We felt as though we were … I think the way I would describe it is that felt like we were under siege. That it was very difficult to go about a normal way of living.

In common with several other research participants, Laura's fears resemble the 'high-fear' narrative, which has come to define this case. Laura represents the typical fears of the middle-class student from this time: she refers to Jacqueline Hill, but does not mention any of the other victims. This is consistent with Hanmer and Saunders' (1984) claim that the murders became a bigger concern for women students in Bradford and Leeds after Barbara Leach, and particularly Jacqueline Hill, were killed which contradicts popular assumptions of women gripped by fear during the five-year period the murders were taking place. Indeed, within this small and varied sample, women's memories of their fears emerged as nuanced and multi-faceted, demonstrating assorted recollections of fearfulness, resistance and disavowal, with notable gradations of fear shaped by class, community and locality. Fear of the 'Ripper' was not isolated to middle-class students as the following extracts from local Leeds women Mary (working as a bus conductor during the murders) and Eileen (working as a secretary) illustrate. In the quote below Eileen discusses fear/lack of fear inconsistently: she discusses how her sense of risk was minimised because of the construction of the 'prostitute-killer', but then how she becomes more concerned and frustrated as the murders progress:

> *Eileen*: Towards the end it got worse and worse. I used to be frightened because I did used to go out with friends through the week and I used to … I did used to have a company car didn't I? If somebody was sacked let's say—they were sacked every two minutes, I was given like a company car to use until they sold it at auction or something so normally I had use of a company car. A lot of times but they used to break down. and I remember a little green thing … I don't know what it was but it used to breakdown every two minutes and I remember being really scared in that thinking shit if it breaks down and its one o clock in the morning and I'm out you know what do I do? And I remember Billy saying to me "lock yourself in the car" and stuff like that and "don't walk anywhere". But um…I wasn't particularly frightened the first couple of murders or something, or attacks. I was horrified by what I read and what I'd heard about what he'd done to them and stuff, what they released for us all to know. I couldn't believe that that … that somebody could actually do that so I wasn't particularly worried about myself at that time but as it got … worse and worse and worse and like Michelle says because it seemed as though he was targeting prostitutes. I still thought in the back of my mind I don't care whether its prostitutes or not you might be walking somewhere and he might think "oh well what's she doing down here she shouldn't be down her at half past

one in the morning she must be a prostitute". And so yeah there was still that realisation at the back of my mind that um yeah I wasn't right happy about it and as … as it went on and on and on and we didn't seem to be finding who it was I think it was not finding who it was put the most pressure on me.

Interviewer: Really?

Eileen: Yeah because I felt like at the end of my tether type of thing with them not getting the bottom of it. It was like oh for god's sake what's going on here somebody somewhere knows something, what the hell's going on? Why can't they get this person?

Mary's account evidences the connections and conflations that can be made between separate crime events and fear even in the space of one recollection. Below, she links the sense of danger she felt during the Leeds riots, which took place on three separate occasions in Chapeltown in 1975, 1981, and 1987 (she is vague about the chronology of the riots and which riots she is referring to specifically), with her fears during the Sutcliffe murders. The riots and the murders are distinct as acts of violence and criminality, but Mary's conflation of her fears in the face of differing criminal events reinforces fear as capricious and complex (Sparks 1992; Girling et al. 2000; Moore and Breeze 2012). As such, women's fearfulness may not in all circumstances, neatly align with a radical feminist analysis:

Mary: I was telling you earlier about when I'd driven right round and that wasn't for the Ripper murders. That was when we had the riots on in Leeds … So yeah, that, that must have been about 1983–1984 I think. The first round of riots. But it's, you see that was one of the first things I said to you when you said would I do the research and I said I remembered how I felt. Now that was sheer, sheer fear was that and it was a very temporary thing—you knew these riots wouldn't last long. But what I associated it with was the fear that I had felt. You know maybe, maybe seven or eight years earlier from, from the Ripper.

Other women expressed a resounding lack of fear and disavowal of the impact of the murders. Rita was thirteen when Wilma McCann, the first woman to be killed by Peter Sutcliffe, was murdered in Chapeltown in November 1975. Rita grew up in Chapeltown and lived there during the time that four women were murdered and a further two women were attacked by Peter Sutcliffe in the area. Yet, as her comments below illustrate, she felt that the murders did not affect herself, friends, family and the wider community in any significant way:

> *Rita*: Nobody in our area was bothered...I'm not saying they weren't
> bothered of course they probably were bothered, but for me, myself,
> my family, my friends, and the people who we worked for we just car-
> ried on as normal. People in the school, everybody at school, just car-
> ried on as normal. Went to Cowper Street Middle School, Earl Cowper
> Middle School, right smack bang in the middle of Chapeltown and
> everybody just carried on as normal you know? It was just...yeah it
> wasn't...it wasn't all that...it wasn't...it wasn't a scary time.

Rita's account is delineated by a strong sense of community and place: stories of her childhood and growing up; discussion of family and friends; frequent references to street names and local landmarks. Rita described Chaptown with great affection, defending its pejorative label-ling as a red-light district (see also, Farrar 1996, 2012). This sense of a close-knit working-class community was also reinforced by Rita's vicarious links to victims Wilma McCann and Jayne MacDonald who she knew through friends and by sight within the neighbourhood. Rita's denial of fear in her telling of these murders can be understood via her positioning within this community and her sense of 'being known' therein (Walklate 1998, 2002). Quoting her best friend from childhood who grew up with her in Chapeltown: "I always felt safe in Chapeltown, there was always somebody". Individuals' connectedness and sense of belonging within their neighbourhoods has been identified as mitigating and confounding fear of crime even in the face of high rates of crime and disorder, objective risk and a clearly defined threat (Walklate 1998, 2002; Moran and Skeggs 2004). Moreover, Rita's account emphasises the complexity of fear and the value of narrative analysis, which offers space for alternative accounts and meanings to emerge (Sandberg et al. 2015).

The complexities of fear narratives were also illustrated within inter-views with two women involved in sex work. These interviews offer alternative accounts of this period, which give voice and visibility to the experiences of sex workers. What is more, these accounts explore the negotiation of fear for two women whose routine experience was circum-scribed by violence and fear. For instance, Kay talked about how she was fostered as a child and then had to support herself from the age of sev-enteen. It was at this point she became involved in sex work. She also discussed her long-term relationship with a violent partner, which had begun around the time she became involved in sex work, and had only recently ended shortly before she was interviewed for this project. Kay was working 'the beat', as she referred to it, around Chapel Town in Leeds in 1975 when Wilma McCann was murdered and continued to do so during the five years the murders were taking place, and was still involved in sex work at the time she was interviewed. When asked about her fears at the time, her response was muted and ambivalent:

> *Interviewer:* So did the murders affect how safe you felt?
> *Kay:* No because you never felt safe anyway!
> *Interviewer:* So you were always...right that's interesting that so you always felt kind of...feared for your safety?
> *Kay:* Oh yeah! Yeah!
> *Interviewer:* And that didn't get worse?
> *Kay:* But...not...maybe slightly, maybe slightly, but no worse than...any customer that might be hard work, or didn't pay you at the end of it, or -
> *Interviewer:* It seemed like part and parcel of ...?
> *Kay:* Give me back my money type of thing you know, beat you up. It's just all part and parcel of the same job.

Kay tells a range stories, which reveal the threat/presence of the Ripper. For example, she discussed how a friend had thought she had been stopped by the murderer; she also recalled being telephoned by a man claiming to be the 'Ripper'. Despite this, Kay did not recall being especially fearful. This was in spite of routine anticipation and negotiation of private and public violence from an abusive partner and clients. Moreover, Kay also endured police harassment, as the police remained intent on arresting and convicting women for soliciting in the red-light districts of Leeds and Bradford. This continued during the murders even though it placed women at even greater risk (Kinnell 2008). In this sense, the threat of the murderer was not exceptional for Kay: the fear of the 'Ripper' was subsumed as 'part and parcel' of male violence as an everyday and longitudinal threat (1997; Painter 1992).

Likewise, Pearl also disclosed a troubled biography of traumatic childhood experiences, homelessness and violence. And, in common with Kay, she was close to the murders in social and situational terms—she knew some of the victims indirectly and recalled seeing Jayne MacDonald on the night she was murdered. Pearl was also conscious that her relationship with fear was complex and problematic as illustrated in extract below:

Pearl: You know you've got to go deeper into it in a way…I had no fear

Interviewer: No fear at all throughout the whole thing?

Pearl: Not that I remember … We all just looked out for each other. None of us had any fear we'd all been pretty messed up women.

Interviewer: Really?

Pearl: Well … normally if that were happening, a normal human being wouldn't go on the street on their own would they? They'd be scared wouldn't they?

The feminist analysis of the Yorkshire Ripper murders positions the killer within a structural analysis, which identifies male violence and women's fear as systemic. This alludes to a unified feminine experience of violence and fear (Haaken 2010)—both in the context of these murders and more widely. However, as Haaken (2010) notes, in the pursuit of a shared history and experience of female oppression, alternative voices and stories are lost if they do not fit the dominant narrative. Working-class women's memories of the murders support this point. In particular, sex workers' reflections on fear—both at the time of the murders and more longitudinally, reveal complex and traumatic biographies delineated by violence and fear which arguably, most closely resemble feminism's claims that women's negotiation of violence and harassment are every day and routine experiences (1997; Valentine 1989, 1992). In this sense, these alternative accounts of fear and violence both disrupt and confirm feminist messages relating to women's experiences of fear and violence.

REFLECTING ON FEMINISM'S NARRATIVES AND COUNTER-NARRATIVES

This chapter has explored the relationship between the Sutcliffe case and feminism in the 1970s. The figure of the Yorkshire Ripper was invoked by feminists as emblematic and constitutive of the threat and actuality of male violence against women within patriarchy. Moreover, police and media discourses of victim-blaming and indifference towards victims predicated on assumptions about feminine respectability and sexual propriety were a further focus for feminist outrage in the face of blatant misogyny, which was especially marked in the framing of women linked to prostitution. Alongside the development of feminist theory, feminist history during this period presents a powerful account of consciousness-raising, local activism (in particular the RTN marches) and a collective experience of women's fear in response to the localised threat of the male serial killer (Hanmer and Saunders 1984; *Spare Rib* 1980; Ceresa 1981; Ward Jouve 1988; Stead 1980; Mackay 2014, 2015). Below Mackay (2015) presents an effective summation of how the murders and public reaction propelled 1970s feminism at the local level and beyond:

> For many women active in the WLM at the time, the national focus and paternalistic, sexist and societal response to these murders gave a very real resonance to the political theory being produced on VAW in that period. (Mackay 2015: 84)

However, the presentation of historical and political/academic narratives as overarching and all-encompassing loses sight of the nuance and complexity of history and narrative. As crime historians Gilman Srebnick and Levy (2005) note, 'all narrative accounts, whether historical or fictional, impose a synthetic order over events that are inherently disordered and culturally disjunctive' (p. 18, her emphasis). They further argue that those with an interest in crime histories are 'faced with working through the meaning' of narratives accounts of crime (fictive and historical) 'endowing them with historical understanding and meaning' (p. 18). Walkowitz (1992) makes this point in regard to Sutcliffe murders, warning that feminism's 'iconography of female victimisation' and the reproduction of 'cultural scripts' which occlude competing interpretations of women's experiences based upon difference may ultimately 'undercut the political impact of feminists' public initiatives (p. 244).

With this in mind, several counter-narratives to the feminist history of the Sutcliffe murders have been explored. Firstly, from those who take issue with feminism's lack of attention to racial oppression and how it intersects with gender to transform lived experiences of oppression, violence against women and racist constructions of Black criminality (Crenshaw 1991; Rice 1990; McCall 2005). Secondly, findings from my own research on the Sutcliffe murders disrupt the overarching accounts of a shared and pervasive feminine fear experience and its relation to the wider feminist analysis of male violence and female fear, with research findings revealing a more complex set of fear experiences based on class and locality, as well as sex workers' specific experiences of fear and violence. Lastly, it has been noted that the voices of sex workers, their campaign groups and pro-sex work feminists are largely absent from the story of feminism and the 'Yorkshire Ripper' (Kinnell 2008). Indeed, the reverberations of the bedding in of these opposing positions on the sale of sex continue to be felt. As Ferris (2015) notes, the Sutcliffe murders 'gave rise to complex political effects' which 'foregrounded feminism's deeply ambivalent relationship to the sex industry' (p. 34) and the further 'politicisation of sexuality' (Walkowitz 1992: 245). To be sure, prostitution/sex work is now an intractable feminist 'fault line' (Mackay 2015)—with opposing sides of the debate laying claim to the welfare and best interests of women (and indeed men).

Janice Haaken's analysis of the history of the 'battered women's movement' illuminates the universalising tendency of radical feminist narratives. In *Hard Knocks: Domestic Violence and the Psychology of Storytelling*, Haaken (2010) interrogates how 'stories' from popular culture and the feminist movement have shaped how we have come to know and understand male violence against women in the domestic sphere and the accompanying academic and activist response provided by feminists. Haaken's does not set out to denigrate the intellectual and practical responses of the women's movement to violence against women in the context of patriarchy. As Haaken maintains 'the critique of gender domination that is at the heart of feminist analysis' must not be lost (p. 44). Rather, she is concerned to work with 'myths and counter-myths' to 'open up a creative space between two opposing claims' (p. 13). For instance, she argues that attempts to reconcile commonality and difference in order to present a unifying story of violence against women may result in the experiences of poor women and women of colour being overlooked if they deviate from the 'stock script'.

Adopting a similar approach, in that both writers recognise the tensions and ambivalences which an engagement with feminist frameworks inheres, Cameron (2018) grapples with the divergent feminist positions on the sale of sex. She aligns herself with the radical feminist position and its critique of heterosexuality, identifying the manner in which it reveals and bears witness to violence against women. Notwithstanding, in something of a unique and optimistic move—given the intense dichotomising with which this debate is generally played out, she acknowledges the issues with the radical feminist analysis of prostitution and heterosexuality more generally, as well as the currency of sex positive arguments. Using psychoanalysis, Cameron (2018) draws on a range of frameworks to present a psychoanalytic account of attachment to specific theoretical and political positions due to their emotive nature, arguing that 'we develop attachments to theory as an investment in … intellectual and political existence' (p. 104). Radical feminism is viewed as especially affecting due to its analytical certainty and passion, and its focus on violence against women, often framed in 'inflammatory' language. For Cameron, this is what causes us to question our feminist position if we do not adhere completely to the arguments. But Cameron then draws attention to 'ambivalent attachments' whereby individuals may identify as radical feminists 'while acknowledging the political utility of sex-positive feminist argumentation' (p. 106) and forming emotional attachments to aspects of sex positive feminism.

> Rather than solving my dilemma concerning ambivalent attachments, this book has made me feel more comfortable with them. My sympathies for radical feminism, notably its cutting criticism of heterosexuality, can coexist with an assertion that sex-positive feminism is often right in its criticisms of radical feminist wrongs. (Cameron 2018: 108)

Cameron reassures that forming ambivalent attachments across these boundaries can be understood via the deployment of psychoanalytical frameworks and that 'ambivalence can be productive' (p. 108) and may be fruitful for feminism. This approach offers reassurance to those who identify with much of what radical feminism has to say but agonise over the conflicts and ambivalences it provokes.

The Sutcliffe murders and their representation demand a strong feminist response and analysis. This type of murder, occurring as it does within the wider context of systemic patriarchal violence and often greeted with indifference or fascination, reminds us of the continuing currency of radical feminist analyses. However, it is also okay to have doubts. The certainty of radical feminist analysis and its tendency to universalise appear to demand an overall commitment to all of the arguments. The themes I have explored in this chapter—race, women's fear of violence and the opposing positions on sex as work and prostitution as violence, evidence the complexity of women's experiences when issues of class and race are taken into account—both within the context of this project and beyond. I have aimed to celebrate and recognise the value of radical feminism, whilst also including alternative histories and voices from this time.

REFERENCES

Agustin, L. (2007). *Sex Work at the Margins: Migration, Labour Markets and the Rescue Industry*. London: Zed Books.

Anthias, N., & Yuval Davis, N. (1993). *Racialised Boundaries: Race, Nation, Gender, Colour and Class and the Anti-Racist Struggle*. London: Taylor and Francis.

Armstrong, L. (2015). From Law Enforcement to Protection? Interactions Between Sex Workers and Police in a Decriminalized Street-Based Sex Industry. *British Journal of Criminology, 57*(3), 570–588.

Aoyama, K. (2008). *Thai Migrant Sex Workers: From Modernisation to Globalisation*. Basingstoke: Palgrave Macmillan.

Barry, K. (1996). *The Prostitution of Sexuality: The Global Exploitation of Women*. New York: New York University Press.

Bindel, J. (2017, October 11). Why Prostitution Should Never Be Legalised. *The Guardian*.

Brooks-Gordon, B. (2008). *The Price of Sex: Prostitution, Policy and Society*. Cullompton: Willan.

Brownmiller, S. (1975). *Against Our Will: Men, Women and Rape*. Harmondsworth: Penguin.

Cameron, J. J. (2018). *Reconsidering Radical Feminism: Affect and the Politics of Heterosexuality*. Washington: University of Washington Press.

Ceresa, D. (1981). It's Women Who Are Under Attack. *Spare Rib*, 107, p. 17.

Chapkis, W. (1997). *Live Sex Acts: Women Performing Erotic Labour*. New York: Routledge.

Cox, C. (1990). Anything Less Is Not Feminism: Racial Difference and the WMWM. *Law and Critique, 1*(2), 237–248.

Crenshaw, K. (1991). Mapping the Margins: Intersectionality, Identity Politics and Violence Against Women of Colour. *Stanford Law Review, 43*(6), 1241–1299.

Dines, G. (2012). A Feminist Response to Weitzer. *Violence Against Women, 18*(4), 512–517.

Dworkin, A. (1976). *Our Blood: Prophecies and Discourses on Sexual Politics*. New York: Harper and Row.

Dworkin, A. (1981). *Pornography: Men Possessing Women*. New York: Perigee.

Ekberg, G. (2004). The Swedish Law That Prohibits the Purchase of Sexual Services: Best Practices for Prevention of Prostitution and Trafficking of Human Beings. *Violence Against Women, 10*(10), 1187–1218.

Farley, M. (2004). "Bad for the Body, Bad for the Heart": Prostitution Harms Women Even If Legalised or Decriminalised. *Violence Against Women, 10*(10), 1087–1125.

Farrar, M. (1996). Migrant Spaces and Settlers' Time: Forming and Deforming an Inner City. In S. Westwood & J. Williams (Eds.), *Imagining Cities: Scripts, Signs and Memory*. London: Routledge.

Farrar, M. (2012). Rioting or Protesting? Losing It or Finding It? *Parallax,* *18*(2), 72–91.

Ferris, S. (2015). *Street Sex Work and Canadian Cities: Resisting a Dangerous Order.* Alberta: University of Alberta Press.

Gilman Srebnick, A., & Levy, R. (2005). *Crime and Culture: An Historical Perspective.* Aldershot: Ashgate.

Gilroy, P. (2002). *There Ain't No Black in the Union Jack: The Cultural Politics of Race and Nation.* London: Routledge.

Girling, Evi, Loader, I., & Sparks, R. (2000). *Crime and Social Change in Middle England: Questions of Order in an English Town.* London: Routledge.

Guest, K. (2006, February 12). Whatever Happened to Feminism's Extreme Sects? *The Independent.*

Haaken, J. (2010). *Hard Knocks: Domestic Violence and the Psychology of Storytelling.* London: Routledge.

Hall, S., Critcher, C., Jefferson, T., Clarke, C., & Roberts, B. (1978). *Policing the Crisis: Mugging, the State and Law and Order.* London: Macmillan.

Hallsgrimdottir, H. G., Phillips, R., Benoit, C., & Walby, K. (2008). Sporting Girls, Streetwalkers and Inmates of Houses of Ill Repute: Media Narratives and the Historical Mutability of Prostitution Stigmas. *Sociological Perspectives,* *51*(1), 119–138.

Hanmer, J., & Saunders, S. (1984). *Well Founded Fear: A Community Study of Violence to Women.* Leeds: Hutchinson.

Hill Collins, P. (1990). *Black Feminist Thought: Knowledge, Consciousness and the Politics of Empowerment.* Boston: Unwin Hyman.

hooks, b. (1982). *Ain't I a Woman.* Boston: Pluto Press.

Jeffreys, S. (1977). The Need for Revolutionary Feminism. *Scarlet Woman, 5.*

Jeffreys, S. (2008). *The Idea of Prostitution.* Melbourne: Spinifex Press.

Jeffreys, S. (2009). *The Industrial Vagina: The Political Economy of the Global Sex Trade.* London: Routledge.

Jones, H., & Cook, K. (2008). *Rape Crisis: Responding to Sexual Violence.* London: Russell House.

Kelly, L. (1987). The Continuum of Sexual Violence. In J. Hanmer & M. Maynard (Eds.), *Women, Violence and Social Control.* London: Macmillan.

Kinnell, H. (2008). *Violence and Sex Work in Britain.* Devon Cullompton: Willan.

Lederer, L. (Ed.). (1980). *Take Back the Night: Women on Pornography.* New York: William Morrow.

Leeds Revolutionary Feminist Group. (1981). Love Your Enemy? *The Debate between Heterosexual Feminism and Political Lesbianism Wires 81,* 5–10.

Lowman, J. (2000). Violence and the Outlaw Status of (Street) Prostitution in Canada. *Violence Against Women, 6,* 987–1011.

Lupton C. (1994). The British Refuge Movement: The Survival of an Ideal? In C. Lupton & T. Gillespie (Eds.), *Working with Violence: Practical Social Work.* London: Palgrave Macmillan.

Mackay, F. (2014). Reclaiming Revolutionary Feminism. *Feminist Review, 106,* 95–103.

Mackay, F. (2015). *Radical Feminism: Feminist Activism in Movement.* London: Palgrave Macmillan.

Mackinnon, C. (1987). Toward Feminist Jurisprudence. *Stanford Law Review, 34,* 703–721.

Mackinnon, C. (1989). *Towards a Feminist Theory of the State.* Cambridge, MA: Harvard University Press.

Marks, L. H., & Neville, L. (2017). Gilead: An Anti-porn Utopia. *Nursing Clio.* https://nursingclio.org/2017/05/15/gilead-an-antiporn-utopia/.

McCall, L. (2005). The Complexity of Intersectionality. *Signs, 30,* 1771–1800.

Moore, S., & Breeze, S. (2012). Spaces of Male Fear: The Sexual Politics of Being Watched. *British Journal of Criminology, 52,* 1172–1191.

Moran, L., & Skeggs, B. (2004). *Sexuality and the Politics of Safety.* London: Routledge.

Morgan, S., & Jenkins, K. (2005). *The Feminist History Reader.* London: Routledge.

O'Neill, M. (2010). Cultural Criminology and Sex Work: Resisting Regulation Through Radical Democracy and Participatory Action Research (PAR). *Journal of Law and Society, 37*(1), 210–232.

Pain, R. (1991). Space, Sexual Violence and Social Control: Integrating Geographical and Feminist Analyses of Women's Fear of Crime. *Progress in Human Geography, 15,* 415–431.

Painter, K. (1992). Different Worlds: The Spatial, Temporal and Social Dimensions of Female Victimisation. In D. Evans, N. Fyfe, & D. Herbert (Eds.), *Crime, Policing and Place: Essays in Environmental Criminology.* London: Routledge.

Pateman, C. (1983). *The Sexual Contract.* Bloomington, IN: Stanford University Press.

Penfold, C., Hunter, G., Campbell, R., & Barham, L. (2004). Tackling Client Violence in Female Street Prostitution: Interagency Working Between Outreach Agencies and the Police. *Policing and Society, 4*(4), 365–379.

Phoenix, J. (2009). *Regulating Sex for Sale: Prostitution, Policy Reform and the UK.* Bristol: Policy Press.

Raymond, J. G. (2004). Prostitution on Demand: Legalising the Buyers as Sexual Consumers. *Violence Against Women, 10*(10), 1156–1186.

Raymond, J. G. (2013). *Not a Choice, Not a Job: Exposing the Myths of the Global Sex Trade.* Dulles: Potomac Books.

Rice, M. (1990). Challenging Orthodoxies in Feminist Theory: A Black Feminist Critique. In L. Gelsthorpe & A. Morris (Eds.), *Feminist Perspectives in Criminology.* Milton Keynes: Open University Press.

Rich, A. (1980). Compulsory Heterosexuality and Lesbian Existence. *Signs, 5*(4), 631–660.

Riger, S., & Gordon, M. (1981). The Fear of Rape: A Study in Social Control. *Journal of Social Issues, 37,* 71–92.

Sandberg, S., Tutenge, S., & Copes, H. (2015). Studies of Violence: A Narrative Criminological Study of Ambiguity. *British Journal of Criminology, 55,* 1168–1186.

Sanders, T. (2009). Controlling the Anti-Sexual City: Sexual Citizenship and the Disciplining of Female Sex Workers. *Criminology and Criminal Justice, 9*(4), 507–525.

Sanders, T. (2016). Inevitably Violent? Dynamics of Space, Governance and Stigma. *Special Issue: Problematizing Prostitution: Critical Research and Scholarship, Studies in Law, Politics and Society, 71,* 93–114.

Sanders, T., & Campbell, R. (2007). Designing Out Vulnerability, Building in Respect: Violence Safety and Sex Work Policy. *The British Journal of Sociology, 58*(1), 1–19.

Scoular, J. (2004). The 'Subject' of Prostitution: Interpreting the Discursive, Symbolic and Material Position of Sex/Work Within Feminist Theory. *Feminist Theory, 5*(3), 343–355.

Spare Rib. (1980). Leeds: Male Violence; Women. Issue 67, p. 302.

Sparks, R. (1992). Reason and Unreason in 'Left Realism': Some Problems in the Constitution of the Fear of Crime. In R. Matthews & J. Young (Eds.), *Issues in Realist Criminology.* London: Sage.

Stanko, E. (1997). Safety Talk: Conceptualising Women's Risk Assessment as a Technology of the Soul. *Theoretical Criminology, 1*(4), 479–499.

Stead, J. (1980, November 5). Now Is the Time to Stand Up and Fight. *The Guardian.*

Valentine, G. (1989). The Geography of Women's Fear. *Area, 21,* 385–390.

Valentine, G. (1992). Images of Danger: Women's Sources of Information About the Spatial Distribution of Male Violence. *Area, 24,* 22–29.

Vanwesenbeeck, I. (2017). Sex Work Criminalisation Is Barking Up the Wrong Tree. *Archives of Sexual Behaviour, 46*(6), 1631–1640.

Walker, S. (1999). The John School: A Diversion from What Is Needed. In N. Lopez-Jones (Ed.), *Some Mother's Daughter: The Hidden Movement of Prostitute Women Against Violence.* California: Crossroads.

Walklate, S. (1998). Crime and Community: Fear or Trust? *The British Journal of Sociology, 49*(4), 550–569.

Walkowitz, J. (1992). *City of Dreadful Delight: Narratives of Sexual Danger in Victorian London.* Chicago: University of Chicago Press.

Ward Jouve, N. (1988). *The Street Cleaner.* New York: Marion Boyars.

Yallop, D. (1993). *Deliver Us from Evil.* Reading: Cox and Wyman.

Yeatman, A. (1994). *Postmodern Revisionings of the Political.* New York: Charman and Hall.

Zheng, T., & Lights, R. (2009). *The Lives of Sex Workers in Post-socialist China.* Minneapolis: University of Minnesota Press.

CHAPTER 5

Remembering and Representing Victims in Research

Abstract Historically, women linked to prostitution have been represented pejoratively in media and crimino-legal discourses which persist in reinforcing marginality and stigma, and legitimating violence against sex workers. The early part of this chapter explores these concerns before drawing upon research findings from oral history interviews focusing on participants' memories of victims. Here I present an alternative set of representations to remedy the invisibility and hyper visibility which often defines the framing of sex workers as victims. While research findings reveal the Othering of women with participants engaging in both conscious and unconscious victim blaming, accounts also highlight more in-depth and humanizing recollections often shaped by social and spatial proximity which connect women to locality and community.

Keywords Media representation · Prostitution and stigma · Sex workers as victims · Invisibility and hypervisibility · Oral history and memory · Social proximity · Spatial proximity · Class and community

© The Author(s) 2018
L. Wattis, *Revisiting the Yorkshire Ripper Murders*,
Palgrave Studies in Victims and Victimology,
https://doi.org/10.1007/978-3-030-01385-1_5

INTRODUCTION

The following two chapters focus on how violence and victimhood have been represented in the Sutcliffe case by exploring research participants' memories of victims from the oral history project in the present chapter, before analysing how a selection of popular criminological texts, which depict the case both directly and indirectly, portray victims, sex workers and violence against women and misogyny more widely. These themes are foregrounded by a number of concerns relating to the historical framing of women, and sex workers specifically, as victims of male violence. Firstly, as Wilson (2007) points out, the figure of the offender dominates popular and academic accounts of serial killing, with victims largely marginalised. Wilson's (2007, 2012) structural analysis of serial killing in late modernity takes a more victim-centred approach, combining a structural analysis of the creation of vulnerability and victims as a consequence of neo-liberalism with a biographical focus on victims' stories. For Wilson, this acts as a counter to the historical absence of victims and/or their dismissive treatment within the stories of serial murder thus far. Likewise, feminist readings of violence and murder in popular culture also highlight a preoccupation and celebration of the male killer (Caputi 1987; Cameron and Frazer 1987; Downing 2013).

Moreover, the news media in particular has a long history of framing female victims of sexual violence and murder in arbitrary terms, often founded upon notions of feminine respectability and sexual propriety. Victims are either ignored or become hyper-visible, framed within tropes of victim-blaming, sensationalism and gratuity, with sex workers subject to particularly negative framings. As Tuchman (2000) has noted, obliteration and condemnation form the dual 'symbolic annihilation' of women within the sphere of representation.

The acknowledged limitations of representations of violence against women broadly informs the chapters to follow, which draw upon the Sutcliffe murders as a case study to explore the remembrance of victims and representation of victimhood and violence against women across a range of representational spheres. This current chapter will begin by exploring how the interplay of class, gender, propriety and stigma combine to produce especially pejorative representations of sex workers in the media and more widely. Drawing upon research findings, which explored memories of the Sutcliffe murders, the chapter will move onto focus on how victims were remembered by research participants, reflecting upon the potential of these findings and wider work in this field for offering up alternative representations and readings of victims—specifically women as victims of male violence.

REPRESENTATIONS OF SEX WORKERS
AND VIOLENCE AGAINST SEX WORKERS

The framing of crime, offenders and victims across news media has long been recognised as arbitrary and unrepresentative in both quantitative and qualitative terms, driven by the imperatives of news values and newsworthiness (Wykes 2001; Reiner 2002; Jewkes 2013) which serve to distort the extent, nature and dynamics of crime and perpetuate particular mythologies around victims and offenders. The suitability of victims in terms of a range of attributes relating to identity, status, vulnerability, appearance and so forth, has a significant bearing on the extent and nature of media attention (Greer 2007). Media narratives dealing with sexual violence and sexually-motivated murder frequently perpetuate and codify assumptions regarding masculinity, femininity and sexual propriety, as well as myths about what constitutes sexual violence and who can be a victim (Greer 2007; Benedict 1992; Lees 1997; Carter and Weaver 2003; Wykes and Welsh 2009). Victims may be afforded visibility within media reporting, but this may merely serve to objectify, denigrate and titillate (Jiwani and Young 2006). Likewise, familiar preoccupations with women's sexuality and respectability reverberate in the investigation and prosecution of rape and other forms of sexual violence such as child sexual exploitation, reflected in the construction of victim credibility and skewed justice outcomes (Smart 1989; Lees 1997; Kelly et al. 2005; Wykes and Welsh 2009). This is in spite of significant reform of legislation relating to sexual offences (Westmarland 2004; Wykes and Welsh 2009) and a recognition across the criminal justice system that the investigation and prosecution of sexual violence and violence against women more generally remains inadequate (HMCPSI and HMIC 2007; CPS 2010).

Arguably, the sex worker as victim occupies the most extreme point in terms of pejorative representations of victims of male violence where the interplay of gender, marginality, stigma and misogyny play out so that the sex worker as victim has long been denied citizenship and victim status (Walkowitz 1982; O'Neill 2010; Wattis 2017). Since the Victorian era, the way in which prostitution, and street prostitution in particular, have been represented across legal, policy and media discourses has been derogatory, reinforcing stigma and abjection (Kinnell 2008; O'Neill 2010; Sanders 2016). In the legal jurisdictions which constitute the United Kingdom, prostitutes have historically been subject to persecution and regulation by legal and criminal justice systems which have exacerbated their vulnerability and victimisation (Walkowitz 1982; Kinnell 2008; Sanders and Campbell 2007). From the Contagious Diseases Acts of the 1860s to the 1957 Wolfenden Report, and the resultant 1959 Street Offences Act in the twentieth Century, policy and legislation has demonstrated a pre-occupation with women's morality and sexuality which served to marginalize and stigmatise the prostitute identity, erode rights and citizenship, and legitimate violence (Walkowitz 1982; Penfold et al. 2004; O'Neill 2010; Sanders 2016). Moreover, the policy shift to a welfarist approach, from the 1980s onwards, with its emphasis on safeguarding and harm minimisation, persisted in framing women in terms of both victimhood and deviance—victims to be saved as well as offenders to be punished (Kinnell 2008; Sanders 2009; O'Neill 2010).

In terms of media representation, the 1888 White Chapel Murders provided an enduring template for successive representations of the murdered prostitute (Walkowitz 1982; Caputi 1987; Warkentin 2010; Downing 2013). Walkowitz's (1982) examination of The White Chapel murders reveals the origins of familiar media tropes of sexual titillation, sensationalism and responsibilisation. For the media, the middle classes and social reformers at the time, the violence itself was overshadowed by the perceived degeneracy and immorality of the victims who were viewed as 'unsympathetic objects of pity' (Walkowitz 1982: 552) and "women of evil life" (*Daily Telegraph*, cited in Walkowitz 1982: 557). As Walkowitz notes, this played out amidst the overarching narrative of prostitution as the 'great social evil' of the time which served to justify indifference and condemnation of impoverished female victims. Much of the reporting overlooks the complexity of women's lives, circumscribed as they were by poverty and destitution, but also by positive relationships and strong connections within the working-class communities of the East End of London (Walkowitz 1982; Warkentin 2010).

Writing about the murdered and disappeared women in Vancouver, Canada in the 1990s and 2000s, many of whom were indigenous and linked to sex work, Jiwani and Young (2006) note these familiar representational tropes where 'representations of Aboriginal women in Vancouver's Downtown Eastside oscillate between invisibility and hyper visibility. Invisible as victims and hypervisible as deviant' (p. 899). Lowman's (2000) earlier work on the Vancouver disappearances highlights how anti-prostitution rhetoric from police, politicians, media and community groups, was an antecedent to the multiple murders of women in Vancouver. For Lowman (2000) this produced a collective 'discourse of disposal' culminating in the introduction of repressive criminal justice legislation, 'creating a social milieu in which violence against prostitutes could flourish' (p. 1003). Lowman (2000) further argues that the deployment of specific metaphors, which frame sex workers as disposable, rubbish, disease, vermin, public nuisance, served to legitimate their murder. This body of Canadian work also highlights the polysemic and complex nature of representations in these cases. For instance, comparing media reporting across time periods, Strega et al. (2014) observe contradictory framings of victims as vermin alongside more sympathetic and humanising accounts of victims which position women in familial relationships as 'mothers, daughters, sisters' (p. 445). The authors argue that it is this reclassification which grants victim status to murdered women. Informed by activism on the part of victims' families and the media's motivation to speak to families, Jiwani and Young refer (2006) to this as counter framing, but question the extent to which it can in any real way, reverse the 'displaced sensationalism' and lack of regard for victims found in much of this reporting.

FRAMING VICTIMHOOD IN THE YORKSHIRE RIPPER CASE

The twentieth century witnessed a number of cases being assigned the Ripper epithet, in what Caputi (1987) refers to as the 'Ripper repetitions'. So for instance, Caputi (1987) identifies the "Dusseldorf Ripper", the "Blackout Ripper", as well as the "Yorkshire Ripper". Subsequent media accounts of 'Ripper style' murders echo the earlier tropes in regard to mythologizing of the male murderer and the denigration of female victims (Caputi 1987; Cameron and Frazer 1987; Downing 2013). Additionally, Bland (1992) has argued that the Ripper myth feeds into popular imagery around the lone man waging war against social and 'moral decay'. In the context of the Yorkshire murders, as the murders progressed so did the myth, with the killer elevated in the popular local imaginary (Yallop 1993). In contrast, across media, police and within the wider culture, victims were by and large treated with prototypical misogyny and a lack of consideration for their biography and humanity, with indifference towards sex workers taken as given (Walkowitz 1992; Wattis 2017; Smith 2013). Indeed, the reciprocal construction of the feminine victim/non-victim by the police and press is especially marked in this case. This is reflected in the police statement below following the murder of Jayne MacDonald:

> He has made it clear that he hates prostitutes. Many people do. We, as a police force, will continue to arrest prostitutes. But the Ripper is now killing innocent girls. That indicates your mental state and that you are in need of medical attention. You have made your point. Give yourself up before another innocent woman dies. (Appeal at a press conference by Superintendent Jim Hobson, West Yorkshire police, 1979, in Smith 2013)

For Smith (2013) the statement above suggests that the murder of prostitutes is a rational act and 'not entirely reprehensible', symptomatic of historical and ongoing marginality and denied citizenship. It resonates with Caputi's (1987) observation that the victimisation of prostitutes is a given within the parameters of femininity laid down within patriarchal cultures where prostitutes are viewed as 'a professional victim, stigmatised and targeted as a member of a sacrificial sex/class … the paradigmatic target of gynocide' (p. 95).

Joan Smith (2013), worked on the Sutcliffe case as a young reporter and recalls overhearing the following remark made by a police officer in reference to Helen Rytka, the nineteen year-old who was murdered by Sutcliffe in Huddersfield in 1978: 'Her fanny was as wet as a paper hanger's bucket' (remark from a senior West Yorkshire detective to a reporter at the Sunday Times). For Smith the lack of regard for the murder victim is palpable: 'It seemed to me that gloating disgust was a curious emotion to feel on contemplation of the mutilated body of a dead teenage girl' (p. 176). Press reports and police statements frequently engaged in 'victim-blaming', referring to murdered 'prostitutes', women who 'like the good life' and 'good-time girls' in contrast to 'innocent' and 'respectable' victims (Bland 1992; Smith 2013). Alongside the emphasis on respectability/ideal victims, media reports also perpetuated discourses of fear and responsibilisation. For example, Bland (1992) identifies a feature in the *Sunday Mirror* from 15th April 1979 entitled 'Checklist for Survival', which warned women not to go out alone at night 'even just to walk a few yards' and not to talk about enjoying sex.

Victim-blaming was not limited to women linked to prostitution, but any woman the police regarded as transgressing the boundaries of tightly proscribed feminine behaviour. Referring to a police dossier on the case containing details of the victims, Smith shows how the police categorized women on the basis of class, lifestyle and perceived respectability. Victims were categorised into two distinct groups: 'innocent victims'; and women of 'loose morals', with crude linkages made between victimhood and sexual propriety: 'Early victims were 'tarts', Ms X was an early victim, therefore she is a 'tart' (p. 172). Class, gender, sexuality and respectability are central in shaping victim blaming discourses and indifference towards women as victims of male violence and murder. The treatment of sex workers as victims within culture and across criminal justice brings into sharp focus the interplay between gender violence, misogyny and representation.

Comparing similar cases involving the murder of sex workers reveals that police attitudes and practice have changed: the police handled the murders of five women involved in prostitution in Ipswich in 2006 far more professionally and sensitively (Harrison and Wilson 2008). In a media analysis of the murders, Warkentin (2010) notes mixed representational frames. Well-worn Ripper formulas were deployed referring to victims as 'vice girls' and 'tarts', but this was overlaid with counter frames in other reports (Jiwani and Young 2006) which produce polysemic and in-depth understandings of the nature of prostitution and the victimisation of marginal, disadvantaged and vulnerable young women. That said, frivolous and gratuitous representation persists in the reporting of the murder of women linked to sex work. The local press reporting of the murders of five young women on Teesside in the North East of England between 1998 and 2003 (three of the murders remain unsolved) repeats familiar tropes—e.g. "teen prostitute", "young prostitute", "fellow prostitute" (Underwood 2006; *The Guardian* 2012; Corrigan 2010).

Remembering and Representing Victims in Research

The research encounter only ever produces partial and ambiguous accounts of the social world for a number of reasons (Miller and Glassner 1997; Sapsford 1996; Seale 1998; Portelli 1998). For example, the study of memory from across a range of disciplines has drawn attention its complexity, fallibility in terms of faulty cognition, as well as individuals' own self-conscious orchestration (Neisser 1982; Thompson 1993; Baddeley 1999). With this in mind, it is important to acknowledge that remembering is not a 'conduit to the past' where 'any given memory is not an inevitable product of a past experience' (Keightley 2008: 57). Indeed, Baddeley (1999) refers to the rehearsal and coding of memories to produce a particular version of the past. Likewise, Thompson (1993) notes how 'memories are 'storied' rather than 'stored' (Thompson 1993: 36), whilst Gemignani (2014) states that 'remembering as a meaningful experience is not about its cognitive retrieval, but its reconstruction' (p. 129). In the extract below, crime historians Gilman Srebnick and Levy (2005) speak to the dilemmas involved in researching and writing people's memories of crime:

> How, I wonder, do the silences and distortions of memory pertain to crime testimony and to the historical analysis of traumatic crimes and criminal events? And, faced with writing the history of such events, we are always contending with questions about voicing subjectivity (again), and multivocality. Where, for example is the voice of the victim, the accused, or the accuser? (Gilman Srebnick and Levy 2005: 9)

Despite their limitations, the stories derived from oral and life history interviews, nevertheless grant us some access to past events (Yow 1994). Drawing upon Bertaux-Wiame, Lummis (1998) maintains that generally, oral testimonies retain 'a solid base of factual information… which remains constant whatever the subsequent experience of the informant…. encouraging for those who want to use oral evidence for an account of the past' (p. 131). For Portelli (1998), accessing an exact account of the past is not the point, the factual veracity of events can be cross-checked against wider sources. Rather, oral testimonies are not concerned merely with historical events per se, but provide the opportunity to interrogate the significance of events by looking at the 'speakers' relationship to their history' and the 'creation of meaning' (pp. 67–69). Portelli clarifies this point below, making the distinction between psychological and factual truths:

The importance of oral history may lie not in its adherence to fact, but rather in its departure from it, as imagination, symbolism and desire emerge… the diversity of oral history consists in the fact that 'wrong' statements are still psychologically true and that this truth may be equally important as factually reliable accounts. (Portelli 1998: 68)

Likewise, Keightley (2008) highlights the multiple 'epistemological potentialities' for social science research of excavating memories to reveal the relationship between individual experiences and collective cultural moments and histories:

Remembering, whether involving individual, social or cultural representation of the past, is a process which involves selections, absences and multiple, potentially conflicting accounts … In acts of representation and communication, multiple social and cultural codes of remembering are performed and reconciled, resisted or rejected in a constant process of locating and relocating the subject in time, space and meaning (p. 59).

Keightley also draws attention to the shoring up of identity via memory and narrative and the value of memory for illuminating how the 'deeply held meanings' of the past operate in the present. Moreover, Keightley is mindful of 'remembering as indivisible from its social context' (p. 58), which alludes to memories as a product of the interaction between groups, institutions and the individual, and which is further filtered in the realm of cultural production and representation in a dialectic between private and public remembering.

The project: *Exploring the Social and Cultural Significance of the Yorkshire Ripper Murders* used oral history interviews to explore the memories of the Sutcliffe case, as well as analysing popular criminological representations of the case. The project investigated women's memories and reflections on their fears from the time (as touched upon in the previous chapter), memories of victims and the details of the case, as well as the impact of the case on everyday experience. Exploring 'local' memories of the Yorkshire Ripper murders resonates with much of the literature on the contingency and selectivity of memory. Indeed, the visible and pervasive presence of these murders and attacks across media and police discourses, as well as their presence within the local cultural imaginary via local folklore and mythology, often manifest as jokes, songs, football terrace chants, reinforces Keightley's observations regarding the interplay between the social, the cultural and the individual in the act and expression of remembering. This is reflected in participants' recollections of victims, as well as broader reminiscences about the case. Moreover, remembering occurs in the context of public/collective memory amidst overarching structures of power and ideology (Grele 1998; Keightley 2008; Hobsbawn and Ranger 1984). This was evident in reflections on victims which linked to gender, class and victimhood. At the same time however, representations of victims as they occurred as part of this research process also offered alternative representations and understandings of victims which both corroborate aforementioned media framings and victim hierarchies, but which also challenged dominant and well-worn news media framings of women who are victims of male violence.

PROXIMITY, IDENTIFICATION AND REMEMBERING

'I Remember Wilma McCann Because of the Name'

> I am trying to connect the reader to that life, in the hope that the victim does not seem distant and anonymous, but is instead humanised and, as a result, given some dignity. Yet there is also more going on here, for in trying to provide these pen pictures of people who are rarely seen within popular accounts of serial killers or in the academic discourse about serial killing, I am attempting to create a different interpretation about who it is who is victimised and in what circumstances. (Wilson 2007: 21)

Participants' memories of Peter Sutcliffe's victims reveal selective and fragmented recollections, whilst other interviewees present multifaceted and nuanced perspectives on victims. Participants did not provide detailed chronologies of victims—a naïve expectation on the part of the researcher to say the least. Rather, participants would instead name one or several women at most with some degree of certainty and detail, often recounting the impact of these murders within and upon their own lives in terms of empathy and/or social and spatial proximity. Indeed, names and locations would often be confused and recollection was overlaid with information from news, true crime and documentaries. As Portelli (1998) observes, 'oral informants are literate' (p. 69) and consequently may themselves engage with a range of written and popular sources as part of remembering. In addition, the interviewer would often prompt further recollection by providing details to research participants in terms of 'corroborating' and working on the 'facts'. This is illustrative of the interview encounter as a co-produced enterprise in which the researcher is acknowledged as 'a

facilitator, collaborator, and "travel companion" in the exploration of experience' (Gemignani 2014: 127). The quote below is typical of ad hoc recollections, in this case prompted by concern for the victim's children:

> *Jessica*: What's-her-name who had kids, who was found at Scott-Hall …
> What were it?
> *Louise*: Wilma McCann?
> *Jessica*: No Wilma, yeah coz that, I remember thinking about that. You
> know and she had kids and like 'aw them poor kids', you know, left
> without a mother … I suppose it were one of first experiences or being
> aware of and reading summat like that. Somebody had been murdered
> and the impact it had on somebody else you know? Not just you see
> something in passing and shrug it off or whatever, but thinking what
> effects that has on like kids and what-have-you.

In the true crime text *Deliver US from Evil*, David Yallop (1993) discusses how the officer in charge of the Wilma McCann murder investigation made much of the fact that Wilma had four children and ensured
the children featured prominently in the newspaper coverage of the
murder in order to garner public sympathy and cooperation. Wilma was
the first woman to be murdered by Sutcliffe, thus predating the realisation amongst police, media and the public that the murder was part of a
series. Jessica's concern over Wilma's children may have been influenced
by the concentrated press coverage featuring Wilma's children. Indeed,
what respondents knew and remembered about victims derives in part
from media reports and true crime documentaries. Having said that, the
local nature of these murders meant that respondents' experience went
beyond engagement with local newspaper reports.

As I Say Particularly Jacqueline Hill … "Well I Do Exactly What She was Doing"

In a similar way, two women who were students at the time of
Jacqueline Hill's murder also offered detailed and powerful recollections of Sutcliffe's final victim Jacqueline Hill, who was murdered in
Leeds in November 1980. Evelyn was studying in Manchester at the
time but would regularly return to her family home in the student area
of Headingley in Leeds; Laura was living in Headingley and studying at
Leeds University when Jacqueline was murdered. Both women recalled
the victim's movements and the location of the murder, as well as reflecting on the impact of the murder upon their own lives:

So I lived at Lupton flats in my first year which was where Jacqueline was murdered ... Yes I suppose the worst time came after Jacqueline Hill's murder.

So it was like the road that comes out of the Arndale Centre: Lupton Flats in the middle and then the other road—Alma Road. And then I think she was found down there. And they'd said in the paper that they thought he'd probably been hanging around for a few days kind of watching—that type of thing.

Laura—Student at Leeds University at the Time of the Murders

I mean I think at first I was aware that there was perhaps some murders, but it was seen as very much connected with prostitutes and red-light ... and didn't seem significant. Not that it wasn't awful but it wasn't as significant to my sort background or lifestyle. But then it became apparent that actually this was a bit you know, more random and the police started coming into schools and playing these tapes and things.

Some of these girls you know ... As I say particularly Jacqueline Hill ... Well I do exactly what she was doing ... I mean I didn't go to university in Leeds but I was repeating what she was doing in Manchester. And so it's the fact that you, you could relate to it I suppose ... Here's somebody who hasn't got a particularly different lifestyle to me and look what's happened ... So it was, that's when it becomes real ... Gosh this could be me sort of thing.

And the normality of the victims as well. No one could believe that you know this was a girl ... It wasn't like she was coming home late at night from a party. She was literally returning from university.

Anna—Studying and Living in Manchester, Family Home in Headingley, Leeds

Both women identified with Jacqueline due to the student lifestyle and identity, and her perceived respectability which for these women, grants her legitimate victim status. In this way, the spatial combines with the social to offer powerful aide memoires. Interestingly, neither women mention Barbara Leach, the student murdered by Sutcliffe in Bradford in September 1979. It is therefore the physical proximity of the murder combined with social identification with the victim, which acts as the most powerful trigger for remembering.

'Whenever It was a Working Woman They Didn't Care! They Just Didn't Bloody Care'

These research findings are mixed in terms of participants' views on victims with some expressing pejorative views, distancing themselves from victims who were "prostitutes" or "not like me" with respondents engaging in both explicit and more subtle and less conscious forms of victim-blaming. That said, a number of participants challenged indifference towards certain victims and victim-blaming discourses. Sometimes, this was explicit—expressed as anger at the arbitrary treatment of sex workers which contrasted with the representational treatment of victims perceived as "respectable":

> There were discussions at the time amongst me and my friends, because the majority of them were prostitutes—were the police doing their jobs properly because they were prostitutes. Were they treating them less than any other person?
>
> *Kay 59, Lived in Harehills Near Chapeltown at the Time of the Murders*

> I remember that one because they were saying she wasn't a prostitute. Well Jayne MacDonald wasn't a prostitute … You know "but she's come from a lovely family"—they all come from nice families you know what I mean. But course I'm older then and I'm thinking here, you know "you bastards!" People have been like stereotyped and you know it was like oh my God, you know just being stereotyped because of where you lived. What gives you? You know to speak ill of the dead or anything like that. But Jacqueline Hill were no better than bloody Wilma McCann just because they lived in different areas or because she went to university … I thought "oh that's awful"—because they made a … of it, how she came from a lovely family and you know she was at university.
>
> *Rita Lived in Chapeltown During the Murders*

Kay was working 'the beat' or red-light district across the boundary of Harehills and Chapeltown in North Leeds from around the time when Wilma McCann was murdered in November 1975. She remembered Wilma clearly because her daughter currently lived in the same neighbourhood where Wilma had lived. In the extract below, she discusses the continued anger in the local community in response to Wilma's murder due to police indifference and failure to act:

Kay: Now she was the one found on Scott Hall fields just up the road there.
Louise: She was yeah. Prince Phillip Playing Fields?
Kay: Yeah that's right. Well my daughter lives on that road so it's still a really sore subject up there—very sore …
Louise: Do people still talk about it?
Kay: People still talk about it. They still hold a massive grudge against the police over it.
Louise: Why?
Kay: Because whenever it was a working woman they didn't care! They just didn't bloody care.

Much of Kay's interview is concerned with the politics of sex work and the police's treatment of sex workers. Indifference towards murder victims is discussed alongside police violence against sex workers: in her interview she talks about women being beaten up by the police and the continuing aggressive policing of street sex work during the murders (see Kinnell 2008 for a discussion of this). This is reflected in the comments below:

"Well you shouldn't be doing it should you?" I had them say that to me … So they didn't care and where the murders where there would be a tape up maybe for a couple of hours, take it away.
They couldn't give a toss honestly! They didn't give a shit. They really didn't. They were still more bothered about getting their quota of cautions for the day.

And later on in the interview:

Kay: The only time it changed, their attitude changed was when the young lass got killed, the young girl.
Louise: Jayne MacDonald?
Kay: Yeah oh there was a massive hoo haa then. Well everybody round here went ape shit because all these women had been killed, murdered, beaten up, attacked—whatever right. Nothing in the paper, not … very little, or teeny little thing on the back page. Until she got murdered and then that was it—all hell broke loose.
Louise: Really? And could you see the change in the way they investigated it?
Kay: Oh God yeah! Yeah! There were so many police cars you couldn't get any work done!
Louise: I heard that from someone who lived in Chapeltown … loads of it was cordoned off.

Kay: That's right, that's right but before that the only coppers you saw were vice.

Kay's memories of victims and her own experiences of the police form part of the wider backdrop to these murders relating to the policing of sex work and the wide disregard for women linked to sex work. It is clear that these overlapping themes are central to her memories from this time in terms of both her identification and familiarity with victims and her sense of injustice at the framing and treatment of victims linked to sex work. Moreover, Kay intersperses her discussion of the past with reflections on the current state of sex work and policing, highlighting Keightley's (2008) point about the manner in which narrative and memory oscillate between past and present. In this way, Kay's combined historical and contemporary commentary provides a lens onto the social and political context of sex work, which speaks to legacies of vulnerability, disenfranchisement and stigmatisation.

Kay's comments regarding Jayne MacDonald, the fifth woman to be murdered by Peter Sutcliffe, reflect the uneven treatment of victims—both explicitly and unconsciously, across media, police, and within the public imagination. Jayne MacDonald was murdered by Peter Sutcliffe in July 1977 walking back to Chapeltown, where she lived and worked, after a night out in Leeds city centre. She was a pretty, sixteen year-old who worked in a supermarket in Chapeltown and as such, was a familiar face in the area. She was also the first murder victim not to be linked to sex work or viewed by the police as a 'good-time girl'. Indeed, it was her murder which prompted the comments from Chief Superintendent Jim Hobson featured earlier on in the chapter. It was assumed that 'she had been 'mistaken for a prostitute' because she was in an area 'frequented by prostitutes' (Kinnell 2008: 6) Consequently, she was afforded the status of 'innocent' and worthy victim with her murder provoking greater concern from the media, police and the wider public (Yallop 1993; Kinnell 2008; Smith 2013).

Jayne was mentioned more frequently than any of the other victims within research interviews and it may be the case that these research findings reflect something of the arbitrary regard for certain victims which typifies this case and defines representation of victims more broadly (Greer 2007; Jewkes 2013). For instance, Gillian made the following comment: 'I think the first time I really tied them in was when the young girl—was it Jayne? She was Chapeltown—between Chapeltown and Scott Hall ... Well with young Jayne ... because that was again very close to home and somewhere I had to pass near'. Gillian mentions that it was this murder which really brought the case to her attention and provoked her concern. In addition, her reference to 'young Jayne'—suggests familiarity and affection for a young woman she did not know and a level of empathy and connection she did not express in relation to any of the other victims. Indeed, Kay was explicit about the changing position of the police following the murder of Jayne MacDonald, but others also picked up on Jayne representing a 'different' type of victim reflected in police and media responses and the recurrent newspaper photograph of the blonde, fresh-faced sixteen year-old (see Kinnell 2008 for a discussion of the emphasis on Jayne's appearance). The construction of youth and innocence channeled through the visual image highlights the 'ideological power' of the image, which Clark-Dillman (2014) argues, provokes assumptions regarding the innocence of the victim and outrage at her death, thus reinforcing the status of legitimate and blameless victim in the local and wider imaginary.

Victimhood, Community and Place

Often for participants, recollections of victims related to vicarious connections to one or two victims, with a strong emphasis on neighbourhood and place. For example, Simon was a retired chef from South Leeds, who grew up in Churwell close to where Emily Jackson, the third woman murdered by Peter Sutcliffe, had lived. During his interview, Simon only ever referred to Emily, discussing at length his shock and disbelief at the revelation that a housewife from the village suburb of South Leeds where he lived was involved in prostitution in the Chapeltown red-light district:

> I don't even know how long it was but it felt as if she wasn't a prostitute ... Somebody from what you're considering to be a better area, they're not going to be over there ... And I think it certainly made a difference to the way in which it was felt around here because it sort of brought it into your own doorstep ... That meant that all the women were in the same boat. They were you know. It could quite easily have been anybody. And until you actually got around to saying she was a prostitute and she was there then it could have been somebody that you knew. Somebody that you really knew who lived close by ... This woman lived in a nice stone-built

house opposite the church and just, I don't know was normal—wasn't ... wasn't a prostitute. So it made a difference until you came to accept that she was there, that's what she was doing. So it's not going to happen to you.

Simon, Retired Chef from South Leeds

There are many things at play here. Simon's vivid memory of Emily relates to both of them living in the same neighbourhood; however, this occurs alongside his difficulty in reconciling that the woman who lived in 'the nice stone-built house opposite the church' was involved in prostitution in the red-light district on the other side of Leeds. Simon's process of distancing himself and the women he knew from Emily serves both as a source of reassurance that the Ripper had not invaded his community and that not all women were in danger. At the same time, he engages in a process of Othering Emily as a prostitute whose presence is out of place in his 'respectable' community. In this sense, Simon's attitude regarding 'respectable' women in contrast to 'prostitutes' echoes well-worn tropes. Again Yallop's (1993) true crime commentary corroborates these recollections, discussing Emily's life as a housewife in South Leeds and how she became involved in prostitution due to spiraling debts and her husband's failing business. Yallop also mentions the shock amongst the community when it was revealed that Emily was the third victim of the killer, and that she had been involved in prostitution.

More subtly, empathy and concern for victims was shaped by relational aspects of women's lives such as acknowledging women's positioning in familial relationships as mothers. This also related to other vicarious connections—knowing women by sight, being friends of friends and so forth. As discussed in the previous chapter, two sex workers were interviewed for the project and unsurprisingly, they mainly remembered women linked to sex work—most of whom they knew by sight or indirectly through friends. So for instance, Pearl started spending a lot of time in Chapeltown with the Afro-Caribbean community from her mid-teens onwards due to a troubled home life and became involved in selling sex in the late 1970s. In the extracts below, she discusses several victims who she knew from the same neighborhood:

Helen Rytka she actually...I let her use my house once yeah so I did know her. I didn't know her really well but I saw her on the beat, she said "I've got nowhere to use, the house is busy what I'm using at the moment". Because people usually let them use a room and give them a pound or something in them days, or a couple of quid. And I said "yeah you can use, I'm just off back out again".

Pearl: Yeah she did but we always used to see Marcella about but she was like a child.
Louise: Yeah so you knew her, you used to see her about?
Pearl: Oh yeah we'd make sure she was alright ...well she, she would get in anybody's car wouldn't she but...
Louise: Oh bless!
Pearl: I know but she was a bit simple. She wasn't what we call a working girl she'd just do it to get a few bob! [Laughter].

Spatial connection and community as played out in the parallel social spaces of Chapeltown is further highlighted in Pearl's memories of Jayne MacDonald:

Well it was the playground where she got killed, there was like a shed there—a hut. They used to call it the shithouse but I hated that name. And we used to break in because the music equipment was in it ... Because she didn't mix with us, she wasn't on the Black scene as much as she lived there. Her boyfriends would have been white and she just lived her kind of town life whereas we lived more the ghetto life.

Pearl's comments, and the interviews with Kay and Pearl as a whole, reveal the positioning of sex workers within networks and communities. Echoing Walkowitz' (1982) exploration of the lives of women murdered in White Chapel in 1888, this contributes to alternative and more in-depth representations of these women's lives, offering counter framing to the sensationalist, indifferent and misogynist discourses which often define police and media representations of murdered sex workers (Jiwani and Young 2006; Warkentin 2010). The importance of socio-spatial connection is also highlighted in Rita's reflections of the murders. In the previous chapter Rita's sense of community was explored as it appeared to mitigate the threat and fear of the murderer. Her positioning in the community and her strong sense of place also appear to shape how she regarded some of the victims. For example, in the extract below, Rita discusses Wilma McCann and Jayne MacDonald:

> Not like it is now no, it was a Grandways store and she worked there and ... she were right distinctive Jayne because she had the right long hair and she had the two blonde streaks which were the fashion at the time you know but she was nice you know? And one of the girls who I went to school with Irene, lived in their street, I think there was some ... they were related somehow, I don't know how and you know they all lived in ... they lived in that street and then years ago when you were kids your mam's mates you always called them Auntie you know? And uh...were one of my mam's friends Pat, we called her Auntie Pat, she lived next door to Wilma McCann, I mean she'd moved by this time when she'd been attacked, or had she? No I don't think she had, I think she still lived there then because she was saying I've lived up here for years and nobody comes to see me and all of a sudden every bugger is coming around you know? Because it was all to be nosy! She was next door but one to Wilma McCann and then up the street Jayne MacDonald lived in the same street! I mean how... ironic is that? You know they lived in the same street, Wilma McCann and Jayne.

Above Rita describes her connections to Jayne MacDonald and Wilma McCann, as well her relationships with other women in her community. Her account is 'explicitly relational' (Phoenix 2008) in its depiction of the working-class community where she is positioned within a network of female relationships, which accounts for her proximity to and memory of specific victims. Indeed, Rita also talked about how she and her best friend would regularly babysit for sex workers in Chapeltown while they 'worked' in the red-light district. Rita recalled how they would earn a couple of pounds, a few cigarettes and the freedom of somebody's house for the night. As such, Rita's narrative offers a rich sense of place and growing up in a close-knit working-class community in the 1970s, which as highlighted above, features her connectedness to several of the women murdered by Peter Sutcliffe.

Participants' reflections on the victims of the Yorkshire Ripper represent a mixed picture, which both conforms to and disrupts the way in which women as victims of male violence and murder are regarded and represented across media, criminal justice and more widely. Research findings reveal the Othering of women with participants engaging in both conscious and unconscious victim blaming via the apportioning of culpability in relation to assumptions about lifestyle and feminine respectability. At the same time however, interviews also include more in-depth and humanizing recollections—often realised through place and community, which position both victims and indeed some of the research participants themselves within relationships and networks within their community. The shortcomings of oral history, narrative and memory are corroborated within these research findings in terms of the impossibility of attempting to access comprehensive and factually accurate accounts of the past (Keightley 2008). These findings nevertheless evoke a sense of place, history and community, which positions often-marginal victims as visible and central within their community. Furthermore, the themes explored in this chapter also aim to contribute to Walklate et al.'s (2015) concern that as criminologists concerned with experiences of violence and victimhood, 'we know what has gone on and to 'know' provides the space for a 'creative cultural victimology' (p. 280). The exploration of victimhood and representation offered here thus allows for alternative framings of victims, as well as a means of remembrance (Wilson et al. 2016) and 'bearing witness' (Walklate et al. 2015).

References

Baddeley, A. D. (1999). *Essentials of Human Memory*. Hove: Psychology Press.

Benedict, H. (1992). *Virgin or Vamp: How the Press Covers Sex Crimes*. Oxford: Oxford University Press.

Bland, L. (1992). The Case of the Yorkshire Ripper: Mad, Bad, Beast or Male? In J. Radford & D. E. H. Russell (Eds.), *Femicide: The Politics of Women Killing*. Buckingham: Open University Press.

Cameron, D., & Frazer, E. (1987) *The Lust to Kill*. Cambridge: Polity.

Caputi, J. (1987). *The Age of the Sex Crime*. Bowling Green: Bowling Green State University Popular Press.

Carter, C., & Weaver, C. K. (2003). *Violence and the Media*. Buckingham: Open University Press.

Clarke Dillman, J. (2014). *Women and Death in Film, Television and News: Dead but Not Gone*. Basingstoke: Palgrave Macmillan.

Corrigan, N. (2010, September 24). Vicky Wasn't the Only One: Harrowing Stories of Teesside's Other Tragic Vice Girls. *The Evening Gazette*.

Crown Prosecution Service. (2010). *Violence Against Women Crime Report*. London: CPS; London: HMSO.

Downing, L. (2013). *The Subject of Murder.* Chicago: University of Chicago Press.

Gemignani, K. (2014). Memory Remembering, and Oblivion in Active Narrative Interviewing. *Qualitative Inquiry, 20*(2), 127–135.

Gilman Srebnick, A., & Levy, R. (2005). *Crime and Culture: An Historical Perspective.* Aldershot: Ashgate.

Greer, C. (2007). News, Media, Victims and Crime. In P. Davies, P. Francis, & C. Greer (Eds.), *Victims, Crime and Society.* London: Sage.

Grele, R. J. (1998). Movement with Aim: Methodological and Theoretical Problems in Oral History. In R. Perks & A. Thomson (Eds.), *The Oral History Reader.* London: Routledge.

Harrison, P., & Wilson, D. (2008). *Hunting Evil: Inside the Ipswich Serial Murders.* London: Sphere.

Jewkes, Y. (2013). *Media and Crime* (2nd ed.). London: Sage.

Jiwani, Y., & Young, M. L. (2006). Missing and Murdered Women: Reproducing Marginality in News Discourse. *Canadian Journal of Communication, 31*, 895–917.

Keightley, E. (2008). Remembering Research: Memory and Methodology in the Social Sciences. *International Journal of Social Research Methodology, 13*(1), 55–70.

Kelly, L., Lovett, J., & Regan, L. (2005). *A Gap or a Chasm? Attrition in Reported Rape Cases. Home Office Research Study.* London: Home Office Research, Development and Statistics Directorate.

Kinnell, H. (2008). *Violence and Sex Work in Britain.* Cullompton, Devon: Willan.

Lees, S. (1997). *Carnal Knowledge: Rape on Trial.* Harmondsworth, UK: Penguin.

Lowman, J. (2000). Violence and the Outlaw Status of (Street) Prostitution in Canada. *Violence Against Women, 6*, 987–1011.

Lummis, T. (1998). Structure and Validity in Oral Evidence. In R. Perks & A. Thomson (Eds.), *The Oral History Reader.* London: Routledge.

Miller, J., & Glassner, B. (1997). The 'Inside' and the 'Outside': Finding Realities in Interviews. In D. Silverman (Ed.), *Qualitative Research: Theory, Method and Practice.* London: Sage.

Neisser, U. (1982). Snapshots or Benchmarks? In U. Neisser (Ed.), *Memory Observed: Remembering in Natural Contexts.* San Francisco, CA: W. H. Freeman and Co.

O'Neill, M. (2010). Cultural Criminology and Sex Work: Resisting Regulation Through Radical Democracy and Participatory Action Research (PAR). *Journal of Law and Society, 37*(1), 210–232.

Penfold, C., Hunter, G., Campbell, R., & Barham, L. (2004). Tackling Client Violence in Female Street Prostitution: Interagency Working Between Outreach Agencies and the Police. *Policing and Society, 4*(4), 365–379.

Phoenix, A. (2008). Analysing Narrative Contexts. In M. Andrews, C. Squire, & Michael Tamboukou (Eds.), *Doing Narrative Research* (pp. 41–56). London: Sage.

Portelli, A. (1998). What Makes Oral History Different? In R. Perks & A. Thomson (Eds.), *The Oral History Reader*. London: Routledge.

Reiner, R. (2002). Media-Made Criminality: The Representation of Crime in the Mass Media. In R. Reiner, M. Maguire, & R. Morgan (Eds.), *The Oxford Handbook of Criminology*. Oxford, UK: Oxford University Press.

Sanders, T. (2009). Controlling the Anti-Sexual City: Sexual Citizenship and the Disciplining of Female Sex Workers. *Criminology and Criminal Justice, 9*(4), 507–525.

Sanders, T. (2016). Inevitably Violent? Dynamics of Space, Governance and Stigma. *Special Issue: Problematizing Prostitution: Critical Research and Scholarship, Studies in Law, Politics and Society, 71*, 93–114.

Sanders, T., & Campbell, R. (2007). Designing Out Vulnerability, Building in Respect: Violence Safety and Sex Work Policy. *The British Journal of Sociology, 58*(1), 1–19.

Sapsford, R. (1996). Reading Qualitative Research. In R. Sapsford (Ed.), *Researching Crime and Criminal Justice*. Milton Keynes: Open University Press.

Seale, C. (1998). *Researching Society and Culture*. London: Sage.

Smart, C. (1989). *Feminism and the Power of the Law*. London: Routledge.

Smith, J. (2013). *Misogynies: Reflections on Myth and Malice*. New York: Fawcett Columbine.

Strega, S., Janzen, C., Morgan, J., Brown, L., Thomas, J., & Carriere, J. (2014). Never Innocent Victims: Street Sex Workers in Canadian Print Media. *Violence Against Women, 20*(1), 6–25.

The Guardian. (2012, July 16). Rachel Wilson Murder: Body Found on Farmland Is Middlesbrough Teenager.

Thompson, P. (1993). Family Myth, Models and Denials in the Shaping of Individual Life Paths. In D. Bertaux & P. Thompson (Eds.), *Between Generations*. Oxford: Oxford University Press.

Tuchman, G. (2000). The Symbolic Annihilation of Women by the Mass Media. In L. Crothers & C. Lockhart (Eds.), *Culture and Politics*. New York: Palgrave Macmillan.

Underwood, M. (2006, February 8). Magic Book Ban on Kellie's Killer. *The Evening Gazette*.

Walkowitz, J. (1982). Jack the Ripper and Myth of Male Violence. *Feminist Studies, 8*(3), 542–574.

Walkowitz, J. (1992). *City of Dreadful Delight: Narratives of Sexual Danger in Victorian London*. Chicago: University of Chicago Press.

Walklate, S., McGarry, R., & Mythen, G. (2015). Trauma, Visual Victimology and the Poetics of Justice. In M. H. Jacobsen (Ed.), *The Poetics of Crime: Understanding and Researching Crime and Deviance Through Creative Sources*. New York: Routledge.

Warkentin, E. (2010). "Jack the Ripper" Strikes Again: The "Ipswich Ripper" and the "Vice Girls He Killed. *Feminist Media Studies, 10*, 35–49.

Wattis, L. (2017). Revisiting the Yorkshire Ripper Murders: Interrogating Sex Work, Gender and Justice. *Feminist Criminology, 12*(1), 1–21.

Westmarland, N. (2004). *Rape Law Reform in England and Wales* (Working Paper No. 7). Bristol: School for Policy Studies.

Wilson, D. (2007). *Serial Killers: Hunting Britons and Their Victims 1966–2006*. Hook, Hampshire: Waterside Press.

Wilson, D. (2012). Late Capitalism, Vulnerable Populations and Violent Predatory Crime. In S. Hall & S. Winlow (Eds.), *New Directions in Criminological Theory*. London: Routledge.

Wilson, D., Yardley, R., & Pemberton, S. (2016). The 'Dunblane Massacre' as a 'Photosensitive Plate'. *Crime, Media, Culture, 13*, 1–14.

Wykes, M. (2001). *News, Crime and Culture*. London: Pluto Press.

Wykes, M., & Welsh, K. (2009). *Violence, Gender and Justice*. London: Sage.

Yallop, D. (1993). *Deliver Us from Evil*. Reading: Cox and Wyman.

Yow, V. (1994). *Recording Oral History: A Guide for the Humanities and Social Sciences*. New York: Sage.

CHAPTER 6

Popular Criminological Representations of the Sutcliffe Case

Abstract This next chapter expands upon the discussion of victims and representation to consider themes of gender, victimhood and representation as they appear within popular criminology. Focusing on depictions of the Sutcliffe murders in four works of true crime and crime fiction, the discussion will explore a number of themes relating to objectification and violence against women, as well as portrayals of sex workers and the police as they appear in the chosen texts. In doing so, the chapter assesses the criminological and political potential of these texts by considering if they offer more progressive and complex representations of women, victims and violence. Conversely, arguments which highlight the way in which these representations may merely reproduce and reinforce women's objectification and subordination are also explored.

Keywords Victims · Representation · Popular criminology · True crime · Crime fiction · Violence and representation

INTRODUCTION

The following chapter builds on themes from the previous chapter relating to the representation of victims by going beyond the news media and looking to popular criminology as a source of alternative representation. Popular criminology is gaining increasing currency amongst academic

© The Author(s) 2018   119
L. Wattis, *Revisiting the Yorkshire Ripper Murders*,
Palgrave Studies in Victims and Victimology,
https://doi.org/10.1007/978-3-030-01385-1_6

criminologists who recognise its potential to develop criminological knowledge and inspire creativity within the discipline (Rafter 2007;
Jacobsen 2014; Wakeman 2013). Moreover, the wide reach, accessibility
and often emotive nature of many forms of popular criminology mean
it has considerable capacity to shape public/popular understandings of
crime and justice (Carrabine 2008; Rafter 2007; Rawlings 1998).

With this in mind, the following discussions focus on how a selection of popular criminological texts, which focus on the Sutcliffe case,
deal with themes of victimhood and violence against women. The
texts included in the chapter are Pat Barker's Blow Your House Down,
David Peace's 1977 and 1980, Gordon Burn's Somebody's Husband,
Somebody's Son and David Yallop's Deliver Us from Evil. Tapping
into wider debates regarding violence and representation, analysis of
these texts assesses the extent to which they offer more progressive and
alternative portrayals of victimhood, violence against women, sex work
and policing in the context of the Sutcliffe case, or are these depictions
of violence yet another a site of titillation, which merely reproduces
powerlessness and subjugation.

The Value of Popular Criminology

The value of attending to crime as culture across a range of representational regimes appears inevitable given the inherent slippage between reality and representation in our experiences of crime. As Carrabine (2008)
notes, the distinction between crime fact and fiction is virtually 'imper-
ceptible'. Commenting on murder specifically, Downing (2013) makes
a similar point, arguing that 'such subject matter seems, almost inevitably, to spawn textual hybridity, creative license, and narrative dissidence
in the texts it inspires. It encourages a blending of myth, "reality" and
imagination' (p. 194). The recognition of crime's 'textual hybridity'
resonates with a cultural turn in criminology (Brown and Rafter 2013),
which stresses the role of culture in engendering crime and the importance of crime as a representational form and key site of cultural production (Linneman 2015). This growing regard for crime as culture alerts
us to the epistemological possibilities of popular criminology for com-
plementing and enriching academic criminology (Brown 2003; Rafter
2007; Wakeman 2013; Hvid Jacobsen 2014). As Wakeman (2013) notes,
mediated texts are 'important vehicles driving and informing popular
understandings' about crime with the potential to 'transcend' academic

criminology and produce alternative epistemologies (p. 225–226). Similarly, Rafter, defining popular criminology as texts ranging from TV, film, crime fiction, video games, true crime, and photography and images of crime, argues that 'ideas developed by popular criminology bring to bear ethical, philosophical and psychological perspectives that are beyond the reach of academic research' (Rafter 2007: 417). Focusing on Crime fiction, Brown (2003) argues that no text should be privileged in reading crime. In her assessment of how the fictive voice stands up alongside social scientific study, Brown further argues for crime fiction's status as a 'valid social document'; distinct but equal to the ethnographic voice as means of engaging with crime, culture and the social:

> Ethnographic narratives which tell people's stories about how crime is situated in culture for them may be read in the same way as fictive texts; crime is real and metaphoric, but so often it is metaphoric. The ethnographic narrative, like the fictive narrative, is an expression of voices, of selves, of the multiplicities of identities. Read as crime texts, they both situate crime in relation to memory and transformations of identity, and the same can be said of the historical record. This is not to deride the usefulness of field research to criminology, but question the privileged claim of 'empirical' criminological research over the fictive voice. The fictive voice refracts the culture through its own generic prism. The research voice offers a different sort of prism, but it is still a prism. (p. 89)

Making similar points about true crime, Linnemann (2015) notes that such texts are 'important sites of cultural production' worthy of 'cultural criminological analysis' (p. 517). For Linnemann these texts represent 'ghost stories … specters of remembrance that transmit and inherit across generations' (p. 517) which inscribe acts of violence and murder into cultural and collective memory. True crime can be defined as cultural products such as novels, magazines, documentary films and television shows which base their narrative on actual criminal events, but which often exhibit the conventions of fictional narratives. As Seltzer (2007) notes, despite being based on 'crime fact', true crime texts often resemble crime fiction and 'manifest a social reality all their own' (p. 517). Indeed, Rossmanith (2014) notes how true crime adopts literary techniques such as scene-setting and first-person narrative found in fiction and drama and, 'in borrowing the narrative techniques of fiction, true crime writers investigate questions of authenticity and epistemology:

they play with notions of 'truth', character's point of view' and voice (p. 100). Rossmanith also considers the relationship between true crime and ethnography, discerning how both sets of writers give themselves over to imagination and engage in empathetic experience. Turning this on its head, Alleyne (2015) notes how ethnographers also deploy 'literary devices like metaphor, plot, characterisation and symbolism to construct texts, including and especially their own ethnographic texts' (p. 20).

Engagement with literary sources beyond the sphere of academic criminology reflects a wider tendency towards interdisciplinarity, creativity and emotion within criminology in order to engage with what has been termed the 'poetics of crime' (Wender 2015; Jacobsen 2014). This has been in response to the perceived stifling tendencies associated with much criminological research and specifically statistical methods (Ferrell et al. 2004; Wender 2015; Jacobsen 2014; Jewkes 2013; Wakeman 2013). Embracing creativity and textual diversity is part of the wider project of cultural criminology, which stresses that culture is intrinsic to crime—both as a means of understanding transgression, but also in terms of exploring its mediated nature (Ferrell et al. 2004). Recognising its scope, ONeill and Seal (2012) define cultural criminology as an examination of 'how crime is constructed, made, understood and experienced' (p. 3). Indeed, this broad remit means that this type of approach not only includes a cultural take on crime in the assumed sense of interrogating mediated texts, but encourages an empirical engagement with the place of crime in culture. Moreover, Seal and O'Neill have noted the scarcity of gendered perspectives and feminist voices within cultural criminology, arguing that in exploring women's lives, combining methods and texts such as fiction, film, historical and biographical research, provides a fuller account of the 'multiple experiences, realities, 'truths', of women's lived experiences and lived relations' and the 'contradictions of female oppression (pp. 73–77). That said, feminist interrogations of culture out with cultural criminology have revealed masculine bias and misogyny as inherent to much cultural production (Cameron and Frazer 1987; Caputi 1987; Mulvey 1975; Smith 2013; Downing 2013). Moreover, feminist work within cultural studies has grappled with the ethical and political dimensions of visual and textual representations of violence against women (McRobbie 2007; Gill 2007; Bronfen 1992; Clover 1992; Clark-Dillman 2014; Jermyn 2015).

The study of the 'Yorkshire Ripper' case in this volume is located within the field of cultural criminology given its focus on history, culture, representation, and popular criminology. In more precise terms, the project contributes to what Ferrell et al. (2015) refer to as 'cultural victimology', whereby the cultural ramifications of victimhood become the key focus. In addition, the analysis herein also offers fresh insights on gender, victimhood and representation, thus contributing to a feminist cultural criminology (O'Neill and Seal 2012).

POPULAR CULTURAL REPRESENTATIONS OF THE 'YORKSHIRE RIPPER' CASE

The remainder of this chapter will explore representations of victimhood and related themes from five popular criminological texts which depict the Sutcliffe case. The analysis includes three texts broadly defined as Crime fiction: Pat Barker's *Blow Your House Down*; David Peace's *Nineteen Seventy-Seven* and *Nineteen Eighty*. This is alongside analysis of two works of true crime: David Yallop's *Deliver Us from Evil*; and Gordon Burn's *Somebody's Husband, Somebody's Son*. These texts were chosen for a number of reasons. David Peace's novels and interviews with the writer were the initial inspiration for this project. Both Burn and Yallop have been valuable resources throughout the research process, offering contrasting commentaries on various aspects of the case in terms Sutcliffe's biography and motivation, socio-historical commentary, victims' stories and details of the police investigation. Lastly, Barker's fiction, which bears a close resemblance to the actual Sutcliffe case, is written from the position of working-class women and victims, and has inspired considerable positive commentary for its depiction of working-class femininity.

Gordon Burn: Somebody's Husband Somebody's Son

Gordon Burn's true crime novel falls within the genres of offender biography, positioned at the 'high-end' of the true crime genre (Rawlings 1998) with works such as Norman Mailer's *Executioner's Song* and Truman Capote's *In Cold Blood*. As discussed in previous chapters, Burn's canon concerns itself with social history, celebrity and popular culture and he is lauded for its interrogation of the links between key events and their social and historical context, as well as the depth and attention to detail evident within his work (Myers 2009). Colebrook (2012) draws attention to this in the comments below:

> Written using a combination of discourses including memoir and realism with cross-cuttings to newspaper clippings, television interviews and familial recollection, this text draws on a wide range of sources to craft a narrative account of the family in which Sutcliffe was brought up, as well as tracing the different worlds in which he lived, observing, identifying and documenting. (Colebrook 2012: 50)

Burn's examination of Peter Sutcliffe's social milieu, wholly focused on the murderer, aims to gain some sense of the role of cultural, structural, regional and biographical factors in shaping Sutcliffe's subjectivity of extreme misogyny and violence (Colebrook 2012; Ward Jouve 1988; Smith 2013). Burn spent three years living in Bingley, Peter Sutcliffe's hometown talking to his friends and family to try and understand his aim. His positioning within the community and the motivation to tell 'the story from the inside out' (Colebrook 2012: 48), along side the depth of his inquiry, imparts this text with an ethnographic quality which resonates with Brown's (2003) championing of crime fiction as valid social document.

Burn's starting point is to provide historical background on Bingley in terms of its working-class heritage, gender relations and its industrial and post-industrial topography. The early part of the book also outlines Sutcliffe's family background and formative years via recollection from friends and family. One of six children, the book reveals how Sutcliffe was close to his mother as a child, bullied at school and was regarded as a strange child and teenager. His father's exaggerated and somewhat abnormal masculinity is also discussed in relation to his cruelty towards women, the patriarchal household and the strange rituals, which featured as part of masculine performance within the Sutcliffe family and peer group. The book also reveals Sutcliffe's abnormal attitudes towards sex and his hatred of women involved in prostitution, as well as his relationship with his wife Sonia. Rawlings (1998) notes that Burn's narrative typifies key elements of the true crime genre in the way it lays out events and interactions as antecedents to Sutcliffe's future actions: 'All of this is presented against the background of his conviction for the murders, and implies the existence of clear, predictive signs of the murders that were to follow' (p. 9). Moreover, the commentary on the murders is embedded in detailed tableaus of place and the minutiae of the daily routines of work, family life and social occasions—family parties and nights in the pub. The realist style and the absence of invented dialogue within the narrative, which is based on accounts from friends and family, means 'that we come to know all these people as we might characters in a novel' (Colebrook 2012: 50). Affinity with those involved in the story and the embedding of the violence within the quotidian and the lives of familiar characters is an affective device for rendering the violence even more disturbing (Rawlings 1998).

David Yallop: Deliver Us from Evil

Drawing upon Rawling's (1998) typology of the true crime genre, Yallop's Deliver Us from Evil can be defined as somewhere between the polemic and the whodunnit. The multiple narrative strands include details of the murders, background on the victims and the police investigation. The book also contains social commentary and evokes a sense of time and place effectively, given it was written in part, during the murders and prior to Peter Sutcliffe's arrest. The dominant theme deals with criticism of the police with a sense of immediacy achieved via the use of transcripts from teleprinter communications between police stations. Yallop documents the catalogue of errors made by the police and positions himself as a self-styled maverick investigator doing a more effective job at identifying characteristics of the murderer prior to his arrest. This resonates with Rawling's (1998) observation that 'so much popular criminology concentrates on the struggle between hunter and hunted' (p. 9). Indeed, Yallop's narrative can be defined in terms of 'mission' in its quest to reveal the 'truth' of the murders. This mainly concerns the murder of Joan Harrison in Preston in 1975 who was initially included in the investigated due to the lifestyle of the victim. When he was caught however, Sutcliffe denied killing Joan Harrison and her murderer has never been apprehended. Yallop thus contends that there may have been two murderers at large during this period, but also that Sutcliffe may have been responsible for additional unsolved murders of women in the North of England during the 1970s.

Yallop's multiple narrative also deploys the perspective of the murderer by way of free indirect speech, which allows the reader access to Sutcliffe's attitudes towards women and possible motivations. Rossmanith (2014) notes that because true crime writers draw upon narrative devices from fiction, they play with notions of 'truth', 'character's point of view' and 'voice' (p. 100). These fictional elements are at their most unrestrained when Yallop assumes the 'voice' of the murderer. This as Seltzer (2007) puts it, is crime fact, which closely resembles crime fiction.

The text is also interspersed with social commentary on prostitution and attitudes towards women, as well as offering some insight into how broader conceptions of sexism, misogyny, sexual harassment and sexual violence link to Sutcliffe's subjevtivity and motivation. Having said that, Yallop's feminist point of view is ambiguous given the gratuitous and sexualised descriptions which also appear in the text (Ward Jouve 1988). In spite of this, Hilary Kinnell (2008) views the text as a valuable resource which she draws on in her own analysis of the lasting legacy of the murders. Moreover, unlike much true crime, Yallop provides detailed descriptions of victims' biographies, the events leading up to attacks and the impact of the attacks and murders on victims' friends and family.

1977 and 1980: David Peace

Combining fact and fiction, David Peace's Red Riding Quartet of crime novels—*Nineteen-Seventy-Four*, *Nineteen-Seventy-Seven*, *Nineteen-Eighty* and *Nineteen-Eighty-Three*, deal with murder, child abuse and police corruption in West Yorkshire during the 1970s and 1980s. Most notably, the novels *Nineteen-Seventy-Seven* and *Nineteen-Eighty* feature the Yorkshire Ripper in a reimagining of the case which includes the 'facts' of the case alongside fictional narratives which play with factual accuracy and chronology. The Ripper murders form the backdrop of Peace's narrative which implicate the police as the main criminal protagonists, engaging in violence, torture and corruption. Like Yallop, Peace also tackles the Joan Harrison case, deploying the real-life uncertainties surrounding Harrison's murder to construct a narrative around the police's involvement in murder, pimping and pornography. The style and narrative structure of these novels and the indictment of the police turns conventional crime and detective fiction on its head as there is no offer of resolution and a return from fear and violence (Young 1996) as the boundaries between good and evil, victim and villain, law and justice become blurred (Shaw 2010, 2011).

David Peace has been described as a macho writer. Indeed, the Red Riding novels are replete with representations of violence against women and men, perpetrated by men (predominantly the police). However, descriptions of women (especially those linked to prostitution) and the depictions of violence, sexual violence and the murder of women are particularly graphic. At the same time, Peace dedicates the novel *1977* to Peter Sutcliffe's victims and is clearly conscious of the cultural and structural dynamics of male violence against women. What is more, as Shaw (2010) argues, the misogynist voice of the novels is a reflection of the time and place in, which the predominantly male, protagonists of these novels are situated. The ambivalence thrown up by such representations will be explored later in this chapter.

Blow Your House Down: Pat Barker

Set in a red-light district in an unnamed Northern city, Pat Barker's novel Blow Your House Down explores the lives of working-class women, who with the exception of one woman, are involved in street prostitution while a killer targeting prostitutes is at large. Rawlinson (2010) has described Barker's work as writing 'small worlds' but she is sociological in that the milieu she creates 'connote or imply' larger-scale socio-economic and cultural conditions. This is certainly true of her portrayal of class and prostitution, which in spite of distancing herself from feminism, offers up a provocative meditation on poor women's oppression and the historical bias and repression of women involved in prostitution. As such, Barker's work exemplifies the progressive value of popular criminology to apply a prism to history and the social (Brown 2003), inviting debate and revealing alternative viewpoints. As Rawlinson (2010) argues:

> We should read Pat Barker because it makes us think as it makes us feel, it causes us to stand back and ponder moral and intellectual dilemmas at the same time as we are drawn into identifying with her characters. (Rawlinson 2010: 14)

Barker has denied that the novel is based on the Sutcliffe murders (Nixon, cited in Rawlinson 2010: 39), but as with Peace's novels, it is clear that 'a historical figure has invaded the fictional frame' (Rawlinson 2010: 29). The similarities between the actual case and Barker's novel are striking given the themes of place, class, gender and violence. The book explores the lives of four working-class women, three of whom are involved in prostitution, in four separate sections. It charts Brenda's entry into prostitution as a lone parent, whose life is circumscribed by poverty, caring responsibilities and limited employment opportunities, whose only other employment option is working at the chicken factory. The book also attends to the legal and social double standards, which working-class women, and particularly those linked to prostitution, are subject to, highlighting sex workers as the sole focus of the criminal justice system and the aggressive policing of soliciting at this time. Chapter 2 focuses on Kath, whose life has unravelled due alcohol abuse and having her children taken into care. The chapter depicts her murder at the hands of the killer and has been criticized as graphic and indeed pornographic (Rawlinson 2010; McRobbie 1984). The final section depicts a further attack by the killer on Maggie who is hit over the head by an unidentified man on the way home from a drink after work. Barker's fictional attack bears a striking resemblance to Peter Sutcliffe's actual attack on Olive Smelt in Halifax in 1975. In both the fictional and actual attacks the victim's husband was initially the main suspect and endured hours of police interrogation.

REPRESENTING MISOGYNY, VIOLENCE AND VICTIMHOOD ACROSS TEXTS

To get a balanced picture, the story of the victims should also be told. The story of the loving home of Jayne MacDonald, whose father died of grief. The story of Emily Jackson, who went in for prostitution because she liked it—no doubt the money was handy too; it also took her mind off the acute pain caused by the death of one of her children. But the easy-going tolerance of her husband, and her own love for her children—like the love of Wilma McCann and Jean Jordan and others for theirs—should be celebrated. As should the heroism of Olive Smelt, who took a job in an old men's home to try and cure herself of the aversion to men her bludgeoning left her scarred with …

… Fiction is probably the only way in which such a celebration could occur. The victims have been hurt too badly not to be spared the limelight of any further discussion. Pat Barker's remarkable novel Blow Your House Down is the fictional answer. (Ward Jouve 1988: 32)

Lisa Downing notes how historically, the figure of the (predominantly male) murderer has been represented as special, as a celebrity, beast, superman—the centre of attention (Downing 2013), with victims (predominantly women) marginalized within popular cultural narratives of fictive and actual crime. For Downing and other feminists, true crime's preoccupation with the offender at the expense of the victim attests to the veneration of the agentic male offender within the patriarchal cultural imaginary (Caputi 1987; Downing 2013). Jouve's quote at the start of this section highlights her faith in fiction, and Barker's novel in particular, to challenge the framing of the women murdered by Peter Sutcliffe, as well as speaking to the representation of sex workers and working-class women more widely. For Ward Jouve, fiction remedies the shallow and sexualized portrayals of the murdered prostitute, granting them humanity and biography with Barker's *Blow Your House Down* exemplifying this. As she further argues, the novel 'gives life and humanity back to the working-class women—prostitutes or not—and some working-class men too, whom the 'Ripper case' had taken it away from' (Ward Jouve 1988: 144).

In general, true crime demonstrates a preoccupation with placing the offender at the centre of the narrative (Rawlings 1998; Biressi 2001), often adopting an ambivalent position towards the violence (often against women) depicted therein. Burn's true crime exploration certainly supports this assessment of the genre. He provides a rich historical and social commentary, which considers the relationship between place, class and gender identity and Sutcliffe's subjectivity and motivation. Nevertheless, this is at the expense of endowing Peter Sutcliffe's victims with an equally in-depth consideration and backstory. In contrast, as well as focusing on the murders and the investigation, Yallop offers detailed background and circumstances of the women attacked and murdered by Peter Sutcliffe. So for instance, the reader learns how Emily Jackson, a housewife from a suburb in South Leeds, became involved in prostitution because of her husband's failing business and mounting debts. Or about Helen Rytka's twin sister Rita and how they had both spent time in care and how they used to look out for each other when out in the red-light district in Huddersfield. How Jean Jordan had come to Manchester from Scotland and was known as 'Scotch Jean'. Yet, Yallop's commentary is variable in terms of the detail and depth afforded to victims. This may have been due to the availability of information on different victims, but it does lead to over-identification and disproportionate concern for certain women. All of whom happen to be women framed as 'innocent', 'respectable' and therefore deserving by police and media. For instance, shop assistant Jayne MacDonald, building society clerk Josephine Whitacker and students Barbara Leach and Jacqueline Hill.

For Joseph (2010), the literary nature of creative non-fiction and its 'greater degree of engagement with its subjects, purportedly lending a richer voice' distinguishes it from other forms of journalism. In this way, narrative devices such as the detailed backstory on Barbara Leach and her relationship with friends and family mean her murder leads to a greater degree of affectivity and empathy. As Rossmanith (2014) observes, literary journalism in the form of true crime differs from more sensationalist media because of its capacity to generate empathy as the narrator/writer gives way to their own imagination. Hartsock sees this as 'an epistemological intention', which aims to close the distance 'between the subjectivity of the journalist and reader on the one hand and an objectified world on the other' (Hartsock, in Rossmanith 2014: 108). Although uneven in its representation, Yallop's text is affective in its depiction of the women attacked and murdered by Peter Sutcliffe and the devastation of these crimes. In so doing, the narrative is affecting, inspiring empathy so that the implications of the murders of these women is fully realised (Rossmanith 2014). It differs from most true crime in this sense and also diverges from news media coverage of 'crime fact' concerning gender and victimhood.

Representations of Sex Workers

Historically, across law and culture, the figure of the prostitute as the embodiment of feminine 'anti-respectability', has been subject to Othering, stigma and violence, reflected in a lack of rights and repressive regulation via the criminal justice system (Walkowitz 1982, 1992; O'Neill 2010; Sanders 2016; Chapkis 1997; Ferris 2015). Popular criminological readings of the Sutcliffe murders both reflect this historical Othering and repression, whilst also presenting more sympathetic and in-depth representations of women's lives. For example, David Peace's portrayal of women linked to prostitution living in the red-light areas of Leeds and Bradford, is dominated by palpable misogyny and graphic and extreme violence against prostitutes. Commenting on the Red Riding quartet, Shaw (2011) notes the peripheral presence of women and the absence of women's voices within the novels merely reflects the cultural conditions of the time, both within the police and more widely. But Peace also reveals the truths of repressive policing of street soliciting in the form of vice squads (Kinnell 2008; Matthews 2005), police disregard for women's well-being and safety, as well the violence committed against sex workers by the police themselves which is mirrored in Yallop's (1993) coverage of actual abuse of women by vice squad officers. That said, graphic depictions of hyper-violence against an already firmly established Other, may also be viewed as problematic and pornographic in the perpetuation of the 'murdered prostitute' trope (McRobbie 1984; O'Neill 2010; Jiwani and Young 2006; Strega et al. 2014; Ferris 2015).

In contrast, Yallop's true crime polemic offers a fuller and more sympathetic representation of women involved in sex work, which is also evident in Barker's fictional portrayal of street sex workers. Both texts demonstrate ethnographic potential in their reading and representation of the lives of marginalized women who have historically been visible as abject non-citizens, alongside the denial of status and recognition as citizens (O'Neill 2010). Kinnell (2008) notes the historical and sociological value of Yallop's text because of its historical proximity, it offering 'a vivid account of the street soliciting areas of West Yorkshire in the 1970s, the way policing of prostitution changed, or did not change, and the emergence of a new kind of feminist activism which sparked widespread protests about violence against women' (Kinnell 2008: 2). Not only does Yallop provide commentary on the policing and regulation of street prostitution, but along with Barker, both texts explore sex workers' lives and their social milieu, which is captured via the humour and camaraderie amongst women in their local pub in the red-light district. Commenting on Barker's novel, Ardis (1991) describes how Barker 'introduces us to the whole community of women who meet for drinks at a local pub before going out on their "beats" (p. 414). Both Yallop and Barker evoke the lived experience of marginalized women, as well as a profound sense of community amongst the women (Auerbach 1978). In the United Kingdom, policy and research agendas adopted welfarist approaches to the regulation of sex work in the late 1980s and 1990s, evident in welfare and harm minimization strategies and the emergence of academic research operating from the position of sex workers themselves (Phoenix 1999; O'Neill 2001, 2010; O'Neill and Campbell 2002, 2006; Agustin 2007; Armstrong 2015). However, these cultural texts predate later policy and research agendas, offering effective counter frames to the construction of sex workers as legal and social pariahs, which humanize women via themes of humour and community, whilst also providing subtle critique of biased legislation and policy.

Indeed, Barker also draws attention to the historical bias of the criminal justice system in its criminalization of women and lack of regard for their safety. This is illustrated in the following exchange between Brenda and Audrey concerning a client who enjoys the risk of attracting the attention of the police: 'Well, let's hope he pays the fucking fine'. (p. 32). The second extract below is a further exchange between the two women and reflects the police's preoccupation with arresting women for soliciting even though there is a murderer at large:

> *Audrey.* 'I wish to God they'd catch the bugger'.
> *Brenda*: 'Too busy catching us'. (p. 32)

Barker's use of sparse and incisive dialogue is efficient at getting to the heart of historical contradictions and hypocrisy with regards the policing of sex work, which persists contemporaneously. Indeed, Barker's vivid description of insanitary and inflexible working conditions at the chicken factory presents as something of a deliberate ploy to demonstrate how sex work might be a more attractive option than working at the factory. Rawlinson (2010) argues that *Blow Your House Down* is sociological in its depiction of power and inequality realised within the axes of gender, class and sexuality. Ardis' (1991) analysis of Barker draws upon Kaplan to highlight how working-class women negotiate gender oppression and the 'powerful nature of class and gender in ordering our social and political imagination' (Kaplan, cited in Ardis 1991: 2). Written as it is from the point of view of the women—some involved in prostitution, some not, it illuminates how these women's lives are circumscribed by both class and patriarchy (Carlen 1988; Skeggs 1997), bringing into sharp relief the scarcity of choices faced by poor women.

Portrayals of the Police

The police are largely invisible in Burn's and Barker's texts, but occupy a central position in Yallop's narrative given a significant proportion of his story is given over to the dynamics and failings of the investigation. A dominant theme running through the narrative is police incompetence, alongside the implication that the narrator has a better grasp on the case than the police. Accordingly, Yallop chronicles the catalogue of mistakes and errors of judgement made by the police during the course of the investigation (Bilton 2006). Yallop is also critical of police's ongoing aggressive approach to soliciting in red-light areas and the use of women as live bait in an attempt to catch the killer, especially given the strategy was an open secret. He also discusses real-life corruption amongst vice squad officers involving the rape of a sex worker. That said, Yallop also recognises variations in police culture and practice in terms of praise for individual officers and more compassionate attitudes towards victims linked to sex work, but this is overshadowed by the popular view of the case as defined by practical and ideological failings (Bland 1992; Bilton 2006; Neyroud and Disley 2007; Maguire 2008; Smith 2013).

In contrast to Yallop's true crime commentary, David Peace's *1977* and *1980* are works of fiction, which draw on crime fact to present an altogether darker and unsettling portrayal of the police with the 'Ripper' serving as a backdrop to examine the police as violent criminals. Reviewing the novels, Meek (2009) notes that 'apart from the Yorkshire Ripper and the odd businessman, the real criminals are the police themselves' who 'rape, pimp, torture and kill with impunity and relish.' Moreover, all of this is delivered in a departure from 'realism' by way of a 'fractured narrative' which deploys the conventions of horror and the surreal in a 'conscious effort to create anxiety' (Wilson 2009). Across the course of all of the four books, the West Yorkshire Police are at the centre of corruption and organized crime with links to a local businessman and local government. This involves complicity in child abuse and murder, several murders committed by the police themselves, the extraction of confessions by torture and the sexual exploitation of women in prostitution and the production of pornography.

Referring to Peace's fictional representation, Shaw argues that the work reveals how 'the internally networked corruption of the West Yorkshire Police is presented as symptomatic of a wider internal corruption in the national police body' (Shaw 2011: 72). When challenged about these portrayals of the police, Peace refers to real-life scandals of police corruption and miscarriages of justice which occurred throughout the 1970s and 1980s (Upson 2001; Newburn 2007; Maguire 2008). Indeed, the widely recognised systemic failings of the Ripper investigation can be located within a series of police 'scandals' originating from the 1960s to the present day, involving police incompetence, corruption and miscarriages of justice, which have led to a decline in public confidence and a 'crisis of legitimacy', whilst also ushering in reform at various points in police history (Newburn 2007; Maguire 2008).

Misogyny and Violence Against Women

'There's a wrestler on telly who looks like an ugly old slag who lives in Bingley, but our Mick's given her one. Our Mick's given everybody one. He'd fuck a pig in knickers. He fucks anything that moves'.
(Peter Sutcliffe's brother Carl commenting on elder Sutcliffe brother Mick's attitude towards women in *Burn's Somebody's Husband, Somebody's Son.*)

Masculinity and misogyny are intrinsic to the Sutcliffe murders: central to the killer's subjectivity and social milieu, as well as the framing of the violence and the victims by the police and media. It is therefore inevitable that they appear in popular representations. Misogyny and masculinity feature heavily in Burn's examination of Sutcliffe and his community, observing that 'women are for frying bacon and screwing' (p. 68). In his commentary on Burn's work, Colebrook (2012) concludes that it was clear that amongst Sutcliffe's family and friends, 'violence and oppression were expected and certainly accepted' (p. 53). Yallop attends more explicitly to the structural nature of violence against women and presents multi-faceted constructions of victims and women within the sex work community. Yet, his narrative is replete with salacious and objectifying descriptions of women (Ward Jouve 1988).

Undoubtedly, the most disturbing portrayals of violence and lack of regard for women occur within David Peace's work. To return to a recurrent theme when considering the ethics of representing violence (Jermyn 2015; Vincent and Naidu 2013; O'Neill and Seal 2012), the extent to which these portrayals are sympathetic to feminism is uncertain, which is rendered more ambiguous by the overarching moral ambiguity of the narrative (Quirk 2009). The text is populated with macho and misogynist male voices and graphic violence. A scene involving the anal rape of a woman by a police officer, which draws parallels with *BYHD*, is particularly brutal and disturbing: even more so given the man involved is the closest the story gets to a heroic character (Rawlinson 2010: 40). Peace has been described as a 'relentlessly masculine' writer and it is most certainly a 'masculine world' he brings forth in his writing (Shaw 2010). Violence against women and the denigration of women as victims more generally via misogynist caricaturing, alongside the marginalization of women's voices, are central features within the narrative. In complete contrast to Barker's 'community of women', Peace offers up:

> A world represented solely through the eyes of men … about a time in
> which men enjoy dominance … female characters are regularly subject
> to semantic derogations … Positioned firmly outside the tightly mascu-
> line structure of Yorkshire, women's lives remain largely unexplored …
> The sexualized female is frequently subject to the murderous thoughts
> of the male gaze or undermined by perceived flaws and faults … … The
> female victim is nothing more than a 'silly slag' [1977, 5] attention
> falling on female beauty rather than on the responsibility of the killer.
> (Shaw 2011: 29–32)

Nicole Ward Jouve (1988) is critical of both Yallop's and Burn's portrayals of women and the masculine voice they adopt in their texts (no
doubt she would have much to say about Peace, had the chronology of
their work aligned), accusing Yallop of revelling in graphic and prurient
imagery and condemning Burn's complicity in reproducing the misogynistic voice of Sutcliffe and the men around him. In contrast, Ward
Jouve praises Barker for granting humanity to Sutcliffe's victims and
working class women more generally, arguing that the book represents a
'critique of the cultural reproduction of violent patriarchy … a voicing of
what is silenced, and a scrupulous revision of a dismissive or exploitative
misrepresentation of prostitutes' (p. 32).

That said, *BYHD* contains the graphic murder of Kath, a woman
involved in prostitution, which is preceded by a disturbing depiction of
anal rape which is narrated from the position/voice of the murderer,
where the reader is forced to assume the murder's point by way of the
use of free indirect speech. As discussed, Barker's novel addresses how
the class/gender nexus circumscribes the lives of working-class women,
as well as challenging one-dimensional constructions of the prostitute
as abject and immoral other. However, its depiction of graphic violence
also provokes ambivalence and unease, calling into question the ethical
position and political worth of representations of this nature. Rawlinson
(2010) acknowledges that Barker is controversial in her engagement with
such explicit representations, but feels they serve the greater good in
alerting audiences to the violent human condition and violence against
women specifically. Like Yallop, Barker uses free indirect speech to place
the reader in a position of collusion with the man who rapes and murders
women. As Rawlinson notes:

> For the reader Barker has created a perspective of the abyss in the abomi-
> nation of an impersonation of the 'Ripper', shifting focalization from pros-
> titute/victim to punter/murderer, and narrating rape and slaughter from
> his point of view. This is controversial because art itself is complicit in vio-
> lence. (Rawlinson 2010: 34)

Caputi (1987) refers to the ubiquitious portrayals of the eroticised murder
of women in representation as 'the pornography of everyday life' (p. 161).
Angela McRobbie (1984) has critiqued Barker's text as pornographic on
the grounds that it represents yet another depiction of the raped and murdered prostitute. Rawlinson is aware of these tensions but concludes that
ultimately, 'Barker's fiction is an interesting if fraught position ... tarrying
with the pornographic in the service of a moral art' (Rawlinson 2010: 41).
He further acknowledges the sociological work of the book in the way it
provokes meditation on violence, victimhood and justice:

> And in Blow Your House Down, the variation of narrative voice and nar-
> rative point of view revises the reader's standpoint on the legal and the
> illegal, visible and invisible, violence on the streets of the modern city.
> (Rawlinson 2010: 43)

Equally, Shaw has been keen to stress Peace's criminological and political
potential, evident in the way he deploys crime fiction to 'refract culture'
and locate criminality within culture (Brown 2003). Peace engages with
etiology via his interrogation of the 'troubled social, political and economic contexts' which engender violence alongside an indictment of the
state as enabling and perpetrating violence. Peace also performs criminological work in disrupting boundaries between victims, perpetrators and
the state, highlighting how 'the line separating good and evil, hunter
and hunted is precariously thin' (Shaw 2010: 73). Likewise, Rawlinson
(2010) notes how the violent male perpetrator in Peace's work is symptomatic 'of the ubiquity, not the singularity, of male monsters ... the
'Ripper's menace is systematically produced throughout the institutions
of law and order' (p. 40). Indeed, Peace's more or less complete focus
on the police as violent criminals is an effective disruption to assumptions about the boundaries between victims, criminals, law and justice
(Young 1996). Radical feminism has made similar points, exposing the

false distinction between the violent male offender, the police and men in general within patriarchal culture, as both perpetrators and enablers of violence against women (Dworkin 1976; Caputi 1987; Smith 2013). Comparing these texts, and especially those of Barker and Peace, both of whom include graphic depictions of sexual violence and the murder of women, albeit from the distinct positions of masculine and feminine subjectivity, provokes familiar debates on gender, violence and representation. Opposing readings thus frame such violence as either a 'species of titillation' or as an attempt to 'reverse the desensitising effects of over-familiarity on our responses to violence and its effects' (Childs, cited in Rawlinson 2010: 37). In common with criminology, Peace asks questions about the boundaries between criminal, victim and the state. More specifically, Peace, in common with feminist analyses, challenges assumptions about the social and spatial dynamics of violence, revealing male violence against women as systemic and operating across the boundaries of the public and the private. Barker grants women humanity and also exposes the dual oppressions of class and gender. Equally, both Yallop and Burn highlight male violence and misogyny as embedded within social structure and the wider culture. All of these texts offer alternative readings and representations of prostitution, justice and victimhood, which at the very least progress from the symbolic annihilation (Tuchman 2000) which characterises much of the news media coverage of the Sutcliffe murders and similar cases involving the murder of sex workers. All of these texts demonstrate how popular criminology can enhance academic epistemologies and provoke fresh emotional and political responses to crime and violence.

However, a commitment to feminism necessitates an ethical and political engagement with the implications of visual and textual violence which inevitably provoke conflicted responses. The constancy of the trope of the murdered and violated woman in the sphere of representation demands such a commitment as so often it is deployed irresponsibly and informed by misogyny. More recently, concerns about textual and visual violence in crime fiction and visual culture have intensified in light of the perceived proliferation, extremity and realism of representations (Jermyn 2015; Clark-Dillman 2014; Hill 2009; Nicholson 2017; Williams 2018). Jermyn (2015) for one is 'tired of negotiating endless media violence against women ... TV crime drama increasingly took the exploration of the brutalized female corpse to be its default prompt, its habitual content, a quotidian mainstay' (p. 14). For Jermyn the female corpse within popular visual culture no longer represents (as she had previously argued) a 'troubling' or disruptive figure—a provocation enabling women to engage with violence and fearfulness vicariously. Rather, these images symbolise a backlash against feminism, which reinforces women's disposability and circumscribes their lives via fear as they regard the murdered and punished woman amidst the contradictions of post-feminist landscapes (Clark-Dillman 2014).

An additional twist in these debates nevertheless, lies in the fact that it is predominantly women who consume popular criminology of this type (Coslett 2014; Browder 2006; Williams 2018), and women who produce the most disturbing images of violence, driven by the commercial imperative that 'dead women sell books' (Hill 2009). This has led some to claim the therapeutic function of these texts in allowing women, who experience fear and anticipate the possibility of victimhood more acutely in patriarchal culture, to engage in fear and victimisation vicariously in a 'safe' place (Coslett 2014; Hemmings 2018; Williams 2018). This is reflected in Browder's (2006) exploration of women who read true crime—much of which features women as murder victims. Browder highlights how these texts offer women a means of dealing with fear, violence and past trauma perpetuated by men, arguing that women:

> [r]ead true crime to help themselves cope with the patriarchal violence they have encountered in the past, and fear in the present … True crimes allow women to gaze into the abyss—both of the terror suffered by crime victims and of their own traumatic memories—and to survive (pp. 928–932).

In light of this, Browder argues that such texts should not simply be written off as anti-feminist, given their therapeutic quality and their capacity for resolution. This reflects Brown's (2003) argument that radical feminist readings of mediated violence against women oversimplify the relationship between patriarchy, misogyny and representation, assuming a coherency of meaning and outcome without proper consideration of polysemy and more complex readings and responses from audiences.

It seems entirely fitting that a project focusing on a murder case involving the serial murder of thirteen women and its representation should end with deliberations on what portrayals of violence against women and our engagement with them mean for gender and power, and the place of such violence (both actual and mediated) within the wider culture. A case such as this (and others like it, which demonstrate very consistent patterns in terms of the representation of victims) compel an engagement with a strong feminist argument. This serves to remind us that violence against women in the sphere of representation and the more recent perpetuation and intensification of mediated images of dead women (Clark Dillman 2014; Jermyn 2015) should not be dismissed. Indeed, the consistency of this trope has implications, which persist even when potential nuance and complexity have been taken into account.

REFERENCES

Agustin, L. (2007). *Sex Work at the Margins: Migration, Labour Markets and the Rescue Industry*. London: Zed Books.

Alleyne, B. (2015). *Narrative Networks: Storied Approaches in a Digital Age*. London: Sage.

Ardis, A. (1991). Political Attentiveness vs. Political Correctness: Teaching Pat Barker's Blow Your House Down. *College Literature, 18*(3), 44–54.

Armstrong, L. (2015). From Law Enforcement to Protection? Interactions Between Sex Workers and Police in a Decriminalized Street-Based Sex Industry. *British Journal of Criminology, 57*(3), 570–588.

Auerbach, N. (1978). *Communities of Women: An Idea in Fiction* (pp. 549–572). Cambridge, MA: Harvard University Press.

Bilton, M. (2006). *Wicked Beyond Belief: The Hunt for the Yorkshire Ripper* (Rev. ed.). London: Harper Perennial.

Biressi, A. (2001). *Crime, Fear and the Law in True Crime Stories*. New York: Palgrave Macmillan.

Bland, L. (1992). The Case of the Yorkshire Ripper: Mad, Bad, Beast or Male? In J. Radford & D. E. H. Russell (Eds.), *Femicide: The Politics of Women Killing*. Buckingham: Open University Press.

Bronfen, E. (1992). *Over Her Dead Body: Death, Femininity and the Aesthetic*. New York: Routledge.

Browder, L. (2006). Dystopian Romance: True Crime and the Female Reader. *The Journal of Popular Culture, 39*(6), 928–953.

Brown, M., & Rafter, N. (2013). Genocide Films, Public Criminology, Collective Memory. *British Journal of Criminology, 53*, 1017–1032.

Brown, S. (2003). *Crime and Law in Media Culture*. Buckingham: Open University Press.

Cameron, D., & Frazer, E. (1987). *The Lust to Kill*. Cambridge: Polity.

Caputi, J. (1987). *The Age of the Sex Crime*. Bowling Green: Bowling Green State University Popular Press.

Carlen, P. (1988). *Women, Crime and Poverty.* Buckingham: Open University Press.

Carrabine, E. (2008). *Crime, Culture and the Media.* Cambridge: Polity.

Chapkis, W. (1997). *Live Sex Acts: Women Performing Erotic Labour.* New York: Routledge.

Clarke Dillman, J. (2014). *Women and Death in Film, Television and News: Dead But Not Gone.* Basingstoke: Palgrave Macmillan.

Clover, C. (1992). *Men, Women and Chainsaws.* Princeton, MA: Princeton University Press.

Colebrook, M. (2012). The Edgier Waters of the Era: Gordon Burn's Somebody's Husband, Somebody's Son. In C. Gregoriou (Ed.), *Constructing Crime: Discourse and Cultural Representations of Crime and 'Deviance'.* Basingstoke: Palgrave Macmillan.

Cosslett, L. (2014, May 21). Why Women Are Hooked on Violent Crime Fiction. *The Guardian.*

Downing, L. (2013). *The Subject of Murder.* Chicago: University of Chicago Press.

Dworkin, A. (1976). *Our Blood: Prophecies and Discourses on Sexual Politics.* New York: Harper and Row.

Ferrell, J., Hayward, K., & Young, J. (2015). *Cultural Criminology: An Invitation* (2nd ed.). London: Sage.

Ferrell, J., Hayward, K., Morrison, W., & Presdee, M. (2004). *Cultural Criminology Unleashed.* New York: Routledge.

Ferris, S. (2015). *Street Sex Work and Canadian Cities: Resisting a Dangerous Order.* Alberta: University of Alberta Press.

Gill, R. (2007). Postfeminist Media Culture: Elements of a Sensibility. *European Journal of Cultural Studies, 10*(2), 147–166.

Hemmings, J. (2018, May 2). No Germain Greer: Women Don't Want to Watch Gratuitous Rapes on TV. *The Guardian.*

Hill, A. (2009, October 25). Sexist Violence Sickens Crime Critic. *The Observer.*

Jacobsen Hviid, M. (2014). *The Poetics of Crime: Understanding and Researching Crime and Deviance Through Creative Sources.* New York: Routledge.

Jermyn, D. (2015). Silk Blouses and Fedoras: The Female Detective, Contemporary TV Crime Drama and the Predicaments of Postfeminism. *Crime, Media, Culture, 13*(3), 259–276.

Jewkes, Y. (2013). *Media and Crime* (2nd ed.). London: Sage.

Jiwani, Y., & Young, M. L. (2006). Missing and Murdered Women: Reproducing Marginality in News Discourse. *Canadian Journal of Communication, 31,* 895–917.

Joseph, S. (2010). Telling True Stories in Australia. *Journalism Practice, 4*(1), 82–87.

Kinnell, H. (2008). *Violence and Sex Work in Britain.* Cullompton, Devon: Willan.

Linnemann, T. (2015). Capote's Ghosts: Violence, Murder and the Spectre of Suspicion. *British Journal of Criminology, 55,* 514–533.

Maguire, M. (2008). Criminal Investigation and Crime Control. In T. Newburn (Ed.), *Handbook of Policing* (2nd ed., pp. 430–465). Cullompton, UK: Willan.

Matthews, R. (2005). Policing Prostitution: Ten years on. *British Journal of Criminology, 45*, 877–895.

McRobbie, A. (2007). Post-feminism and Popular Culture. *Feminist Media Studies, 4*(3), 255–264.

McRobbie, A. (1984, June 8). 'Cross Winds', Review of Pat Barker, Blow Your House Down. *New Statesman*.

Meek, J. (2009, August 6). *Polly the Bleeding Parrot, London review of Books*.

Mulvey, L. (Autumn 1975). Visual Pleasure and Narrative Cinema. *Screen, 16*(3), 6–18.

Myers, B. (2009, July 22). Gordon Burn Was One of the Greatest Writers of His Age. *The Guardian*.

Newburn, T. (2007). Understanding Investigation. In T. Newburn, T. Williamson & A. Wright (Eds.), *Handbook of Criminal Investigation* (pp. 1–11). Cullompton, UK: Willan.

Neyroud, P., & Disley, E. (2007). The Management, Supervision and Oversight of Criminal Investigations. In T. Newburn, T. Willamson & A. Wright (Eds.), *Handbook of Criminal Investigation*. Cullompton, UK: Willan.

Nicholson, R. (2017, August 7). True Crime Makes Great TV. But Must It Linger on Women's Corpses? *The Guardian*.

O'Neill, M. (2001). *Prostitution and Feminism: Towards a Politics of Feeling*. Cambridge: Polity Press.

O'Neill, M. (2010). Cultural Criminology and Sex work: Resisting Regulation Through Radical Democracy and Participatory Action Research (PAR). *Journal of Law and Society, 37*(1), 210–232.

O'Neill, M., & Campbell, R. (2002). *Working Together to Create Change*. Available at http://www.safetysoapbox.com.

O'Neill, M., & Campbell, R. (2006). Street Sex Work and Local Communities: Creating Discursive Spaces for Genuine Consultation and Inclusion. In R. Campbell & M. O'Neill (Eds.), *Sex Work Now* (pp. 33–61). Cullompton: Willan.

O'Neill, M., & Seal, L. (2012). *Transgressive Imaginations: Crime, Deviance and Culture*. Basingstoke: Palgrave Macmillan.

Phoenix, J. (1999). *Making Sense of Prostitution*. Basingstoke: Palgrave Macmillan.

Quirk, J. (2009, February 28). Northern Exposure. *The Guardian*.

Rafter, N. (2007). Crime, Film and Criminology: Recent Sex Crime Movies. *Theoretical Criminology, 11*(3), 403–420.

Rawlings, P. (1998). True Crime. *British Criminology Conferences*, Vol. 1. www.britsoc.org/volume1/010.pdf. Accessed 5 March 2014.

Rawlinson, M. (2010). *Pat Barker*. Basingstoke: Palgrave Macmillan.

Rossmanith, K. (2014). Plots and Artefacts: Courts and Criminal Evidence in the Production of True Crime Writing. *Australian Feminist Law Journal, 40*(1), 97–111.

Sanders, T. (2016). Inevitably Violent? Dynamics of Space, Governance and Stigma [Special Issue]. *Problematizing Prostitution: Critical Research and Scholarship, Studies in Law, Politics and Society, 71*, 93–114.

Seltzer, M. (2007). *True Crime: Observations on Violence and Modernity*. New York: Routledge.

Shaw, K. (2010). *David Peace: Texts and Contexts*. Brighton: Sussex Academic Press.

Shaw, K. (Ed.). (2011). *Analysing David Peace*. Cambridge: Cambridge Scholars.

Skeggs, B. (1997). *Formations of Class and Gender: Becoming Respectable*. London: Sage.

Smith, J. (2013). *Misogynies: Reflections on Myth and Malice*. New York: Fawcett Columbine.

Strega, S., Janzen, C., Morgan, J., Brown, L., Thomas, J., & Carriere, J. (2014). Never Innocent Victims: Street Sex Workers in Canadian Print Media. *Violence Against Women, 20*(1), 6–25.

Tuchman, G. (2000). The Symbolic Annihilation of Women by the Mass Media. In L. Crothers & C. Lockhart (Eds.), *Culture and Politics*. New York: Palgrave Macmillan.

Upson, N. (2001, August 20). Hunting the Yorkshire Ripper. *New Statesman*.

Vincent, L., & Naidu, S. (2013). The Representation of Violence Against Women in Margie Orford's Clare Hart Novels. *African Safety Promotion Journal, 11*(2), 48.

Wakeman, S. (2013). 'No One Wins. One Side Just Loses More Slowly': The Wire and Drug Policy. *Theoretical Criminology, 18*, 224–239.

Walkowitz, J. (1982). Jack the Ripper and Myth of Male Violence. *Feminist Studies, 8*(3), 542–574.

Walkowitz, J. (1992). *City of Dreadful Delight: Narratives of Sexual Danger in Victorian London*. Chicago: University of Chicago Press.

Ward Jouve, N. (1988). *The Street Cleaner*. New York: Marion Boyars.

Wender, J. (2015). 'The Phenomenology of Arrest: A Case Study in Poetics of Police-Citizen Encounters. In M. H. Jacobsen (Ed.), *The Poetics of Crime: Understanding and Researching Crime and Deviance through Creative Sources*. London: Ashgate.

Williams, Z. (2018, May 1). Are Women Responsible for All the Sexual Violence on Screen? *The Guardian*.

Wilson, T. (2009). *Red Riding Quartet Review*. http://Capturescrime.blogspot.co.uk/2009101/review-red-riding-quartet-david-peace.html. Accessed 10 November 2014.

Yallop, D. (1993). *Deliver Us from Evil*. Reading: Cox and Wyman.

Young, A. (1996). *Imagining Crime: Textual Outlaws and Criminal Conversations*. London: Sage.

CHAPTER 7

Conclusion: Applying a Creative Feminist Approach to Exploring Crime History

Abstract In the concluding chapter I reiterate the value of crime history and studying key criminal events as a lens onto a wider range of criminological issues. For instance, this book's focus on the Yorkshire Ripper case has inspired the exploration of crime, place and history; feminist history; gender, structure and serial murder; and the framing of female victims across representational schemas. The chapter also emphasises the value of an interdisciplinary approach which integrates popular criminology, crime history, academic criminology and cultural studies to develop the criminological imagination. Feminist analyses have been pivotal to this project and I conclude by stressing the importance of these perspectives, whilst also acknowledging the tensions and contradictions provoked by an engagement with feminist knowledges.

Keywords Crime history · Criminological imagination · Feminist perspectives

INTRODUCTION

Studying a specific criminal event (albeit a very high-profile one) opens up a range of criminological possibilities. The discussions in the preceding chapters attest to this. Indeed, the Sutcliffe case not only extends the opportunity to revisit the relationship between masculinity and the

© The Author(s) 2018
L. Wattis, *Revisiting the Yorkshire Ripper Murders*,
Palgrave Studies in Victims and Victimology,
https://doi.org/10.1007/978-3-030-01385-1_7

serial murder of women, but as discussions in this volume highlight, it also inspires reflection on crime, place and history, feminism, as well as the way in which victims, misogyny and violence emerge within both the popular and criminological imaginary. More widely, discussions in the book speak to a number of related gendered concerns: violence against women; women's fear of crime; the historical repression and abjection of the prostitute figure. Moreover, analyzing a high profile case such as this, which has been the focus of considerable popular criminological attention, inevitably invites an interdisciplinary and intertextual approach (Downing 2013), and reinforces the value of popular criminology to academic criminology (Rawlings 1998; Rafter 2007; Carrabine 2008; Wakeman 2013). It is thus argued that drawing upon popular criminological texts—true crime and crime fiction, alongside academic criminology, contributes to a more creative criminology, which embraces both the figurative and the real in attempts to enhance criminological epistemologies and understandings of crime, violence and culture (Wakeman 2013; Jacobsen 2014; Wender 2015).

I use this final chapter to revisit key themes by drawing them together under several broadly overlapping headings: the importance of history to studies of crime and violence; feminism; violence and serial murder; and the representation of violence and victims.

'History Matters'

The subheading above comes from Carrabine (2008), who stresses the importance of a historical perspective in considering the origins of the print media and its relationship to contemporary representations of crime and violence (see also Brown's 2003 exploration of the relationship between the onset of modernity and the emergence of the modern media). Crime history has now developed as a sub-genre of criminology which Godfrey et al. (2009) define in the following way: 'crime history has attempted to understand the processes and interactions between how people perceived crime and its impact at particular moments in history' (p. 13). Godfrey et al. (2009) progress to argue for the advantages of 'historically contextualized criminology', which recognises the impact of the past on the present and moves away from temporal 'parochialism', defined as criminology's tokenistic engagement with some notion of 'the past' (Burke 1992, cited in Godfrey et al. 2009). This is not lost on Wilson et al. (2016) who also focus on recent crime history in their interrogation of the mass shooting of

16 schoolchildren in the Scottish city of Dunblane in 1996. Taking issue with academic criminology's silence on Dunblane, their aim in this article is to 'remember' and honour the truth' of this atrocity and by way of their concept of the 'criminological autopsy', to interrogate the past to comprehend, as far as is possible, the killer's motivation and to search for clues in order to prevent mass murder in the future.

This volume and the wider project upon which it is based, engages with crime history by way of its focus on a past criminal event which invites engagement with a historical perspective on a number of interlocking themes (Wilson et al. 2016). For instance, can this series of murders and attacks be viewed as an isolated event in terms of their socio-historical context and the nature of the crime or do they fit within a pattern of similar crimes, or within the broader context of violence against women? Serial killing is rare and the serial murder of thirteen women in the North of England over a five-year period in the 1970s even more so. However, as socio-structural analyses of serial murder maintain, we ignore history, culture and structure at our peril (Grover and Soothill 1999). The concentration of serial murder in the latter part of the Twentieth Century and its links to modernity and late capitalism also bear out the way in which 'history matters' in studies of crime.

In terms of the police investigation and media coverage, there is evidence to suggest that this was a crime of its time. It is unlikely that given advances in police investigative techniques and the ubiquity of CCTV, a man could continue to murder women in this manner over a period of five years. For instance, between October and December 2006 when five sex workers were murdered in the English city of Ipswich, the murderer Steve Wright was arrested within two months of the discovery of the first victim's body (Harrison and Wilson 2008). That said, the murder of vulnerable and marginalised women connected to street prostitution and the manner in which they are framed representationally, demonstrates historical continuities in terms of misogyny, violence against women and the historical Othering of women connected to prostitution (Walkowitz 1982; Warkentin 2010). For instance, police attitudes towards street sex workers and the repressive policing of street prostitution during the Sutcliffe murders forms part of the repression of prostitutes in law and justice since the Victorian period (Walkowitz 1992; O'Neill 2010). Furthermore, as Kinnell (2008) points out, the framing of violence against sex workers by radical feminism during the Sutcliffe murders has cast a long shadow in terms of policy and public attitudes towards the figure of the prostitute, violence against sex workers and contemporary approaches to the regulation of street prostitution.

Chapter 2 dealt specifically and explicitly with the historical context of the Sutcliffe murders, interrogating the case as a crime of time and place whereby Peter Sutcliffe's subjectivity and motivation are explored as a product of 1970s Northern masculine culture. Likewise, similar cultural traits were evident in police culture from the time and can in part, account for investigative failings on the case (Bland 1992; Smith 2013). Drawing upon a range of texts from history, criminology, true crime, fiction and cultural studies (reflecting an overall commitment to an intertextual and interdisciplinary approach to 'reading crime') this chapter interrogated the socio-historical context in which this crime took place. In doing so, it highlighted the Sutcliffe case as constitutive and symptomatic of a decade characterized by social, economic and political crisis, racism, gender inequality and sexual exploitation emanating from the celebrity culture at the time. At the same time however, the discussion reinforced the way in which misogyny, violence against women and femicide transcend history and place, albeit shaped by specific socio-historical contexts.

FEMINISM, VIOLENCE AND SERIAL MURDER

The focus on the Sutcliffe case inevitably necessitates some engagement with broader analyses of serial killing. Chapter 3 acknowledged the dominance of individual, psychologically orientated perspectives on serial murder, but was more interested in locating this violence in its structural and cultural contexts, exploring the role modernity and late capitalism/neo-liberalism have played in engendering serial murder. So for instance, Haggerty's (2009) work on the parallels between modernity and the subjectivity of the serial murderer were explored. Likewise, Wilson's (2007, 2012) victim-centred approach to serial murder which implicates the neo-liberal order in creating more available victims due to the intensification of vulnerability and marginality was also considered. What is more, this focus on structure and the 'necessary conditions' for serial killing has occurred alongside academic analysis of the growing cultural popularity of the figure of the serial killer. The cultural presence and appeal of the serial killer increased significantly in the latter half of the Twentieth Century to the point of elevation to celebrity status (Jenkins 1994; Seltzer 1998;

Schmid 2005). This occurred in the midst of a cultural landscape in thrall to mediated violence more generally (Hobsbawn 1995; Seltzer 1998; Brown 2003; Ray 2011; Carrabine 2008; Jewkes 2013). Work on the cultural life of the serial killer reveals how the mediated version residing in popular culture has taken on a life of its own—both in terms of exaggerated incidence, as well as stoking up the mythological persona of the offender.

These structural and cultural analyses concentrate on class and the political economy rather than gender in accounting for motivation. There are parallels here with the discipline of criminology more generally where there has been a history of fixating on the experience of the male offender without acknowledging offending as gendered and the offender as predominantly male (Cain 1989; Gelsthorpe and Morris 1990; Walklate 2004). This is not altogether true of the structural work on serial killing (see Grover and Soothill; Wilson 2007). Having said that, structural explanations ultimately privilege the political economy and the impact of the current economic order in shaping motivation and victim vulnerability (Wilson 2007, 2012; Hall and Wilson 2014). Equally, key work focusing on the serial killer in culture—from Jack the Ripper through to those offenders who occupy the cultural landscape of the Twentieth Century (real and imagined) often do not name the fetishized and celebrated killer in culture as male (Seltzer 1998; Schmid 2005). To quote Cain (1989), 'the criminological gaze cannot see gender; the criminological discourse cannot speak men and women (Cain 1989, cited in Walklate 2004: 21).

In contrast, feminist analyses of violence against women and the murder of women by men—politicized in feminist analysis as femicide, focuses squarely and explicitly on the male perpetrator (Dworkin 1981; Hollway 1981; Cameron and Frazer 1987; Radford and Russell 1992; Jeffries 2013). With regards serial murder specifically, feminist analyses take issue with the depoliticisation of the sex or lust murderer in both popular and academic culture, whose masculinity is obscured by individual and pathological explanations of deviance and the veneration of the masculine murdering subject with (Caputi 1987; Cameron and Frazer 1987; Hollway 1981; Downing 2013; Warkentin 2010). Feminist analyses identify misogynist masculinity as driving the serial murder of women and the representation of victims. Indeed, within the sphere of representation and popular culture, feminist writers name the figure of the murderer, celebrated and lionized across history and culture as a male figure (Caputi 1987; Cameron and Frazer 1987; Downing 2013). The cultural vilification of significantly smaller numbers of female offenders certainly bears this out (Wykes and Welsh 2009; Jewkes 2013; Downing 2013). And whilst it is acknowledged that misogyny cannot account for all instances of serial murder, the quest for transcendence and exceptionality (identified essentially as traits of masculinity) are evident across the biographies and subjectivities of male killers—both real and fictional, who are often received favourably within the wider culture (Cameron and Frazer 1987; Downing 2013).

Chapter 3 spent some time considering the contribution of structural and cultural approaches to understanding serial murder—both feminist analyses and those prioritizing the role of social transformation and the political economy in fostering violence and serial killing (actual and mediated) and exacerbating vulnerability. These distinct explanatory frameworks are often sequestered from one another as they carry out distinct theoretical work on violence and serial killing, calling forth the figure of offender and victim differently. Greater integration of the structural frameworks on serial murder and indeed studies of violence more generally, would expand understandings and address some of the complexities of etiology and representation.

For instance, integrated analyses illuminate how patriarchy and violence against women operate within the context of neo-liberalism and provide a counter to the accusation that feminism is now in collusion with the neo-liberal project (Fraser 2013; Campbell, n.d.; Schwartz 2013; Walby 2011). For example, work on disappeared women in Latin and South America—the mass femicide of poor, migrant women in the Mexican city of Cuidad Juarez in the late 1990s and 2000s, demonstrates how neo-liberalism's lack of regard for poor workers, who are deemed disposable within neo-liberal labour markets, was manifest in the lack of care afforded to poor young women. However, this lack of regard intersperses with patriarchal misogyny so that the mass rape, torture and murder of women is carried out with impunity (Ensalaco 2006; Jeffries 2013; Schmidt Camacho 2010). Likewise, in the sphere of representation, Clarke-Dillman (2014) has drawn attention to the proliferation of visual images of dead women within the cultural landscapes of the recent 2000s.

Referring to the commentaries on the actual murders in Ciudad Juarez, for Dillman (2014) the profusion of dead women in visual culture, depicted with intensified realism, reinforces women's disposability in the context of globalised, neo-liberal labour markets.

That said, although this case reinforces the salience of feminist analyses for understanding crime and violence, the discussions in this volume also reveal some of the dilemmas and tensions which feminist frameworks inhere. Firstly, in common with academic narratives more generally (Sandberg et al. 2015), the feminist project to name gender and violence against women as political and to offer a universal analysis, often loses sight of the complexity and nuance of narrative and the human experience (Walkowitz 1992; Haaken 2010). Chapter 4 dealt with these themes exploring the links between the Sutcliffe case and the development of feminism in response to the murders and the discourses of indifference and victim blaming which surrounded them. Feminist history from the time presents a compelling account of activist responses to the murders and a unified experience of women's fear in the face of the threat from the male murderer, which fits with the overarching radical feminist analysis of violence against women in the context of patriarchy. This alludes to a unified feminine experience of violence and fear (Haaken 2010)—both in the context of these murders and more widely. However, as Haaken (2010) notes, in the pursuit of a shared history and experience of oppression, alternative voices and stories are lost if they do not fit the dominant narrative. Criticisms of radical feminism's insensitivity to race (Cox 1990; Bhavnani and Coulson 2005), and the fact that sex workers and their advocates were denied a voice in this history, (Kinnell 2008) bear out Haaken's notions of lost voices.

This brings me to the second point which also links to the Sutcliffe case—that of the debate over the meaning and implications of the sale of sex. Radical feminist analyses of systemic male violence include prostitution as a reflection of male heterosexual, patriarchal power and as violence against women in and of itself, which should be eradicated via abolition (Pateman 1983; Jeffreys 2008, 2009; Barry 1996). To paraphrase Sheila Jeffreys, a staunch opponent of prostitution, it is the very idea of prostitution as a legitimate activity, which allows its existence and acceptance. In contrast, those who adopt the sex worker or 'sex positive' position advocate for the rights and recognition of sex workers via research and activism, favouring decriminalization as a means to secure sex workers' rights and citizenship, and to ensure the safety and well-being of those involved in the sex industry. It has been argued that these opposing positions, often referred to as the sex wars' were entrenched in the UK context around the time of the Sutcliffe murders in the midst of radical feminist activity, which was at the time fine-tuning its analysis of violence, sexual violence and patriarchy. The ideological battle over the meaning of prostitution established at this time (Walkowitz 1982; Ferris 2015), remains a consistent fault line across feminism (Mackay 2015).

READING VIOLENCE AND VICTIMISATION

This project highlights how a focus on even one past criminal event invites a range of criminological possibilities, many of which have been explored within this volume. To conclude, I want to reiterate the commitment of this project to reading crime across texts and academic disciplines. A number of academics from across disciplinary boundaries have picked up on this. For instance, from the perspective of cultural studies, Downing (2013) notes, the study of murder is inevitably intertextual, 'it encourages a blending of myth, "reality" and imagination' (p. 194). Her cultural and historical examination of the murdering subject as a celebrated figure (almost exclusively male and definitely so in the representational sphere) is something of a manifesto for reading crime by way of cultural texts.

The recognition that academic criminology needs to engage more fully with popular criminology defined as the range of cultural representations of crime emanating from popular culture such as film, fiction, true crime, television crime dramas (Rafter 2007) has gathered momentum amongst academic criminologists (Young 1996; Rawlings 1998; Brown 2003; Rafter 2007; Carrabine 2008; Seal and O'Neill 2012; Wakeman 2013; Jacobsen 2014; Walklate and Jacobsen 2017). Various arguments in support of this popular/cultural turn highlight the significantly longer reach of popular criminology and relatedly, that it is from popular culture that various publics gain their understandings of the 'crimino-legal complex' (Young 1996; Brown 2003). This is in comparison to the significantly more limited reach of academic publications, which even in the face of the impact agenda and the proliferation of academic blogs and journalistic think pieces, academic discourse rarely makes it out of its own community. Moreover, the engagement with popular criminology also speaks to debates regarding public criminology and the relationship between academic criminology and the public and political sphere (Loader and Sparks 2011; Brown and Rafter 2013).

Cultural texts are provocative devices which do important affective work in making us think and feel differently about crime, criminal subjects and victims (Brown 2003; Rafter 2007; Seal and O'Neill 2012; Wakeman 2013)—both for the academic criminologist and the wider publics who engage with popular criminology in visual and textual forms. Indeed, 'reading' crime (Brown 2003) by way of popular criminology inspires new ways of regarding crime, violence, victimization and so forth, because it provokes a fresh set of psychological and emotional responses. Engagement with such texts also invites debate on ethical and political concerns (Rafter 2007) with the potential to challenge conservative and stereotypical assumptions and 'restrictive portrayals', offering 'radical democratic possibilities' (O'Neill and Seal 2012: 1). In addition, fictional and true crime prisms can be ethnographic, sociological and criminological and as such, offer great possibility as historical, social and political documents (Brown 2003; Wakeman 2013). In essence, popular criminology has great epistemological potential for enhancing understandings of crime (Carrabine 2008).

In the context of this study, analysis of popular criminological texts underlines the value of fiction and true crime for contemplating violence against women, the figure of the prostitute and the distinctions between criminal, victim and the state. Indeed, Chapter 6 examined the portrayals of victims in true crime and crime fiction. It also considered the framing of policing, sex workers and violence against women and misogyny. In doing so, it offered alternative representational possibilities, which challenge gratuitous, simplistic and misogynist framings of marginalized women and male violence against women.

However, engagement with popular criminology also requires a critical approach, which asks questions about the nature of the representations. Just as texts may offer alternative, 'counter-hegemonic' or 'democratic' ways of imagining crime, offenders, victims and violence (O'Neill and Seal 2012), they may also reinforce limited and conservative assumptions regarding the nature of crime, offending and victimisation, as well as legitimating and perpetuating powerlessness and inequality via cultural production. This has not been lost on those academics concerned with the study of culture (Horkheimer and Adorno 1972; Hall and Jefferson 1976; Hall et al. 1978), who in a range of analyses, highlight the reproduction and maintenance of class-based power and the Othering of social groups within the sphere of culture. As McRobbie (2007) puts it: 'Relations of power are indeed made and re-made within texts of enjoyment and rituals of relaxation' (p. 262).

In relation to this project specifically, the implications of representing misogyny and graphic violence against women as it appears in texts covering the Sutcliffe case were discussed in Chapter 6. Between them, these texts contain graphic portrayals of sexual violence, murder, misogynist voices and prurient images of women. Consequently, they provoke tensions relating to the ethics of representation and the politics and purpose of mediated portrayals of violence against women in popular cultural production (McRobbie 2007; Jermyn 2015; Clarke-Dillman 2014; Carrabine 2008; Brown 2003; Villalon 2012; Vincent and Naidu 2013). Do such texts, as Jacobs (2010) has argued, merely reproduce powerlessness as they 'invite fantasy and an objectification of the female victims' (Jacobs 2010: 43). On the other hand, does mediated violence serve a purpose in rendering violence visible and offering reassurance and resolution (Munt 1994; Browder 2006)?

A commitment to feminism necessitates an ethical and political engagement with the implications of visual and textual violence which will inevitably provoke conflicted responses. Representational violence is yet another example of the way in which feminist knowledges provoke tension and ambivalence (Cameron 2018). Indeed, as many of the discussions in this book have highlighted, a commitment to feminism and feminist knowledge is not an easy political and academic choice, requiring an emotional, as well as intellectual engagement (Cameron 2018). Considerations of class, race and the politicization of sex work/prostitution in this volume connect to wider debates and highlight the difficulties in negotiating feminism and its 'faultlines' (Mackay 2015). Having said that, the focus of this project—a case involving the murder of thirteen women motivated by misogyny and framed by an unambiguous disregard for poor and marginalized connected to prostitution reminds of us the need for robust and unswerving feminist responses. This project has both embraced and challenged radical feminist approaches, whilst remaining fully aware that violent patriarchal societies require feminist frameworks to analyse gender, power and violence.

REFERENCES

Barry, K. (1996). *The Prostitution of Sexuality: The Global Exploitation of Women*. New York: New York University Press.

Bhavnani, K., & Coulson, M. (2005). Transforming Socialist Feminism: The Challenge of Racism. *Feminist Review, 80*, 87–97.

Bland, L. (1992). The Case of the Yorkshire Ripper: Mad, Bad, Beast or Male? In J. Radford & D. E. H. Russell (Eds.), *Femicide: The Politics of Women Killing*. Buckingham: Open University Press.

Browder, L. (2006). Dystopian Romance: True Crime and the Female Reader. *The Journal of Popular Culture, 39*(6), 928–953.

Brown, M., & Rafter, N. (2013). Genocide Films, Public Criminology, Collective Memory. *British Journal of Criminology, 53*, 1017–1032.

Brown, S. (2003). *Crime and Law in Media Culture*. Buckingham: Open University Press.

Cain, M. (1989). Feminists Transgress Criminology. In M. Cain (Ed.), *Growing Up Good*. London: Sage.

Cameron, D., & Frazer, E. (1987). *The Lust to Kill*. Cambridge: Polity.

Cameron, J. J. (2018). *Reconsidering Radical Feminism: Affect and the Politics of Heterosexuality*. Washington: University of Washington Press.

Caputi, J. (1987). *The Age of the Sex Crime*. Bowling Green: Bowling Green State University Popular Press.

Carrabine, E. (2008). *Crime, Culture and the Media*. Cambridge: Polity.

Clarke Dillman, J. (2014). *Women and Death in Film, Television and News: Dead But Not Gone*. Basingstoke: Palgrave Macmillan.

Cox, C. (1990). Anything Less Is Not Feminism: Racial Difference and the WMWM. *Law and Critique, 1*(2), 237–248.

Downing, L. (2013). *The Subject of Murder*. Chicago: University of Chicago Press.

Dworkin, A. (1981). *Pornography: Men possessing Women*. New York: Perigee.

Ensalaco, M. (2006). Murder in Ciudad Juarez: A Parable of Women's Struggle for Human Rights. *Violence Against Women, 12*(5), 417–440.

Ferris, S. (2015). *Street Sex Work and Canadian Cities: Resisting a Dangerous Order*. Alberta: University of Alberta Press.

Fraser, N. (2013). *Fortunes of Feminism: From State Managed Capital to Neo-Liberal Crisis*. London: Verso.

Gelsthorpe, L., & Morris, A. (Eds.). (1990). *Feminist Perspectives in Criminology*. Buckingham: Open University Press.

Godfrey, B. S., Lawrence, P., & Williams, C. A. (2009). *History and Crime*. London: Sage.

Grover, L., & Soothill, K. (1999). British Serial Killing: Towards a Structural Explanation. In *The British Criminology Conferences: Selected Proceedings* (Vol.

2). Papers from the British Criminology Conference, Queens University, Belfast, 15–19 July 1997. This volume published March 1999. Editor: Mike Brogden.

Haaken, J. (2010). *Hard Knocks: Domestic Violence and the Psychology of Storytelling*. London: Routledge.

Haggerty, K. (2009). Modern Serial Killers. *Crime, Media, Culture, 5,* 168.

Hall, S., & Jefferson, T. (1976). *Resistance Through Rituals: Youth Subcultures in Post-War Britain*. London: Routledge.

Hall, S., & Wilson, D. (2014). New Foundations: Pseudo-Pacification and Special Liberty as Potential Cornerstones for a Multi-level Theory of Homicide and Serial Murder. *European Journal of Criminology, 11*(5), 635–655.

Hall, S., Critcher, C., Jefferson, T., Clarke, C., & Roberts, B. (1978). *Policing the Crisis: Mugging, the State and Law and Order*. London: Palgrave Macmillan.

Harrison, P., & Wilson, D. (2008). *Hunting Evil: Inside the Ipswich Serial Murders*. London: Sphere.

Hobsbawn, E. (1995). *Age of Extremes: The Short Twentieth Century 1914–1991*. London: Abacus.

Hollway, W. (1981, October). I Just Wanted to Kill a Woman' Why? The Ripper and Male Sexuality. *Feminist Review, 9,* 33–40.

Horkheimer, M., & Adorno, T. W. (1972). *The Dialectic of the Enlightenment*. New York: Herder and Herder.

Jacobs, J. (2010). *Memorialising the Holocaust: Gender, Genocide and Collective Memory*. London: I.B. Tauris.

Jacobsen Hviid, M. (2014). *The Poetics of Crime: Understanding and Researching Crime and Deviance Through Creative Sources*. New York: Routledge.

Jeffreys, S. (2008). *The Idea of Prostitution*. Melbourne: Spinifex Press.

Jeffreys, S. (2009). *The Industrial Vagina: The Political Economy of the Global Sex Trade*. London: Routledge.

Jeffries, F. (2013). Documentary Noir in the City of Fear: Feminicide, Impunity and Grass Roots Communication in Ciudad Juarez. *Crime Media Culture, 9*(3), 301–317.

Jenkins, P. (1994). *Using Murder: The Social Construction of Serial Homicide*. New York: Routledge.

Jermyn, D. (2015). Silk Blouses and Fedoras: The Female Detective, Contemporary TV Crime Drama and the Predicaments of Postfeminism. *Crime, Media, Culture, 13*(3), 259–276.

Jewkes, Y. (2013). *Media and Crime* (2nd ed.). London: Sage.

Kinnell, H. (2008). *Violence and Sex Work in Britain*. Cullompton: Willan.

Loader, I., & Sparks, R. (2011). *Public Criminology*. London: Routledge.

Mackay, F. (2015). *Radical Feminism: Feminist Activism in Movement*. London: Palgrave Macmillan.

McRobbie, A. (2007). Post-feminism and Popular Culture. *Feminist Media Studies, 4*(3), 255–264.

Munt, S. (1994). *Murder by the Book? Feminism and the Crime Novel.* London: Routledge.

O'Neill, M. (2010). Cultural Criminology and Sex Work: Resisting Regulation Through Radical Democracy and Participatory Action Research (PAR). *Journal of Law and Society, 37*(1), 210–232.

O'Neill, M., & Seal, L. (2012). *Transgressive Imaginations: Crime, Deviance and Culture.* Basingstoke: Palgrave Macmillan.

Pateman, C. (1983). *The Sexual Contract.* Bloomington, IN: Stanford University Press.

Radford, J., & Russell, D. (1992). *Femicide: The Politics of Woman Killing.* New York, NY: Twayne.

Rafter, N. (2007). Crime, Film and Criminology: Recent Sex Crime Movies. *Theoretical Criminology, 11*(3), 403–420.

Rawlings, P. (1998). True Crime. *British Criminology Conferences* (Vol. 1). www.britsoc.org/volume1/010.pdf. Accessed 5 March 2014.

Ray, L. (2011). *Violence and Society.* London: Sage.

Sandberg, S., Tutenge, S., & Copes, H. (2015). Studies of Violence: A Narrative Criminological Study of Ambiguity. *British Journal of Criminology, 55,* 1168–1186.

Schmid, D. (2005). *Natural Born Celebrities: Serial Killers in American Culture.* London: University of Chicago Press.

Schmidt-Camacho, A. S. (2010). Ciudadana X: Gender Violence and the Denationalisation of Women's Rights in Ciudad Juarez, Mexico. In R. L. Fregoso & C. Bejarano (Eds.), *Terrorising Women: Feminicide in the Americas.* Washington: Duke University Press.

Schwartz, M. (2013). Kicking Back, Not Leaning. *Dissent, 60*(3), 713–722.

Seltzer, M. (1998). *Serial Killers: Death and Life in America's Wound Culture.* London: Sage.

Smith, J. (2013). *Misogynies: Reflections on Myth and Malice.* New York: Fawcett Columbine.

Villalon, R. (2012). Accounts of Violence Against Women: The Potential of Realistic Fiction. In D. King & C. L. Smith (Eds.), *Men Who Hate Women and Women Who Kick Their Asses: Stieg Larrson's Millennium in Feminist Perspective.* Nashville, TN: Vanderbilt University Press.

Vincent, L., & Naidu, S. (2013). The Representation of Violence Against Women in Margie Orford's Clare Hart Novels. *African Safety Promotion Journal, 11,* 48.

Wakeman, S. (2013). 'No One Wins. One Side Just Loses More Slowly': The Wire and Drug Policy. *Theoretical Criminology, 18,* 224–239.

Walby, S. (2011). *The Future of Feminism.* Cambridge: Polity.

Walklate, S. (2004). *Crime and Justice* (2nd ed.). Cullompton: Willan.

Walklate, S., & Jacobsen Hviid, M. (Eds.). (2017). *Liquid Criminology: Doing Imaginative Criminological Research*. London: Routledge.

Walkowitz, J. (1982). Jack the Ripper and Myth of Male Violence. *Feminist Studies, 8*(3), 542–574.

Walkowitz, J. (1992). *City of Dreadful Delight: Narratives of Sexual Danger in Victorian London*. Chicago: University of Chicago Press.

Warkentin, E. (2010). "Jack the Ripper" Strikes Again: The "Ipswich Ripper" and the "Vice Girls" He Killed. *Feminist Media Studies, 10*, 35–49.

Wender, J. (2015). The Phenomenology of Arrest: A Case Study in Poetics of Police-Citizen Encounters. In M. H. Jacobsen (Ed.), *The Poetics of Crime: Understanding and Researching Crime and Deviance Through Creative Sources*. London: Ashgate.

Wilson, D. (2007). *Serial Killers: Hunting Britons and Their Victims 1966–2006*. Hampshire Hook: Waterside Press.

Wilson, D. (2012). Late Capitalism, Vulnerable Populations and Violent Predatory Crime. In S. Hall & S. Winlow (Eds.), *New Directions in Criminological Theory*. London: Routledge.

Wilson, D., Yardley, R., & Pemberton, S. (2016). The 'Dunblane Massacre' as a 'Photosensitive Plate'. *Crime, Media, Culture, 13*, 1–14.

Wykes, M., & Welsh, K. (2009). *Violence, Gender and Justice*. London: Sage.

Young, A. (1996). *Imagining Crime: Textual Outlaws and Criminal Conversations*. London: Sage.

Young, J. (1999). *The Exclusive Society: Social Exclusion, Crime and Difference in Late Modernity*. London: Sage.

BIBLIOGRAPHY

Agustin, L. (2007). *Sex Work at the Margins: Migration, Labour Markets and the Rescue Industry*. London: Zed Books.

Alleyne, B. (2015). *Narrative Networks: Storied Approaches in a Digital Age*. London: Sage.

Amis, M. (2000). *Experience*. London: Jonathan Cape.

Anthias, N., & Yuval Davis, N. (1993). *Racialised Boundaries: Race, Nation, Gender, Colour and Class and the Anti-Racist Struggle*. London: Taylor and Francis.

Aoyama, K. (2008). *Thai Migrant Sex Workers: From Modernisation to Globalisation*. Basingstoke: Palgrave Macmillan.

Ardis, A. (1991). Political Attentiveness Vs. Political Correctness: Teaching Pat Barker's Blow Your House Down. *College Literature, 18*(3), 44–54.

Armstrong, L. (2015). From Law Enforcement to Protection? Interactions Between Sex Workers and Police in a Decriminalized Street-Based Sex Industry. *British Journal of Criminology, 57*(3), 570–588.

Atkinson, R., & Parker, S. (2011, July 7–9). *The Autotomic City: The Strategic Ejection of Unruly Urban Space*. International RC21 Conference on Urban Order, Crime and Citizenship, Amsterdam.

Auerbach, N. (1978). *Communities of Women: An Idea in Fiction* (pp. 549–572). Cambridge, MA: Harvard University Press.

Baddeley, A. D. (1999). *Essentials of Human Memory*. Hove: Psychology Press.

Bailoni, M. (2014). *The Effects of Thatcherism in the Urban North of England*. Metropolitics.eu. www.metropolitiques.eu/The-effects=of-Thatcherism-in-the-html.

Barbaret, R. (2014). *Women, Crime and Criminal Justice: A Global Enquiry*. Abingdon: Routledge.

© The Editor(s) (if applicable) and The Author(s),
under exclusive license to Springer Nature Switzerland AG 2018
L. Wattis, *Revisiting the Yorkshire Ripper Murders*, Palgrave Studies
in Victims and Victimology, https://doi.org/10.1007/978-3-030-01385-1

157

Barlow, C. (2015). Silencing the Other: Gendered Representations of Co-accused Women Offenders. *The Howard Journal of Criminal Justice, 54*(5), 469–488.

Barry, K. (1996). *The Prostitution of Sexuality: The Global Exploitation of Women.* New York: New York University Press.

Bartol, C. R., & Bartol, A. M. (2008). *Criminal Behaviour a Psychosocial Approach* (8th ed.). New York: Pearson.

Beckett, A. (2010). *When the Lights Went Out: What Really Happened to Britain in the Seventies.* London: Faber and Faber.

Benedict, H. (1992). *Virgin or Vamp: How the Press Covers Sex Crimes.* Oxford: Oxford University Press.

Bennell, C., Bloomfield, S., Emeno, K., & Mussolino, E. (2013). Classifying Serial Sexual Murderers: An Attempt to Validate Keppel and Walter's 1999 Model. *Criminal Justice and Behaviour, 40*(11), 5–23.

Bennett, C. (2017, May 21). We Learn Nothing from Ian Brady's Murder: We're Just Fetishising Him. *The Guardian.*

Bhavnani, K., & Coulson, M. (2005). Transforming Socialist Feminism: The Challenge of Racism. *Feminist Review, 80*, 87–97.

Bilton, M. (2006). *Wicked Beyond Belief: The Hunt for the Yorkshire Ripper* (Rev. ed.). London: Harper Perennial.

Bindel, J. (2017, October 11). Why Prostitution Should Never Be Legalised. *The Guardian.*

Biressi, A. (2001). *Crime, Fear and the Law in True Crime Stories.* New York: Palgrave Macmillan.

Blackburn, R. (1993). *The Psychology of Criminal Conduct: Theory, Research and Practice.* Chichester: Wiley.

Bland, L. (1992). The Case of the Yorkshire Ripper: Mad, Bad, Beast or Male? In J. Radford & D. E. H. Russell (Eds.), *Femicide: The Politics of Women Killing.* Buckingham: Open University Press.

Bolland, E. (n.d.). Emma Bolland: (Short Paper For Occursus 'Post-traumatic Landscapes Symposium'). *Every Place a Palimpsest* (Part Two).

Bottoms, A. E., & Wiles, P. (1997). Environmental Criminology. In M. Maguire, R. Moran, & R. Reiner (Eds.), *Oxford Handbook of Criminology.* Oxford: Clarendon Press.

Bottoms, A. E., Mawby, R. I., & Walker, M. A. (1987). A Localised Crime Survey in Contrasting Areas of a City. *British Journal of Criminology, 27*, 125–154.

Boyle, K. (2017). Hiding in Plain Sight. *Journalism Studies, 19*(11), 1562–1578.

Bronfen, E. (1992). *Over Her Dead Body: Death, Femininity and the Aesthetic.* New York: Routledge.

Brooks-Gordon, B. (2008). *The Price of Sex: Prostitution, Policy and Society.* Cullompton: Willan.

Browder, L. (2006). Dystopian Romance: True Crime and the Female Reader. *The Journal of Popular Culture, 39*(6), 928–953.

Brown, R. (2012). 'Armageddon Was Yesterday—Today We Have a Serious Problem': Pre and Postmillennial Tropes for Crime and Criminality by David Peace and Stieg Larsson. In C. Gregoriou (Ed.), *Constructing Crime: Discourse and Cultural Representations of Crime and 'Deviance'*. Basingstoke: Palgrave Macmillan.

Brown, S. (2003). *Crime and Law in Media Culture*. Buckingham: Open University Press.

Brown, M., & Rafter, N. (2013). Genocide Films, Public Criminology, Collective Memory. *British Journal of Criminology, 53*, 1017–1032.

Brownmiller, S. (1975). *Against Our Will: Men, Women and Rape*. Harmondsworth: Penguin.

Bruley, S. (2016). Women's Liberation at the Grass Roots: A View from Some English Towns, c.1968–1990. *Women's History Review, 25*(5), 723–740.

Burgess-Proctor, A. (2006). Intersections of Race, Class, Gender and Crime: Future Directions for Feminist Criminology. *Feminist Criminology, 1*, 27–47.

Burn, G. (2004). *Somebody's Husband, Somebody's Son*. London: Viking.

Byford, L. (1981). *The Yorkshire Ripper Case: Review of the Police Investigation of the Case by Lawrence Byford, Esq., C.B.E., Q.P.M., Her Majesty's Inspectorate of Constabulary*. London: Home Office.

Cain, M. (1989). Feminists Transgress Criminology. In M. Cain (Ed.), *Growing Up Good*. London: Sage.

Cameron, D., & Frazer, E. (1987). *The Lust to Kill*. Cambridge: Polity.

Cameron, J. J. (2018). *Reconsidering Radical Feminism: Affect and the Politics of Heterosexuality*. Washington: University of Washington Press.

Canter, D. (2000). Offender Profiling and Psychological Differentiation. *Journal of Criminal and Legal Psychology, 5*, 23–46.

Canter, D. (2001). *Criminal Shadows: The Inner Narratives of Evil*. Texas City: Authorlink Press.

Canter, D. V., & Wentink, N. (2004). An Empirical Test of Holmes and Holmes's Serial Murder Typology. *Criminal Justice and Behavior, 31*, 489–515.

Canter, D. V., Laurence, J. A., Alison, E., & Wentink, N. (2004). The Organized/Disorganized Typology of Serial Murder: Myth or Model? *Psychology, Public Policy and Law, 10*(3), 293–320.

Caputi, J. (1987). *The Age of the Sex Crime*. Bowling Green: Bowling Green State University Popular Press.

Carlen, P. (1988). *Women, Crime and Poverty*. Backingham: Open University Press.

Carrabine, E. (2008). *Crime, Culture and the Media*. Cambridge: Polity.

Carter, C., & Weaver, C. K. (2003). *Violence and the Media*. Buckingham: Open University Press.

Castells, M. (1996). *The Rise of the Network Society*. Oxford: Blackwell.

Ceresa, D. (1981). It's Women Who Are Under Attack. *Spare Rib, 107*, p. 17.

Chan, W. (2001). *Women, Murder and Justice*. Basingstoke: Palgrave Macmillan.

Chapkis, W. (1997). *Live Sex Acts: Women Performing Erotic Labour*. New York: Routledge.

Clarke Dillman, J. (2014). *Women and Death in Film, Television and News: Dead but Not Gone*. Basingstoke: Palgrave Macmillan.

Clover, C. (1992). *Men, Women and Chainsaws*. Princeton, MA: Princeton University Press.

Colebrook, M. (2012). The Edgier Waters of the Era: Gordon Burn's Somebody's Husband, Somebody's Son. In C. Gregoriou (Ed.), *Constructing Crime: Discourse and Cultural Representations of Crime and 'Deviance'*. Basingstoke: Palgrave Macmillan.

Cooke, R. (2016, July 16). Somebody's Husband, Somebody's Son: An Unflinching Look at the Yorkshire Ripper. *The Guardian*.

Corradi, C., Marcuello Servos, M., & Boira, S. (2016). Theories of Femicide and Their Significance for Social Research. *Current Sociology, 64*(7), 975–995.

Corrigan, N. (2010, September 24). Vicky Wasn't the Only One: Harrowing Stories of Teesside's Other Tragic Vice Girls. *The Evening Gazette*.

Cosslett, L. (2014, May 21). Why Women Are Hooked on Violent Crime Fiction. *The Guardian*.

Cox, C. (1990). Anything Less Is Not Feminism: Racial Difference and the WMWM. *Law and Critique, 1*(2), 237–248.

Crenshaw, K. (1991). Mapping the Margins: Intersectionality, Identity Politics and Violence Against Women of Colour. *Stanford Law Review, 43*(6), 1241–1299.

Cresswell, D. M., & Hollin, C. R. (1994). Multiple Murder: A Review. *British Journal Criminology, Delinquency and Deviant Social Behaviour, 22*, 395–414.

Crown Prosecution Service. (2010). *Violence Against Women Crime Report*. London: CPS; London: HMSO.

Currie, E. (2009). *The Roots of Danger: Violent Crime in Global Perspective*. Upper Saddle River, NJ: Prentice Hall.

Curtis, L. (2002). *Jack the Ripper and the London Press*. New Haven: Yale University Press.

D'Cruze, S., Jackson, L. A., & Rowbotham, J. (2005). Gender, Crime and Culture in the Twentieth-First Century: Conversations Between Academics and Professionals. *History Workshop Journal, 60*, 139–151.

D'Cruze, S., Walklate, S., & Pegg, S. (2006). *Murder: Social and Historical Approaches to Understanding Murder and Murderers*. Cullompton: Willan.

Daly, M. (1973). *Beyond God the Father: Towards a Philosophy of Women's Liberation*. Boston: Beacon Press.

Davies, D. (2016). *In Plain Sight: The Life and Lies of Jimmy Saville*. London: Quercus.

Davis, M. (1990). *City of Quartz: Excavating the Future in Los Angeles*. New York: Verso.

Department of Health. (2005). *Responding to Domestic Abuse*. London: HMSO.

Derrida, J. (1994). *Specters of Marx: The State of the Debt, the Work of Mourning and the New International*. New York and London: Routledge.

Dines, G. (2012). A Feminist Response to Weitzer. *Violence Against Women, 18*(4), 512–517.

Dorling, D. (2004). Prime Suspect: Murder in Britain. In C. Pantazis, S. Tombs, & D. Gordon (Eds.), *Beyond Criminology: Taking Harm Seriously*. London: Pluto Press.

Douglas, J. E., Burgess, A. W., & Ressler, R. K. (1992). *Crime Classification Manual: A Standard System for Investigating and Classifying Violent Crime*. New York: Simon & Schuster.

Douglas, J. E., Ressler, R. K., Burgess, A. W., & Hartman, C. R. (1986). Criminal Profiling from Crime Scene Analysis. *Behavioural Sciences and Law, 4*, 401–421.

Downes, D., & Rock, P. (2007). *Understanding Deviance: A Guide to the Sociology of Crime and Rule Breaking*. Oxford: Oxford University Press.

Downing, L. (2013). *The Subject of Murder*. Chicago: University of Chicago Press.

Dworkin, A. (1976). *Our Blood: Prophecies and Discourses on Sexual Politics*. New York: Harper and Row.

Dworkin, A. (1981). *Pornography: Men Possessing Women*. New York: Perigee.

Egger, S. A. (1984). A Working Definition of Serial Murder and the Reduction of Linkage Blindness. *Journal of Police Science and Administration, 12*(3), 348–357.

Ekberg, G. (2004). The Swedish Law That Prohibits the Purchase of Sexual Services: Best Practices for Prevention of Prostitution and Trafficking of Human Beings. *Violence Against Women, 10*(10), 1187–1218.

Ellis, A. (2015). *Men, Masculinities and Violence: An Ethnographic Approach*. London: Routledge.

Ellison, G., & Weitzer, R. (2015). The Dynamics of Male and Female Street Prostitution in Manchester, England. *Men and Masculinities, 20*(2), 181–203.

Ensalaco, M. (2006). Murder in Ciudad Juarez: A Parable of Women's Struggle for Human Rights. *Violence Against Women, 12*(5), 417–440.

Evans, D., Fyfe, N., & Herbert, D. (Eds.). (1992). *Crime, Policing and Place: Essays in Environmental Criminology*. London: Routledge.

Farley, M. (2004). "Bad for the Body, Bad for the Heart": Prostitution Harms Women Even If Legalised or Decriminalised. *Violence Against Women, 10*(10), 1087–1125.

Farrar, M. (1996). Migrant Spaces and Settlers' Time: Forming and Deforming an Inner City. In S. Westwood & J. Williams (Eds.), *Imagining Cities: Scripts, Signs and Memory*. London: Routledge.

Farrar, M. (2012). Rioting or Protesting? Losing It or Finding It? *Parallax, 18*(2), 72–91.

Ferguson, E. (2004, February 15). There's Nobody Home. *The Guardian*.

Ferrell, J., Hayward, K., & Young, J. (2015). *Cultural Criminology: An Invitation* (2nd ed.). London: Sage.

Ferrell, J., Hayward, K., Morrison, W., & Presdee, M. (2004). *Cultural Criminology Unleashed*. New York: Routledge.

Ferris, S. (2015). *Street Sex Work and Canadian Cities: Resisting a Dangerous Order*. Alberta: University of Alberta Press.

Flanders, J. (2011). *The Invention of Murder*. London: Harper Press.

Fox, J. A., & Levin, J. (2005). *Extreme Killing: Understanding Serial and Mass Murder*. London: Sage.

Fraser, N. (2013). *Fortunes of Feminism: From State Managed Capital to Neo-Liberal Crisis*. London: Verso.

Gadd, D. (2000). Masculinities, Violence and Defended Psychosocial Subjects. *Theoretical Criminology, 4*(4), 429–449.

Gadd, D., & Jefferson, T. (2007). *Psychosocial Criminology: An Introduction*. Los Angeles, CA: Sage.

Gelsthorpe, L., & Morris, A. (Eds.). (1990). *Feminist Perspectives in Criminology*. Buckingham: Open University Press.

Gemignani, K. (2014). Memory Remembering, and Oblivion in Active Narrative Interviewing. *Qualitative Inquiry, 20*(2), 127–135.

Gill, R. (2007). Postfeminist Media Culture: Elements of a Sensibility. *European Journal of Cultural Studies, 10*(2), 147–166.

Gilman Srebnick, A., & Levy, R. (2005). *Crime and Culture: An Historical Perspective*. Aldershot: Ashgate.

Gilroy, P. (2002). *There Ain't No Black in the Union Jack: The Cultural Politics of Race and Nation*. London: Routledge.

Girling, Evi, Loader, I., & Sparks, R. (2000). *Crime and Social Change in Middle England: Questions of Order in an English Town*. London: Routledge.

Glaser, B., & Strauss, A. (1967). *The Discovery of Grounded Theory: Strategies for Qualitative Research*. Hawthorne, NY: Aldine de Gruyter.

Godfrey, Barry S., Lawrence, P., & Williams, C. A. (2009). *History and Crime*. London: Sage.

Godwin, G. M. (2008). *Hunting Serial Predators*. Sudbury, MA: Jones & Bartlett.

Gordon, A. (2008). *Ghostly Matters: Haunting and the Sociological Imagination*. University of Minnesota Press.

Greer, C. (2007). News, Media, Victims and Crime. In P. Davies, P. Francis, & C. Greer (Eds.), *Victims, Crime and Society*. London: Sage.

Grele, R. J. (1998). Movement with Aim: Methodological and Theoretical Problems in Oral History. In R. Perks & A. Thomson (Eds.), *The Oral History Reader*. London: Routledge.

Grover, L., & Soothill, K. (1999). British Serial Killing: Towards a Structural Explanation. *The British Criminology Conferences: Selected Proceedings* (Vol. 2). Papers from the British Criminology Conference, Queens University, Belfast, 15–19 July 1997. This volume published March 1999. Editor: Mike Brogden.

Guest, K. (2006, February 12). Whatever Happened to Feminism's Extreme Sects? *The Independent*.

Haaken, J. (2010). *Hard Knocks: Domestic Violence and the Psychology of Storytelling*. London: Routledge.

Haggerty, K. (2009). Modern Serial Killers. *Crime, Media, Culture, 5*, 168.

Hale, C. (1996). Fear of Crime: A Review of the Literature. *International Review of Victimology, 4*(2), 79–150.

Hall, S. (2012). *Theorising Crime and Deviance: A New Perspective*. London: Sage.

Hall, S., Critcher, C., Jefferson, T., Clarke, C., & Roberts, B. (1978). *Policing the Crisis: Mugging, the State and Law and Order*. London: Palgrave Macmillan.

Hall, S., & Jefferson, T. (1976). *Resistance Through Rituals: Youth Subcultures in Post-War Britain*. London: Routledge.

Hall, S., & MacLean, C. (2009). A Tale of Two Capitalisms: Preliminary Spatial and Historical Comparisons of Homicide rates in Western Europe and the USA. *Theoretical Criminology, 13*, 303–319.

Hall, S., & Wilson, D. (2014). New Foundations: Pseudo-Pacification and Special Liberty as Potential Cornerstones for a Multi-level Theory of Homicide and Serial Murder. *European Journal of Criminology, 11*(5), 635–655.

Hall, S., & Winlow, S. (2015). *Revitalising Criminological Theory: Towards a New Ultra-Realism*. London: Routledge.

Hall, S., Winlow, S., & Ancrum, C. (2008). *Criminal Identities and Consumer Culture: Crime, Exclusion and the Culture of Narcissism*. Cullompton: Willan.

Hallsgrimdottir, H. G., Phillips, R., Benoit, C., & Walby, K. (2008). Sporting Girls, Streetwalkers and Inmates of Houses of Ill Repute: Media Narratives and the Historical Mutability of Prostitution Stigmas. *Sociological Perspectives, 51*(1), 119–138.

Hanmer, J., & Saunders, S. (1984). *Well Founded Fear: A Community Study of Violence to Women*. Leeds: Hutchinson.

Harrison, P., & Wilson, D. (2008). *Hunting Evil: Inside the Ipswich Serial Murders*. London: Sphere.

Hayward, K. (2012). Cultural Geography, Space and Crime. In S. Hall & S. Winlow (Eds.), *New Directions in Criminological Theory*. London: Routledge.

Heidensohn, F., & Gelsthorpe, L. (2007). Gender and Crime. In M. Maguire, R. Morgan, & R. Reiner (Eds.), *The Oxford Handbook of Criminology* (4th ed.). Oxford: Oxford Press.

Hemmings, J. (2018, May 2). No Germain Greer: Women Don't Want to Watch Gratuitous Rapes on TV. *The Guardian*.

Her Majesty's Crown Prosecution Service Inspectorate and Her Majesty's Inspectorate of Constabulary. (2007). *Without Consent: A Report on the Joint Review on the Investigation and Prosecution of Rape Offences*. London: Home Office.

Hickey, E. W. (1990). The Etiology of Victimization in Serial Murder. In S. A. Egger (Ed.), *Serial Murder: An Elusive Phenomenon*. New York: Praeger.

Hickey, E. W. (2013). *Serial Murders and Their Victims* (6th ed.). Wadsworth: Cengage Learning.

Highsmith, P. (1984). Fallen Women. *London Review of Books, 6*(11), 20–22.

Hill, A. (2009, October 25). Sexist Violence Sickens Crime Critic. *The Observer*.

Hill Collins, P. (1990). *Black Feminist Thought: Knowledge, Consciousness and the Politics of Empowerment*. Boston: Unwin Hyman.

Hill Collins, P. (1991). Towards an Afro-Centric Feminist Epistemology. In P. Hill Collins (Ed.), *Black Feminist Thought: Knowledge, Consciousness, Empowerment*. New York: Routledge.

Hinch, R., & Hepburn C. (1998). Researching Serial Murder: Methodological and Definitional Problems. *Electronic Journal of Sociology, 3*(2), 1–11.

Hobsbawn, E. (1995). *Age of Extremes: The Short Twentieth Century 1914–1991*. London: Abacus.

Hobsbawm, E., & Ranger, E. (1984). *The Invention of Tradition*. Cambridge: Cambridge University Press.

Hollway, W. (1981, October). 'I Just Wanted to Kill a Woman' Why? The Ripper and Male Sexuality. *Feminist Review, 9*(1), 33–40.

Holmes, R. M., & Deburger, J. (1988). *Serial Murder*. London: Sage.

Holmes, R. M., & Holmes, S. T. (1996). *Profiling Violent Crimes: An investigative Tool*. Thousand Oaks: Sage.

hooks, b. (1982). *Ain't I a Woman*. Boston: Pluto Press.

Horkheimer, M., & Adorno, T. W. (1972). *The Dialectic of the Enlightenment*. New York: Herder and Herder.

Hubbard, P., & Whowell, M. (2008). Revisiting the Red Light District: Still Neglected, Immoral and Marginal? *Geoforum, 39*(5), 1743–1755.

Ingala Smith, K. (2013). *This Thing About Male Victims*. https://kareningalasmith.com/2013/04/29/this-thing-about-male-victims.

Jacobs, J. (2010). *Memorialising the Holocaust: Gender, Genocide and Collective Memory*. London: I.B. Tauris.

Jacobsen Hviid, M. (2014). *The Poetics of Crime: Understanding and Researching Crime and Deviance Through Creative Sources*. New York: Routledge.

Jarvis, B. (2007). Monsters Inc.: Serial Killers and Consumer Culture. *Crime, Media, Culture, 3*(2), 326–344.

Jefferson, T. (1998). "Muscle", "Hard Men" and "Iron" Mike Tyson: Reflections on Desire, Anxiety and the Embodiment of Masculinity. *Body and Society, 4*(1), 77–98.

Jefferson, T. (2002). Subordinating Hegemonic Masculinity. *Theoretical Criminology, 6,* 63–88.

Jeffreys, S. (1977). The Need for Revolutionary Feminism. *Scarlet Woman,* 5.

Jeffreys, S. (2008). *The Idea of Prostitution.* Melbourne: Spinifex Press.

Jeffreys, S. (2009). *The Industrial Vagina: The Political Economy of the Global Sex Trade.* London: Routledge.

Jeffries, F. (2013). Documentary Noir in the City of Fear: Feminicide, Impunity and Grass Roots Communication in Ciudad Juarez. *Crime, Media Culture, 9*(3), 301–317.

Jenkins, P. (1988). Serial Murder in England, 1940–1985. *Journal of Criminal Justice, 16,* 1–15.

Jenkins, P. (1994). *Using Murder: The Social Construction of Serial Homicide.* New York: Routledge.

Jenks, C. (2003). *Transgression.* London: Routledge.

Jermyn, D. (2015). Silk Blouses and Fedoras: The Female Detective, Contemporary TV Crime Drama and the Predicaments of Postfeminism. *Crime, Media, Culture, 13*(3), 259–276.

Jewkes, Y. (2013). *Media and Crime* (2nd ed.). London: Sage.

Jiwani, Y., & Young, M. L. (2006). Missing and Murdered Women: Reproducing Marginality in News Discourse. *Canadian Journal of Communication, 31,* 895–917.

Jones, H., & Cook, K. (2008). *Rape Crisis: Responding to Sexual Violence.* London: Russell House.

Joseph, S. (2010). Telling True Stories in Australia. *Journalism Practice, 4*(1), 82–87.

Keightley, Emily. (2008). Remembering Research: Memory and Methodology in the Social Sciences. *International Journal of Social Research Methodology, 13*(1), 55–70.

Kelleher, M. D., & Kelleher, C. L. (1998). *Murder Most Rare: The Female Serial Killer.* Westport, CT: Praeger.

Kelly, L. (1987). The Continuum of Sexual Violence. In J. Hanmer & M. Maynard (Eds.), *Women, Violence and Social Control.* London: Palgrave Macmillan.

Kelly, L., Lovett, J., & Regan, L. (2005). *A Gap or a Chasm? Attrition in Reported Rape Cases. Home Office Research Study.* London: Home Office Research, Development and Statistics Directorate.

Keppel, R. D., & Walter, R. (1999). Profiling Killers: A Revised Classification Model for Understanding Sexual Murder. *International Journal of Offender Therapy and Comparative Criminology, 43,* 417–437.

Keyes, J. (2011). "No Redemption": The Death of the City in the Work of David Peace. In K. Shaw (Ed.), *Analysing David Peace.* Cambridge: Cambridge Scholars.

Kimpton Nye, L. (n.d.). Feminist Collectives. *Spare Rib* (online archive). British Library. https://www.bl.uk/spare-rib/articles/feminist-collectives.

King, A. (2006). The Serial Killer and the Postmodern Self. *History of Human Sciences, 19*(3), 109–125.

Kinnell, H. (2008). *Violence and Sex Work in Britain.* Devon Cullompton: Willan.

Koskela, H. (1997). 'Bold Walk and Breakings': Women's Spatial Confidence Versus Fear of Violence. *Gender, Place and Culture, 4,* 301–319.

Langstraat, J. W. (2006). *The Urban Regeneration Industry in Leeds: Measuring Sustainable Urban Regeneration Performance Earth & Environment, 2,* 167–210.

Lederer, L. (Ed.). (1980). *Take Back the Night: Women on Pornography.* New York: William Morrow.

Leeds City Council. (2016). *Leeds Economy Handbook.*

Leeds Revolutionary Feminist Group. (1981). Love Your Enemy? *The Debate between Heterosexual Feminism and Political Lesbianism Wires 81,* 5–10.

Lees, S. (1996). *Carnal Knowledge: Rape on Trial.* Harmondsworth: Penguin.

Lewis, J., & Townsend, A. (1989). *The North-South Divide: Regional Change in Britain in the 1980s.* London: Paul Chapman.

Leyton, E. (1986). *Hunting Humans: The Rise of the Modern Multiple Murderer.* Toronto: McClelland and Stewart.

Linnemann, T. (2015). Capote's Ghosts: Violence, Murder and the Spectre of Suspicion. *British Journal of Criminology, 55,* 514–533.

Loader, I., & Sparks, R. (2011). *Public Criminology.* London: Routledge.

Lowman, J. (1992). Street Prostitution Control: Some Canadian Reflections on the Finsbury Park Experience. *The British Journal of Criminology, 32*(1), 1–17.

Lowman, J. (2000). Violence and the Outlaw Status of (Street) Prostitution in Canada. *Violence Against Women, 6,* 987–1011.

Lummis, T. (1998). Structure and Validity in Oral Evidence. In R. Perks & A. Thomson (Eds.), *The Oral History Reader.* London: Routledge.

Lupton, C. (1994). The British Refuge Movement: The Survival of an Ideal? In C. Lupton & T. Gillespie (Eds.), *Working with Violence. Practical Social Work.* London: Palgrave Macmillan.

MacDonald, R., & Marsh, J. (2005). *Disconnected Youth: Growing Up in Britain's Poorest Neighbourhoods.* Basingstoke: Palgrave Macmillan.

MacDonald, R., Shildrick, T., Webster, C., & Simpson, D. (2005). Growing Up in Poor Neighbourhoods: The Significance of Class and Place in the Extended Transitions of Socially Excluded Young Adults. *Sociology, 39*(5), 873–891.

Mackay, F. (2014). Reclaiming Revolutionary Feminism. *Feminist Review, 106,* 95–103.

Mackay, F. (2015). *Radical Feminism: Feminist Activism in Movement.* London: Palgrave Macmillan.

Mackinnon, C. (1987). Toward Feminist Jurisprudence. *Stanford Law Review, 34,* 703–721.

Mackinnon, C. (1989). *Towards a Feminist Theory of the State.* Cambridge: Harvard University Press.

MacKinnon, C. (1993). *Only Words.* Cambridge: Harvard University Press.

Maguire, M. (2008). Criminal Investigation and Crime Control. In T. Newburn (Ed.), *Handbook of Policing* (2nd ed., pp. 430–465). Cullompton, UK: Willan.

Maguire, P. (2011). Politics and Class in the 1970s/80s. In K. Shaw (Ed.), *Analysing David Peace.* Cambridge: Cambridge Scholars.

Maher, L. (1997). *Sexed Work: Gender, Race and Resistance in a Brooklyn Drug Market.* Oxford: Oxford University Press.

Marks, L. H., & Neville, L. (2017). Gilead: An Anti-porn Utopia. *Nursing Clio.* https://nursingclio.org/2017/05/15/gilead-an-antiporn-utopia/.

Matthews, R. (2005). Policing Prostitution: Ten years on. *British Journal of Criminology, 45,* 877–895.

Merck, M. (1981, July). Sutcliffe: What the Papers Say. *Spare Rib, 10.*

McCall, L. (2005). The Complexity of Intersectionality. *Signs, 30,* 1771–1800.

McRobbie, A. (1984, June 8). 'Cross Winds', Review of Pat Barker, Blow Your House Down. *New Statesman.*

McRobbie, A. (2007). Post-feminism and Popular Culture. *Feminist Media Studies, 4*(3), 255–264.

Meek, J. (2009, August 6). *Polly the Bleeding Parrot, London review of Books.*

Miller, J. (2010). Commentary on Heidensohn's 'The Deviance of Women': Continuity and Change over Four Decades of Gender, Crime and Social Control. *British Journal of Sociology, 61,* 134–139.

Miller, J., & Glassner, B. (1997). The 'Inside' and the 'Outside': Finding Realities in Interviews. In D. Silverman (Ed.), *Qualitative Research: Theory, Method and Practice.* London: Sage.

Miller, J., & Mullins, C. (2011). The Status of Feminist Theories in Criminology. In F. T. Cullin, J. P. Wright, & K. R. Blevins (Eds.), *Taking Stock: The Status of Criminological Theory.* New Brunswick and London: Transaction Publishers.

Miller, L. (2014). Serial Killers: I. Subtypes, Patterns, and Motives. *Aggression and Violent Behavior, 19,* 1–11.

Moore, S., & Breeze, S. (2012). Spaces of Male Fear: The Sexual Politics of Being Watched. *British Journal of Criminology, 52,* 1172–1191.

Moran, L., & Skeggs, B. (2004). *Sexuality and the Politics of Safety.* London: Routledge.

Morgan, S., & Jenkins, K. (2005). *The Feminist History Reader.* London: Routledge.

Morrison, W. (1995). *Theoretical Criminology: From Modernity to Postmodernism.* London: Cavendish.

Morrissey, B. (2003). *When Women Kill: Questions of Agency and Subjectivity.* New York: Routledge.

Mortimer, J. (1984). *Famous Trials,* originally edited by H. Hodge and J. Hodge (1981). Harmondsworth: Penguin.

Mulvey, L. (1975, Autumn). Visual Pleasure and Narrative Cinema. *Screen, 16*(3), 6–18.

Munt, S. (1994). *Murder by the Book? Feminism and the Crime Novel.* London: Routledge.

Myers, B. (2009, July 22). Gordon Burn Was One of the Greatest Writers of His Age. *The Guardian.*

Naffine, N. (1997). *Feminism and Criminology.* Cambridge: Polity.

Neisser, U. (1982). Snapshots or Benchmarks? In U. Neisser (Ed.), *Memory Observed: Remembering in Natural Contexts.* San Francisco, CA: W. H. Freeman.

Newburn, T. (2007). Understanding Investigation. In T. Newburn, T. Williamson & A. Wright (Eds.), *Handbook of Criminal Investigation* (pp. 1–11). Collumpton, UK: Willan.

Newburn, T., & Stanko, E. (1994). *Just Boys Doing Business: Men, Masculinities and Crime.* London: Routledge.

Neyroud, P., & Disley, E. (2007). The Management, Supervision and Oversight of Criminal Investigations. In T. Newburn, T. Willamson & A. Wright (Eds.), *Handbook of Criminal Investigation.* Cullompton, UK: Willan.

Nicholson, R. (2017, August 7). True Crime Makes Great TV. But Must It Linger on Women's Corpses? *The Guardian.*

Office for National Statistics. (2016). *Homicide: Findings from Analyses Based on the Homicide Index Recorded by the Home Office Covering Differing Aspects of Homicide.* London: Office for National Statistics.

O'Hagan, A. (2012, November 8). Light Entertainment: Andrew O'Hagan Writes About Child Abuse and the British Public. *London Review of Books.* https://www.lrb.co.uk/v34/n21/andrew-ohagan/light-entertainment.

O'Neill, M. (2001). *Prostitution and Feminism: Towards a Politics of Feeling.* Cambridge: Polity.

O'Neill, M. (2010). Cultural Criminology and Sex Work: Resisting Regulation Through Radical Democracy and Participatory Action Research (PAR). *Journal of Law and Society, 37*(1), 210–232.

O'Neill, M., & Campbell, R. (2002). *Working Together to Create Change.* http://www.safetysoapbox.com.

O'Neill, M., & Campbell, R. (2006). Street Sex Work and Local Communities: Creating Discursive Spaces for Genuine Consultation and Inclusion. In R. Campbell & M. O'Neill (Eds.), *Sex Work Now* (pp. 33–61). Willan: Cullompton.

O'Neill, M., & Seal, L. (2012). *Transgressive Imaginations: Crime, Deviance and Culture.* Basingstoke: Palgrave Macmillan.

Orr, D. (2015, August 15). Jack the Ripper Is an Invented Villain but His Victims Were Real: A Museum to These Crimes Is a Disgrace. *The Guardian.*

Pain, R. (1991). Space, Sexual Violence and Social Control: Integrating Geographical and Feminist Analyses of Women's Fear of Crime. *Progress in Human Geography, 15,* 415–431.

Painter, K. (1992). Different Worlds: The Spatial, Temporal and Social Dimensions of Female Victimisation. In D. Evans, N. Fyfe, & D. Herbert (Eds.), *Crime, Policing and Place: Essays in Environmental Criminology.* London: Routledge.

Passerini, L. (1992). *Memory and Totalitarianism.* Oxford: Oxford University Press.

Pateman, C. (1983). *The Sexual Contract.* Bloomington, IN: Stanford University Press.

Peace, D. (1999). *Nineteen Seventy Four.* London: Serpents Tail.

Peace, D. (2000). *Nineteen Seventy Seven.* London: Serpents Tail.

Peace, D. (2001). *Nineteen Eighty.* London: Serpents Tail.

Peace, D. (2002). *Nineteen Eighty-Three.* London: Serpents Tail.

Penfold, C., Hunter, G., Campbell, R., & Barham, L. (2004). Tackling Client Violence in Female Street Prostitution: Interagency Working Between Outreach Agencies and the Police. *Policing and Society, 4*(4), 365–379.

Phoenix, A. (2008). Analysing Narrative Contexts. In M. Andrews, C. Squire, & Michael Tamboukou (Eds.), *Doing Narrative Research* (pp. 41–56). London: Sage.

Phoenix, J. (1999). *Making Sense of Prostitution.* Basingstoke: Palgrave Macmillan.

Phoenix, J. (2009). *Regulating Sex for Sale: Prostitution, Policy Reform and the UK.* Bristol: Policy Press.

Pilar Blanco, M. D., & Pereen, E. (2013). Possessions: Spectral Places/Introduction. In M. D. Pilar Blanco & E. Pereen (Eds.), *The Spectralities Reader.* London: Bloomsbury.

Polk, K. (1998). *When Men Kill.* Cambridge: Cambridge University Press.

Polkinghorne, D. (2007). Validity Issues in Narrative Research. *Qualitative Inquiry, 13*(4), 471–486.

Portelli, A. (1998). What Makes Oral History Different? In R. Perks & A. Thomson (Eds.), *The Oral History Reader.* London: Routledge.

Presser, L. (2009). The Narratives of Offenders. *Theoretical Criminology, 13,* 177–200.

Purcell, C., & Arrigo, B. (2006). *The Psychology of Lust Murder.* Burlington, MA: Elsevier.

Quinet, K. (2007). The Missing Missing: Toward a Quantification of Serial Murder Victimization in the United States. *Homicide Studies, 11,* 319–339.

Quinet, K. (2011). Prostitutes as Victims of Serial Homicide: Trends and Case Characteristics, 1970–2009. *Homicide Studies, 15,* 74–100.

Quirk, J. (2009, February 28). Northern Exposure. *The Guardian.*

Radford, J. (1992). Introduction. In J. Radford & D. Russell (Eds.), *Femicide: The Politics of Woman Killing.* New York, NY: Twayne.

Radford, J., & Russell, D. (1992). *Femicide: The Politics of Woman Killing.* New York, NY: Twayne.

Rafter, N. (2007). Crime, Film and Criminology: Recent Sex Crime Movies. *Theoretical Criminology, 11*(3), 403–420.

Ramsland, K. (2005). *The Human Predator: A Historical Chronicle of Serial Murder and Forensic Investigation.* New York, NY: The Berkley Publishing Group.

Rawlings, P. (1998). True Crime. *British Criminology Conferences* (Vol 1). www.britsoc.org/volume1/010.pdf. Accessed 5 March 2014.

Rawlinson, M. (2010). *Pat Barker.* Basingstoke: Palgrave Macmillan.

Ray, L. (2011). *Violence and Society.* London: Sage.

Raymond, J. G. (1998). Prostitution as Violence Against Women. *Women's Studies International Forum, 21*(1), 1–9.

Raymond, J. G. (2004). Prostitution on Demand: Legalising the Buyers as Sexual Consumers. *Violence Against Women, 10*(10), 1156–1186.

Raymond, J. G. (2013). *Not a Choice, Not a Job: Exposing the Myths of the Global Sex Trade.* Dulles: Potomac Books.

Reilly, N. (2008). *Women's Human Rights: Seeking Gender Justice in a Globalising Age.* Cambridge: Polity.

Reiner, R. (2002). Media-Made Criminality: The Representation of Crime in the Mass Media. In R. Reiner, M. Maguire, & R. Morgan, Rod, (Eds.), *The Oxford Handbook of Criminology.* Oxford: Oxford University Press.

Ressler, R. K., Burgess, A. W., & Douglas, J. E. (1988). *Sexual Homicides: Patterns and Motives.* Lexington, MA: Lexington Books.

Rice, M. (1990). Challenging Orthodoxies in Feminist Theory: A Black Feminist Critique. In L. Gelsthorpe & A. Morris (Eds.), *Feminist Perspectives in Criminology.* Milton Keynes: Open University Press.

Rich, A. (1980). Compulsory Heterosexuality and Lesbian Existence. *Signs, 5*(4), 631–660.

Riger, S., & Michael, G. (1981). The Fear of Rape: A Study in Social Control. *Journal of Social Issues, 37,* 71–92.

Rivera, M. (2005). La historia de las mujeres que nombran el mundo en femen-ino [The History of Women Who Name the World by Using the Female Gender]. *Acta Historica et Archaeologica Mediaevalia, 26*, 1155–1164.

Roberts, B. (2002). *Biographical Research*. Buckingham: Open University Press.

Roberts, Y. (2015, April 15). 'Ooh You Were Awful': Why I Can't Look Back on the Sexist Seventies With Kindness. *The Observer*.

Rossmanith, K. (2014). Plots and Artefacts: Courts and Criminal Evidence in the Production of True Crime Writing. *Australian Feminist Law Journal, 40*(1), 97–111.

Runciman, D. (2013). The Crisis of British Democracy: Back to the '70s or Stuck in the Present? *Institute for Public Policy Research*. https://www.ippr/juncture/the-crisis-of-british-democracy-back-to-70s-or-stuck-in-the-present.

Salfati, C. G., James, A. R., & Ferguson, L. (2008). Prostitute Homicides: A Descriptive Study. *Journal of Interpersonal Violence, 23*, 505–543.

Samuel, R., & Thompson, P. (1990). *The Myths We Live By*. London: Routledge.

Sandberg, S., Tutenge, S., & Copes, H. (2015). Studies of Violence: A Narrative Criminological Study of Ambiguity. *British Journal of Criminology, 55*, 1168–1186.

Sanders, T. (2009). Controlling the Anti-Sexual City: Sexual Citizenship and the Disciplining of Female Sex Workers. *Criminology and Criminal Justice, 9*(4), 507–525.

Sanders, T. (2016). Inevitably Violent? Dynamics of Space, Governance and Stigma. *Special Issue: Problematizing Prostitution: Critical Research and Scholarship, Studies in Law, Politics and Society, 71*, 93–114.

Sanders, T., & Campbell, R. (2007). Designing Out Vulnerability, Building in Respect: Violence Safety and Sex Work Policy. *The British Journal of Sociology, 58*(1), 1–19.

Santtila, P., Pakkanen, T., Zappalà, A., Bosco, D., Valkama, M., & Mokros, A. (2008). Behavioural Crime Linking in Serial Homicide. *Psychology, Crime and Law, 14*(3), 245–265.

Sapsford, R. (1996). Reading Qualitative Research. In R. Sapsford (Ed.), *Researching Crime and Criminal Justice*. Milton Keynes: Open University Press.

Schmid, D. (2005). *Natural Born Celebrities: Serial Killers in American Culture*. London: University of Chicago Press.

Schmidt-Camacho, A. S. (2010). 'Ciudadana X: Gender Violence and the Denationalisation of Women's Rights in Ciudad Juarez, Mexico. In R. L. Fregoso & C. Bejarano (Eds.), *Terrorising Women: Feminicide in the Americas*. Washington: Duke University Press.

Schwartz, M. (2013). Kicking Back, Not Leaning. *Dissent, 60*(3), 713–722.

Scoular, J. (2004). The 'Subject' of Prostitution: Interpreting the Discursive, Symbolic and Material Position of Sex/Work Within Feminist Theory. *Feminist Theory, 5*(3), 343–355.

Seal, L. (2010). *Women, Murder and Femininity: Gender Representations of Women Who Kill*. Basingstoke: Palgrave Macmillan.

Seale, C. (1998). *Researching Society and Culture*. London: Sage.

Seltzer, M. (1998). *Serial Killers: Death and Life in America's Wound Culture*. London: Sage.

Seltzer, M. (2007). *True Crime: Observations on Violence and Modernity*. New York: Routledge.

Sen, A. (1990). *More Than 100 Million Women Are Missing*. http://www.nybooks.com/articles/archives/1990/dec/20/more-than-100-millionwomen-are-missing/. Accessed 1 April 2014.

Shaw, K. (2010). *David Peace: Texts and Contexts*. Brighton: Sussex Academic Press.

Shaw, K. (Ed.). (2011). *Analysing David Peace*. Cambridge: Cambridge Scholars.

Skeggs, B. (1997). *Formations of Class and Gender: Becoming Respectable*. London: Sage.

Smart, C. (1976). *Women, Crime and Criminology*. London: Routledge and Kegan Paul.

Smart, C. (1989). *Feminism and the Power of the Law*. London: Routledge.

Smith, J. (2013). *Misogynies: Reflections on Myth and Malice*. New York: Fawcett Columbine.

Smith, M., Bondi, L., & Davidson, J. (Eds.). (2005). *Emotional Geographies*. Aldershot: Ashgate.

Smith, K., Coleman, K., Eder, S., & Hall, P. (2011). *Homicides, Firearm Offences and Intimate Violence*. London: Home Office HMSO.

Soothill, K. (1993). The Serial Killer Industry. *Journal of Forensic Psychiatry, 4*(2), 342–354.

Soothill, K. (1996). Murder: The Importance of the Structural and Cultural Conditions. *Journal of Forensic Medicine, 3*, 161–165.

Spare Rib. (1980). Leeds: Male Violence; Women. Issue 67, p. 302.

Sparks, R. (1992). Reason and Unreason in 'Left Realism': Some Problems in the Constitution of the Fear of Crime. In R. Matthews & J. Young (Eds.), *Issues in Realist Criminology*. London: Sage.

Sparks, R., Girling, E., & Loader, I. (2001). Fear and Everyday Urban Lives. *Urban Studies, 38*(5–6), 885–898.

Stanko, E. (1987). Typical Violence, Normal Precaution: Men, Women and Interpersonal Violence in England, Wales, Scotland and the USA. In J. Hanmer & M. Maynard (Eds.), *Women, Violence and Social Control*. London: Palgrave Macmillan.

Stanko, E. (1990). *Everyday Violence: How Women and Men Experience Physical and Sexual Danger*. Pandora Press.

Stanko, E. (1997). Safety Talk: Conceptualising Women's Risk Assessment as a Technology of the Soul. *Theoretical Criminology, 1*(4), 479–499.

Stead, J. (1980, November 5). Now Is the Time to Stand Up and Fight. *The Guardian.*

Strega, S., Janzen, C., Morgan, J., Brown, L., Thomas, J., & Carriere, J. (2014). Never Innocent Victims: Street Sex Workers in Canadian Print Media. *Violence Against Women, 20*(1), 6–25.

Tatar, M. (1995). *Lustmord: Sexual Murder in Weimar Germany.* Princeton: Princeton University Press.

The Guardian. (2012, July 16). Rachel Wilson Murder: Body Found on Farmland Is Middlesbrough Teenager.

Thompson, P. (1993). Family Myth, Models an Denials in the Shaping of Individual Life Paths. In D. Bertaux & P. Thompson (Eds.), *Between Generations.* Oxford: Oxford University Press.

Treadwell, J., & Garland, J. (2011). Masculinity, Marginalisation and Violence: A Case Study of the English Defence League. *British Journal of Criminology, 11*(5), 1171–1193.

Tuchman, G. (2000). The Symbolic Annihilation of Women by the Mass Media. In L. Crothers & C. Lockhart (Eds.), *Culture and Politics.* New York: Palgrave Macmillan.

Underwood, M. (2006, February 8). Magic Book Ban on Kellie's Killer. *Evening Gazette.*

Upson, N. (2001, August 20). Hunting the Yorkshire Ripper. *New Statesman.*

Valentine, G. (1989). The Geography of Women's Fear. *Area, 21,* 385–390.

Valentine, G. (1992). Images of Danger: Women's Sources of Information About the Spatial Distribution of Male Violence. *Area, 24,* 22–29.

Vanwesenbeeck, I. (2017). Sex Work Criminalisation Is Barking Up the Wrong Tree. *Archives of Sexual Behaviour, 46*(6), 1631–1640.

Villalon, R. (2012). Accounts of Violence Against Women: The Potential of Realistic Fiction. In D. King & C. L. Smith (Eds.), *Men Who Hate Women and Women Who Kick Their Asses: Stieg Larrson's Millennium in Feminist Perspective.* Nashville, TN: Vanderbilt University Press.

Vincent, L., & Naidu, S. (2013). The Representation of Violence Against Women in Margie Orford's Clare Hart Novels. *African Safety Promotion Journal, 11,* 48.

Vronsky, P. (2004). *Serial Killers: The Method and Madness of Monsters.* New York: Berkley Books.

Wacquant, L. (2008). *Urban Outcasts: A Comparative Sociology of Advanced Marginality.* Cambridge: Polity.

Wakeman, S. (2013). 'No One Wins. One Side Just Loses More Slowly': The Wire and Drug Policy. *Theoretical Criminology, 18,* 2, 224–239.

Wakeman, S. (2014). Fieldwork, Biography and Emotion: Doing Criminological Auto-Ethnography. *British Journal of Criminology, 54,* 705–721.

Walby, S. (2011). *The Future of Feminism.* Cambridge: Polity.

Walby, S., & Allen, J. (2004). *Domestic Violence, Sexual Assault and Stalking: Findings from the British Crime Survey.* London: Home Office Research, Development and Statistics Directorate.

Walker, S. (1999). The John School: A Diversion from What Is Needed. In N. Lopez-Jones (Ed.), *Some Mother's Daughter: The Hidden Movement of Prostitute Women Against Violence.* California City: Crossroads.

Walklate, S. (1998). Crime and Community: Fear or Trust? *The British Journal of Sociology, 49*(4), 550–569.

Walklate, S. (2001). Fearful Communities? *Urban Studies, 38*(5–6), 929–939.

Walklate, S. (2004). *Crime and Justice* (2nd ed.). Cullompton Devon: Willan.

Walklate, S., & Jacobsen Hviid, M. (Eds.). (2017). *Liquid Criminology: Doing Imaginative Criminological Research.* London: Routledge.

Walklate, S., McGarry, R., & Mythen, G. (2014). Trauma, Visual Victimology and the Poetics of Justice. In M. H. Jacobsen (Ed.), *The Poetics of Crime: Understanding and Researching Crime and Deviance Through Creative Sources.* New York: Routledge.

Walkowitz, J. (1982). Jack the Ripper and Myth of Male Violence. *Feminist Studies, 8*(3), 542–574.

Walkowitz, J. (1992). *City of Dreadful Delight: Narratives of Sexual Danger in Victorian London.* Chicago: University of Chicago Press.

Ward Jouve, N. (1988). *The Street Cleaner.* New York: Marion Boyars.

Ward Jouve, N. (2010, May 29). Bradford Murders Show Area Still Beset by Death, 30 Years After Ripper Case. *The Guardian.*

Warkentin, E. (2010). "Jack the Ripper" Strikes Again: The "Ipswich Ripper" and the "Vice Girls He Killed. *Feminist Media Studies, 10,* 35–49.

Wattis, L. (2017). Revisiting the Yorkshire Ripper Murders: Interrogating Sex Work, Gender and Justice. *Feminist Criminology, 12*(1), 1–21.

Wattis, L., Green, E., & Radford, J. (2011). 'Women Students' Perceptions of Crime and Safety: Negotiating Fear and Risk in an English Post-industrial Landscape. *Gender, Place and Culture, 18*(6), 749–767.

Webber, C. (2010). *Psychology and Crime.* London: Sage.

Webster, C. (2006). Race, Space and Fear: Imagined Geographies of Racism, Crime, Violence and Disorder in Northern England. *Capitalism and Class, 80,* 95–122.

Wender, J. (2015). The Phenomenology of Arrest: A Case Study in Poetics of Police-Citizen Encounters. In M. H. Jacobsen (Ed.), *The Poetics of Crime: Understanding and Researching Crime and Deviance Through Creative Sources.* London: Ashgate.

Westmarland, N. (2004). *Rape Law Reform in England and Wales* (Working Paper No. 7). Bristol: School for Policy Studies.

Wiest, J. B. (2011). *Creating Cultural Monsters: Serial murder in America.* Boca Raton, FL: CRC Press.

Williams, E. (1967). *Beyond Belief.* London: Pan.

Williams, Z. (2018, May 1). Are Women Responsible for All the Sexual Violence on Screen? *The Guardian.*

Wilson, D. (2007). *Serial Killers: Hunting Britons and Their Victims 1966–2006.* Hampshire Hook: Waterside Press.

Wilson, D. (2012). Late Capitalism, Vulnerable Populations and Violent Predatory Crime. In S. Hall & S. Winlow (Eds.), *New Directions in Criminological Theory.* London: Routledge.

Wilson, D. (2013). *Mary Ann Cotton: Britain's First Female Serial Killer.* Hook Hants: Waterside Press.

Wilson, D., Yardley, R., & Pemberton, S. (2016). The 'Dunblane Massacre' as a 'Photosensitive Plate'. *Crime, Media, Culture, 13,* 1–14.

Winder, R. (1991, April 27). When Murder Is Not Enough. *The Independent.*

Wilson, T. (2009). *Red Riding Quarlet Review.* http://Capturescrime.blogspot.co.uk/2009101/review-red-riding-quarlet-david-peace.html. Accessed 10 November 2014.

Winlow, S. (2001). *Badfellas.* Oxford: Berg.

Wykes, M. (2001). *News, Crime and Culture.* London: Pluto Press.

Wykes, M., & Welsh, K. (2009). *Violence, Gender and Justice.* London: Sage.

Yallop, D. (1993). *Deliver Us from Evil.* Reading: Cox and Wyman.

Yeatman, A. (1994). *Postmodern Revisionings of the Political.* New York: Charman and Hall.

Young, A. (1996). *Imagining Crime: Textual Outlaws and Criminal Conversations.* London: Sage.

Young, J. (1999). *The Exclusive Society: Social Exclusion, Crime and Difference in Late Modernity.* London: Sage.

Young, J. (2011). *The Criminological Imagination.* Cambridge: Polity.

Yow, V. (1994). *Recording Oral History: A Guide for the Humanities and Social Sciences.* New York: Sage.

Zheng, T., & Lights, R. (2009). *The Lives of Sex Workers in Post-socialist China.* Minneapolis: University of Minnesota Press.

INDEX

Printed by Printforce, the Netherlands